SHAWN

SHAWN

by

URI GELLER

℗1990 Published by Goodyer Associates Limited
3rd floor, 25 Market Place, Nuneaton, Warwickshire

ISBN NO. 1 871406 09 9

Printed and bound in Great Britain
by
Billing & Son Limited, Hylton Road, Worcester

Previous books by the author:

URI GELLER: MY STORY
THE GELLER EFFECT
URI GELLER'S FORTUNE SECRETS

Books about the author:

URI
URI GELLER EL DESCUBIERTO
THE GELLER PAPERS
THE GELLER PHENOMENON
THE STRANGE STORY OF URI GELLER
THE AMAZING URI GELLER
THE MAGIC OF URI GELLER
THE SEARCH FOR SUPERMAN
SUPERMINDS
MYSTERIOUS POWERS
THE TRUTH ABOUT URI GELLER
THE METAL BENDERS
GELLERISM REVEALED
URI GELLER FUP ELLER FAKTA

To Aba and Hava Above

ACKNOWLEDGEMENT

To my loved ones Hanna, Natalie, Daniel, Muti, Shipi, Arie and to all my true friends who return friendship with friendship and love with love.

Uri Geller
April 1990

CONTENTS

1

CRYSTAL

The planet to which Nonomine had been exiled was not accessible to astral travellers or galactic castaways, nor even to the human imagination. Even the idea of exile did not perfectly apply to his situation then, for the place chosen for Nonomine was one of unsurpassable beauty and comfort. Sending him there had not been meant as punishment, since any form of rebellion was considered a step on the road to the penultimate wisdom, the wisdom that God's creatures can be *close* to God but can never *be* God.

On this planet of rainbow crystals and shimmering falls of ether vapours where three turquoise moons shed magnificent light, Nonomine lived outside the confines of time, abandoning his spirit to take what shapes it pleased. And so he himself, only vague in outline, allowed himself to become part of the nature of his exile, become turquoise light, refracted vapours, or be lost for long beats of the cosmic heart on the sparkling crystal plains and iridescent rock faces with no will to determine his shape or appearance.

By doing this he was acting in the way that those who had sent him here expected him to. This particular planet, for its magnificent treasures of nature, was considered particularly absorbable. When it had been made part of a certain individual, that individual had advanced considerably.

In the white-hot winds that alternated with icy gales in long cycles, Nonomine gave up almost all of his being that was still coarse and physical. He released it, even tried to release the active, positive male principle by which he was governed in this phase of his life and there, too, he succeeded. He became ozone and gale, light, vapour, crystal - and if there had been anyone there to touch him or to be enveloped by him, such a person would not have been able to identify what it was that was touched except by its common appearance as an object or phenomenon of nature.

By Earth time, Nonomine spent more than two centuries on the crystal planet. But, of course, Nonomine had merely heard of Earth and its time. It meant little to him. In those two hundred years a great deal had happened on Earth. A thing called technology had developed and had been perfected to the point where humans sent probes through their local system of planets. Crude as these probes were - human technology having developed a method called rocket propulsion - they carried polluted debris to the far reaches of the solar system. A great deal of useless information was conveyed back to Earth through instruments which were either deposited on the hitherto virginal surfaces of planets, or placed in orbit about them, or worse, allowed to continue on course into infinity to be drawn into the orbit of some distant, incalculable world to crash there and litter it, perhaps to annihilate whatever population might be there.

But of all this the exiled Nonomine knew nothing. When finally he coalesced, following an abrupt, shocking impulse, he found his persona as Nonomine intact, resplendent with energy and new knowledge. The crystal vapours were part of the new man now, and this new Nonomine confronted the messenger who had been sent to authenticate a message to him - a message he had already received - the message that urged him to become himself again. He was instructed to go to Earth ..... Terra.

Concerning the nature of his mission: it was conveyed to him that the Terrans had not yet learned that the road to mastery of the natural forces began with the restraint of power. Incapable of recognizing or grasping the subtle examples of this principle, which abounded in their own natural environment, they needed more dramatic demonstrations. These, Nonomine would improvise out of situations that would develop naturally simply by the juxtaposition of his presence with the ordinary reality of Terra. It was not a pleasant mission, though Nonomine recognised that it signified the end of exile. Being asked to enter any time-sphere in the galaxy was an honour, of course. It meant that one was considered tough, and the benefits for advancement that went along with immersion in time were enormous.

The messenger was of the female principle and, having had only the wind for companionship during his stay here, Nonomine displayed his ardour fully in unmistakable fashion and was granted an immediate merger. The two essences came together and it was only in that quick union that all the lonely sadness of his sojourn on the crystal planet struck him and he realized that, yes, there was vengeance in the condition of exile, even if his judges had provided sweet balm at the moment they had revealed the full severity of their verdict. There was a surge of angry rebellion in him and consequently in her. But the messenger's vast oceanic passivity absorbed even that and finally allowed both of them the full bliss of ethereal union in a state of advanced purity.

When they separated, his exile already lay far behind him. In the absence of time it was action and thought that determined any condition of living and gradually his thought now turned to Terra, where he was bound. The messenger informed him of certain hazards of entry into the world of Terra. It had been decided to introduce him as a fully-grown Terran rather than as a baby; and for this purpose a human-like body had been created and placed ready, a receptacle which Nonomine might enter at the right harmony of conditions. Soon.

The two adjoined each other on the crystal planet as she told Nonomine about Terra.

She communicated to him that time and money were the two elements that governed Terra. The third was names. He would need a name and one would be given to him. During the initial period of orientation he should allow his mind to be impregnated with impressions, take in the seed of human words and ideas and do nothing to disturb them in their fold. For a while of time in that place, there, Nonomine would be a container, a receptacle. Then he would bring forth his own ideas. That would be the second stage. In the third stage he would put these ideas into action in their world. Much of his power would be set aside but enough would remain. Finally, the councillors would occupy themselves directly with his work and make the decisions necessary to complete it.

Then she passed on to him details about human beings.

Their bodies were adaptable in a very limited way. They were heavy, muscular, slow. They yielded certain minimal pleasures. They were easily damaged, expensive to repair. What was called money was held in high regard on Terra and it would be necessary for him to obtain money as part of the learning process. It would not be difficult to get money, but certain difficulties would arise out of having it.

Usually those on Terra who had money had no time, and those who had time had no money. To have both time and money was a considerable accomplishment which made Terrans envious, often to the point where they would plot to steal either, or both, or even a body's life.

Nonomine began to realize that being sent to Terra was much more unpleasant than the exile behind him. It did not especially impress him that apparently this was done not exclusively for his own good but that his presence there was meant to accomplish something for the Terrans. As he absorbed the messenger's thoughts he began to see himself in the lighter, higher harmonies of his galactic home which he might see again if he acquitted himself well of his tasks on Terra. He began to shape that characteristic warbling whistle, that acoustic giggle which was heard in all the friendly conversations where he came from. The messenger stopped transmitting. She had heard this before. Nonomine was homesick, and so she warbled back at him. They trilled and whistled in their spatial giggle. They lingered there, two beautiful wavering shapes of light, on the rainbow crystal planet, jabbering, gossiping, whispering, tumbling into and out of new energies within themselves, refreshing familiar stories. They were brother and sister. They were one.

Even before she saw that she had provided the service and rendered the message with which she had been entrusted, Nonomine felt the first stirring of the gale and he indicated this to her. In the distance, where purple hues suffused the turquoise moonlight, the crystal plain glared in sudden flashes of ice and the vapours became sheets sent crashing to the ground before the approaching storm. The messenger's shape contracted. Nonomine told her to leave now. He, too, would have to leave.

Facing the approaching gale, feeling now for the first time the ferocious impact of freezing ether on his near-corporeal self - not now willing to let himself disintegrate - he turned and spun his thoughts toward Terra. He was no longer in exile. And so his mind drew him away through the chill of the crystal gale, into the chill of the great galactic deserts, through the spaces that his fine body would feel empty and forbidding, toward his destination on Terra, toward the human body of a Terran. That, too, so the messenger had informed him, was warm. But it could easily be chilled. Nor was it fine enough to abandon itself to cold or heat and reintegrate to function as itself.

A Terran, she had warbled with delight, would melt on the crystal planet. Melt or freeze, never to feel warmth again.

As his mind spun Nonomine toward Earth a picture grew before him, an ineradicable imprint. It showed two creatures unfamiliar to him, resting side by side on what he perceived but did not interpret as sun-dappled grass in a peaceful forest clearing. It was a pictorial imprint, a transitional image of a lion and a lamb. It was clear to him that the lion would not hurt the lamb.

2

CRASH

Theoretically speaking, it should have been no great news media sensation for an aeroplane to crash in the Swiss Alps. The mountains were very high and the weather sometimes very bad. This was usually compensated for by the pilots, who were very experienced. Still, the crash that occurred in the Valais region, up on the granite flanks of the Durstli Massif, stirred up more public and private excitement than even the crashing of a Norwegian charter plane there four years ago. The aircraft had gone off course, carrying some ninety-seven Scandinavian sun-seekers not to Spain but to icy death in the eternal snows of a mountain chain just north of the Durstli. So now, again, the Deadly Durstli, as the English-language papers on the continent had begun to call it, was in the news.

There were a number of circumstances surrounding the crash which did not smoothly fit into the pattern that is routine for such events. For one thing, what looked like a news blackout was immediately suspected by the more alert among the newsmen covering the event. Between the time of the crash sometime after midnight on a Monday morning in early March and the first eye-witness accounts, almost twenty-four hours elapsed. While the wire services had relied on stringers in such places as Geneva, Lausanne and Montreux, it quickly became evident that these men did not produce satisfactory news.

All the routine questions remained unanswered. For example: What type of plane had crashed? How many people had been aboard? Where did they come from? Where were they going? Were there any survivors? How many injured? Where precisely had the wreckage been located? What had been the cause of the crash? Perhaps the most significant detail that developed was that the local police of Durstlimas, Switzerland, not only blocked all pertinent inquiry, but by midmorning the Durstli Pass was occupied by armed troops and traffic to Italy re-routed through neighboring passes. It seemed that even if a determined man, relying on what scant information could be squeezed out of the locals, had set out to find the wreckage himself, he would have run into mountain troops equally determined to stop him.

When an eyewitness was produced, he turned out to be a member of the Ski Guard, a young man with a familiar, weather-beaten face and intelligent, not to say cunning, eyes and his story was extremely suspicious to say the least. According to him, he had been camping out, had been awakened in the clear, starry night by a tremendous crash and thunderous explosion nearby and had immediately set out to investigate. On the Swiss side of the Durstli, at an altitude of more than 13,000 feet, he found that a plane had crashed in the small mountain community of Morgendurst, Valais, a jumble of ancient buildings that clung precariously to the rock folds of the great massif.

According to this witness, the airplane had hit the Durstli at an angle, slid sideways and down through the snowy plateau directly into the village. It had sideswiped a number of sheds and ended up squarely in a building that served simultaneously as the Morgendurst post office and local branch of the Schweizer Bankverein, the Society of Swiss Banks. Of course, at that hour of the morning the bank had been closed and apparently there had been no survivors on the plane.

The story was badly garbled and unconvincing. In desperation, the cynical newsmen were obliged to turn for news to the police, who had provided what was supposed to pass for a lucid information sheet on the crash. Every reporter now rewrote this according to his imagination and using his favourite "facts" as provided on the sheet. The result was a disturbing variety of reports - so disturbing, in fact, that at least one paper, the *Inter-Europe News* out of Paris, decided to send one of their better men, a certain Patrick Young, to look into this mystery. Young flew to Geneva, and from there took the train which carried him with Swiss punctuality and efficiency in just a little under three hours and thirty minutes to Durstlimas.

Young was late, of course, too late for a scoop. His colleagues in various ways had given up and were in the process of turning into regular clients of the local bars and restaurants, especially a place called the Trocadero. Young, who had a minor reputation for a certain flair and ability with the ladies, was greeted with a great deal of friendly derision. He spent a couple of hours exposing himself to facts and fancy. He read the police sheet he was given, shaking his head and grinning. He drank two more beers, checked into the Hotel de la Poste, took a shower and promptly fell asleep. When he woke it was late in the afternoon. He splashed his face with cold water, unnecessarily combed his curly red hair, and decided to go and talk to the postmaster.

Young had had some experience with mountain folk. He'd spent a little time around ski lifts and ski lodges and he figured that since the plane had demolished the Morgendurst post office, the postmaster of Durstlimas, from where all mail was expedited up to Morgendurst, might have a little bit of the inside track on this situation. In this excellent hunch he turned out to be dead right.

The postmaster of Durstlimas, a squirrel-faced little man named Antoine Delacroix, indeed had the inside track on the matter, but he had been securely briefed not only by his friend, the local Chief of Police who also doubled as first lieutenant and one third of the entire police force (not counting a secretary and switchboard operator), but by two gentlemen from the Swiss National Security Police. Mountain troops were stationed in Durstlimas and more had arrived during the day following the crash and when Patrick Young, in his best Swiss-German, inquired as to the true cause of all this commotion, Antoine Delacroix's reply was significant more for what it did not contain than for what it did.

Antoine said that it would do no good to pry into this accident. It was, well, just an unlucky thing and the world should forget about it and not stir it up.

Young emphasized that he wanted nothing less than to stir up whatever "it" was, but he had a professional obligation to get all the facts as they could be ascertained. Delacroix looked up at the gangly reporter and shook his head, saying that sometimes, by the cross we must all bear, there simply were no facts or, worse, that the facts did not properly fit the world and were too confusing to be passed on to people who would not understand them anyway. This mundane postmaster quickly lost himself in the vaguest double-talk which to Young seemed to border on the mystical. Strange, strange indeed! It was another accident, one of a minor sort, which finally saved Young's reputation as a go-getter. On the way out of the little post office, deep in thought, employing his usual wobbly gait designed to consume lots of ground at a leisurely pace, he walked into and over a dumpy woman on a bicycle. As she slid and fell, he was by her side instantly, helping her up, brushing her clothes, offering his sincerest apologies.

The woman, smiling and unhurt, even slightly amused by his embarrassment, turned out to be the postmaster's wife and Young had enough presence of mind to comfort her with a well-formulated question along the lines of what the hell was going on up there in Morgendurst?

"Well," she informed him, blushing just a little, "I don't know what the men are up to this time - it's carnival time, you know - but this is silly enough. There is no town of Morgendurst, certainly there is no post office up there. Some years ago there was a plan to develop that high plateau for especially daring ski tourists and it was called Morgendurst and some of us down here called it "Gelddurst" (thirst for money) but nothing ever came of that, you can be sure. If there is a whole town there now it was built last night, but there isn't, I know! Everybody else who lives here knows it, too. Just that this is the story they're passing out for the reporters."

Patrick Young smiled a genuine smile of gratitude and ambled right on over to the police station, which was very busy. The Chief of Police gave him three minutes, only to tell him that the fact sheet would be updated in the morning, that a search and rescue party had reached Morgendurst and that by noon tomorrow it might even be possible to ferry some of the newsmen up there to take a look around for themselves.

Young trusted the Chief as little as he had trusted Delacroix and as soon as there was a pause in the official's slightly breathless delivery, he calmly inserted that he knew for a fact there was no town of Morgendurst, never had been. Yes, there'd been a project once, some sort of ski development, which had fallen through. Now there was nothing up there, no more than a name, anyway. No post office, either. And so, even if there had been a plane crash in that area, the wreckage could not have slid into the post office, so at least that part of the fact sheet was fantasy. Could it be, he inquired, that the young Ski Guard had suffered from exposure, or taken a fall, and that there had been no plane crash at all?

The Chief of Police blushed but made a swift recovery, taking the reporter by an elbow and leading him directly into a room where the two men from the Swiss National Security Police sat grouped around a small, colourless desk that was full of tiny wormholes. One of them was on the telephone. He seemed to be confirming that he had understood certain instructions. Then he hung up. Both these men looked exceedingly dull and very efficient. The Police Chief told them that this man, Patrick Young, a reporter for *Inter-Europe News*, was questioning the existence of the town of Morgendurst and in fact the entire official version of the plane crash. Having said this, the Chief left just slowly enough to avoid the suspicion of flight. Young was left behind with the two dull-looking gentlemen.

One of them asked him for his credentials and Young showed them. They nodded. They told him that this entire affair was difficult, no, unprecedented, and contained the seeds of great embarrassment, even international embarrassment and, therefore, he must understand that all they would now tell him would have to be treated with great delicacy and discretion. Did he understand?

Patrick Young, controlling his urge to leap forward and embrace these two sturdy fellows, mumbled his assurances of discretion.

They said, "It will be necessary for you to impose certain limitations on the scope of your reportage in this matter, a certain amount of censorship. If you wish we will talk with your supervisors...."

He said yes, he wished they would but wouldn't it be appropriate to tell him first what was going on? They looked at each other, came close to a unified sigh, and then the one who had been talking on the telephone, after briefly touching his thin moustache, began to, as Patrick later called it, spill the beans.

"There is no town of Morgendurst," he confided, "or rather there wasn't until thirty-six hours ago or so. Now there is. There's a town up there now, including a post office and a branch of Société de Banque Suisse. And precisely - if you can believe this and we allow for your consternation, sir, because we were shocked, too, when we heard this - precisely into this post office bank crashed an airplane." He pointed at a map spread on the table which indicated no town or village whatsoever.

"No, not a jet, Mr Young, no modern jet, not at all. A Pampini. A 1938 twelve-seat Pampini."

Young wished to know, as much to maintain check on his powers of reasoning as to learn more, what a Pampini was.

He was told: "A Pampini, Mr Young, is an Italian airplane of which only six were built and none survived. We have made inquiries with the Italian Museum of the History of Aeronautics in Milan. The Pampini was an impossible bird, an ornamental thing. It never got off the ground. It hopped. Salvatore Pampini spent nine of his last eleven years in jail for fraud, even though his plane became a collector's toy almost immediately. Two of these crazy constructions were wrecked purposely by their owners, the other four attended a reunion of collectors toward the end of World War II and burned down in a fire, probably arson. But the Pampini that flew into the mountain near what was once to be called Morgendurst seems to have been mechanically perfect. Oh, and one other thing - there were no survivors because there were no passengers. No pilot, no navigator, no onboard personnel, not a soul. No one in the new town, either. Those, Mr Young, are the facts and you can understand now why we have tried to guard these facts."

"Yes," said Patrick Young, "because these are no facts at all."

"Precisely," they agreed.

3

ARRIVAL

While it took the Swiss Federal Government almost a week to formulate a plausible position regarding these phenomenal occurrences in the Alps, *Inter-Europe News* profited from their man Young's persistent endeavors. Under Young's by-line, *Inter-Europe News* was allowed, within certain confinements, to leak the true facts of the Morgendurst crash to the world, and the big wire services felt obliged to quote this relatively obscure, sensational paper as gospel in this matter.

In co-operation with the Swiss National Security Police, Young and his editors had worked out a story which allowed as much of the factual background to emerge as was possible without causing immediate danger of a public panic reaction. Patrick Young himself had said to his editor, "I frankly don't give a damn about their panic or anybody else's. What panic are they talking about, anyway? Why should anybody panic? But if this is how they want it, fine, why not? If you ask me, they're braiding the rope with which they're going to hang themselves!"

The story was simply that a very small town, a village called Morgendurst, high up in the Durstli Massif, had been abandoned some years ago because it had become unsafe. Later it was buried under an avalanche, but recent changes in climate, including a particularly mild warm wind, had freed it from snow and so it seemed to have "appeared" overnight. To compound this simple phenomenon, an antique airplane, probably remote-controlled by a still-anonymous Italian collector, a souped-up, rewired '38 Pampini, had flown into the mountainside and slid into the newly surfaced town of Morgendurst, right into the former post office and bank. It was the best they could do and it was mighty fishy, but surprisingly the public accepted it. There was an immediate influx of the idle and the curious into Durstlimas.

By the time the Swiss Government broke the silence to corroborate the *Inter-Europe News* story, newsmen had been taken up to the newly discovered town and given a cautious tour of the premises. Naturally, Patrick Young was at the head of the first batch and, breathing with a little difficulty through his smoker's lungs at this altitude, he made so many notes that his wrist hurt. Some of these were:

People, people, no trace of people! Never were no people here! This is all new! The Pampini! A ghost plane! Propellers, intact! How could that be after such a crash! Post-office bank interior doesn't fit! Looks like U.S. desert outpost bank interior! Signs in garbled mixture of English-French-German. This is no Swiss bank! In the Pampini again. No radar, no remote-control gear! What a plane! This thing could never have flown!

Exclamation marks covered his note sheet. Back down in the Hotel de la Poste, Patrick Young sat down to file a new report. By this time he had become clearly the leader of the newsmen and they were watching his every move. New facts were arriving every day. Had there been people up in that ghost town, had there been victims, all would have been forgotten, blown over by now. Idly he touched the keys of his Olivetti portable and ran off a line which he read with some surprise. There it said: "*They should have brought in some corpses so we could have all been happy*!" Another exclamation mark.

"*Even a single good body would have done the trick*!" It was not an original thought, he knew, and though the body was provided for him that very afternoon in an almost casual twist of developments, it did not bring the relief he had predicted but intensified the mystery and propelled the crash story to the front pages of even the most reputable publications in the West.

The body was found half a mile southeast of the crash site, almost entirely buried in snow, frozen stiff. It was entirely nude, a well-proportioned young man, certainly an athlete, with medium length blond hair and a face much too handsome to be cast in icy silence forever. Incredibly, within an hour after being pulled from the clutch of the Durstli, the corpse began to show signs of life, its colour changed, it began to breathe. A miracle was being witnessed by all, including a young, pale-faced priest who had been called to save what could be saved, if anything. In a little while the corpse felt sufficiently strong to accept small spoonfuls of hot tea. His cheeks turned pink, his blue eyes regained their lustre and he sat up. A medic, provided free of charge by the platoon sergeant stationed in Durstlimas, thought it better not to press the foundling with questions as to his name, his place of origin or his connection with the crash. Naturally enough, the newsmen now saw an opportunity, each of them, to recover some of the ground they had lost to Patrick Young and the *Inter-Europe News*, and they began to make up a name that would fit the young survivor.

While he recovered under the medic's supervision, they converged on the Trocadero for their daily brainstorming session and went right at it with: the Swiss Snowman, the Durstli Monster, Mr Frozen White, and Mr Yah-Yah, because he had croaked something that sounded like Yah-Yah when they asked him if he wanted hot tea. None of this impressed Patrick Young as particularly serviceable. He had retired to his room and he was thinking. Again! He felt, there is more to this man than meets the eye! That young man should not have survived! Not a scratch on him. Almost four days in the snow and ice, it should have killed him certainly! Then at last Patrick Young had to confess to himself, in the privacy of his little chamber at the Hotel de la Poste, that his clumsy colleagues at the Trocadero might indeed be right concerning at least one point: namely, that if there were an explanation to any of this, it would have to be sought in the realm of the supernatural.

4

ORANGE

It was Patrick Young who came up with a name that stuck for the good-looking young foundling. There had been a change in the nurses who had been brought up to Durstlimas to help supervise his recovery, and a new nurse named Emma was introduced to the patient. She walked through the door, her hand flew to her mouth, her eyes stared and she exclaimed, "*Schön*!" Young was there to record the event and provide the Anglo-American equivalent: Shawn. For poor nurse Emma, the first word, Beautiful!, was more than ominous. She fell head over heels in love with the foundling and a few days later became the first babbling convert to a new cult of love at whose centre Shawn pontificated with the innocence of all true saints and leaders of men.

For now the only apparent survivor of the Durstli crash sat up in his bed, dressed in white hospital linen, devouring enormous amounts of food: yoghurt, *Müsli*, potatoes, meat, bread, eggs - whatever was put before him. The public, as represented by newsmen from many parts of Europe, was cautiously admitted to his room but only Patrick Young had been granted a privileged station. That Shawn had indeed been aboard the antique Pampini, that he had actually piloted it, was now no longer doubted by anyone.

With this in mind, the buzzing host of investigative reporters and photographers whenever admitted, threw a hundred questions at the patient, who smiled and flexed the smooth musculature of his pectorals but said little or nothing. In fact, it could not be ascertained what language he spoke. What little he uttered was certainly neither French, German, English, nor Italian, for that matter. Psychiatrists and psychologists who had come up to undo the Gordian Knot of Shawn's psyche left considerably less confident than they had arrived. It seemed that he not only suffered from amnesia but was also illiterate, which compounded the case.

Surprisingly and encouragingly, it was English to which Shawn took most easily and Patrick Young immediately developed a primitive system of communication so that, in a week, Shawn mastered basic English, especially the words: "food", "drink", "sleep", "light", "air". However, long before the words "love" or "sex" had been imparted to him, an incident occurred which showed that he was indeed more a man of action than of words.

The nurse, Emma, was found running stark naked through the pre-dawn cold of Durstlimas, raving and screaming. She was taken back to the hospital and sedated, then she told the following story: "I went in for the three o'clock check up. The boy was awake. He smiled at me. I smiled back at him. You know how he is, when he smiles you smile too. I went over to his bed to take his temperature, but instead he took my hand and my own temperature went up very fast. I felt hot and red in the face. I don't know what he did, but when he touched me I could not control myself. I tore off my clothes. I slipped into bed with him. He put his arm around me and I showed him how to make love to me. I think he has never made love to anyone. After that I remember nothing."

Asked if she was afraid of him, she said, "Afraid? Why should I be afraid of the man I love? I'm proud that I went to him. I want to love him always. I want to be his wife. I want to be anything to be with him. He showed me the meaning of the word 'love', and I will never forget it."

Despite this testimonial there was an abbreviated court hearing at the police station, but nothing came of it. Shawn didn't seem to understand. Having been sufficiently stabilised to be allowed out of bed, he moved cautiously in his environment, communicating often through Patrick, who was getting to know him better than anyone else.

By this time, some two weeks after the crash, efforts were being made to bring the wreckage of the Pampini down the mountainside, but what would become of the newly sprouted town of Morgendurst remained uncertain. The mayor of Durstlimas suggested it might be made into a tourist attraction, which it was fast becoming anyway. The mysterious tone which had crept into all communications about the crash had attracted not only the idle and the curious but professional space freaks and psychic investigators, who smelled in the

Durstli incident the most important parapsychological development in modern history. It was this particular angle which finally brought the U.S. into the fray at full speed.

The President of the American Society for the Investigation of Extraterrestrial Phenomena, Inc. (ASIEP), Mr Jack Baldwin, arrived with a staff of three and announced that he would set up a permanent base camp where all evidence coming off the Durstli mountainside could be examined and evaluated firsthand. It was his opinion, presented in no uncertain terms, that: "We have here a mystery that tends in the direction of our particular field of interest and we'll do our best to find out what's behind this thing. That is what we are here for!"

There seemed to be nothing extra-worldly about the foundling himself. He had been outfitted with colourful ski clothes, striking red pants, a sky-blue shirt, a quilted yellow jacket and imitation sealskin après-ski boots. At first glance he could easily pass for one of those young daredevil ski instructors who catered wholesale to stout German tourist ladies and their even stouter husbands. In fact he looked so striking in his outfit, so much the part, that the first commercial offer wasn't long in coming.

A Monsieur Francois Clivaz who represented an outfit named Zip-Ski of Geneva managed to communicate rather easily with Shawn that he would need a little pocket money to get around and that he, Francois Clivaz, was empowered to offer him the sum of 10,000 Swiss francs in return for participating in a photographic session on the slopes and the results would soon grace all the good picture papers and magazines of Switzerland and France.

It was through the catalytic offer of Monsieur Clivaz that the relationship between Shawn and Patrick Young took a turn toward business. Shawn asked Young, still mainly through sign language, what all this meant and Young was quick to instruct him that it meant money and that money was good. There and then, Monsieur Clivaz handed a fine gold-embossed pen to Shawn, which the latter took much as a big ape would, though he handled it with greater delicacy. In fact, there was something in the young man's face which transcended his apparent unfamiliarity with the alphabet, something so intense, so quick, so slickly instinctive that it had a frightening dimension.

Shawn looked terribly intelligent. Along with this impression went a habit of losing himself in thought, of appearing at least to be so totally absent-minded that one did not like to disturb him, fearing some sort of unknown and unpredictable shock. Still, whenever he was called or addressed, he responded instantly, as if his thoughts had never been "away." And so, while he absently held the pen, he let Patrick Young guide his hand to the preliminary contract drawn up for them on Zip-Ski stationery, and with just the slightest hesitation he appended an "X" to indicate his approval. Young himself signed in witness of the authenticity of this signature.

The next day the Zip-Ski photo team arrived, led by a slim young Frenchman and a young woman with wavy brown hair who immediately fell in love with Shawn as soon as she aimed her lens. Her condition did not become apparent until later when she appeared in the Trocadero around midnight, totally nude and wandered from table to table among the newsmen, apparently unaware of her appearance, to their great delight. She, too, was taken to the hospital, sedated, and told pretty much the same story as Emma the nurse had, though her language was more refined, especially when it came to describing Shawn's emotional impact on her.

She said, "I am a liberated woman and I consider myself independent in matters of love and sex. Naturally, I was curious to see who this wild man of the mountain was who had so miraculously survived an awful plane crash. I expected to find him incapacitated in some way, of course, but he is extremely healthy, I assure you. Still, in view of my conduct in the Trocadero bar, it must be understood that it was I who was the aggressor. Beautiful Shawn did nothing - not at first, that is. It was I who tore off my clothes, I who attacked him. I did not know - I could not help myself. Something came over me. Do you understand? His eyes are hypnotic, his voice is a velvet rope with which he binds his victims. No, I take back that word. I was not a victim. Does a victim dissolve in tears of ecstasy? Does a victim beg for more and more and is given more and more? No, I was no victim. Shawn liberated me. I love him as fire loves the flame. Without him I am nothing, I am ashes. He can do with me as he pleases."

When Patrick Young cautiously informed her that she was not alone with her attitude and introduced Emma to her, the beautiful young photographer said, "Emma and I know each other through love for this man. There can be no jealousy between us. In this we are one, are we not, Emma?" And Emma nodded and began to weep.

Her photographs were magnificent. Shawn was a natural

subject. Tall, slim-waisted, broad-shouldered, with the reflexes of a cat. And if all this tended to stereotype him as a nature-boy, the awesome concentration of intelligence in his face, albeit rarely spoken, made it difficult to underestimate him. So he was an illiterate! Tarzan, too, had had some difficulty with the printed word at first.

Patrick Young slowly began to make his influence felt. He pointed out to the various representatives of government, science, medicine and commerce that Shawn was his own man, even though it might take time to determine who this man was or had been. Obviously he had been born somewhere on the globe, obviously there were parents, and with all the publicity around him, his family were bound to step forward soon to identify him. Meanwhile it would be at least courteous, after what he'd been through, to give him a little breathing space. To a question of who he Patrick Young was, he simply replied, "a friend."

It was easy for Young to persuade his editors to give him additional time and expense money to cover the foundling exclusively. This was just the kind of stuff *Inter-Europe News* had thirsted for in vain for years. Every other day now, Young's reports were meted out to an eager public, but Patrick himself was already developing other plans. He had recognized a potential bonanza in the young savage out of the Durstli glacier. The Zip-Ski money was only a beginning, and a modest one at that. There were all kinds of possibilities: books, movies, TV, personal appearances. Shawn had, to say the least, an intriguing personality and he, Patrick, was sitting at the source, so to speak. With this in mind he began to take a greater direct interest in his charge.

It had been decided that Shawn should go to Geneva to the Institut International de Neuropsychologie for a series of tests, so naturally Young accompanied him on the train ride. The reporter had been careful enough to make reservations for an entire compartment. Now he drew the curtains and began to drill, or try to drill, his mystery man, whose English had developed encouragingly, though complex intellectual concepts still gave him some trouble.

Patrick started by explaining to Shawn, in simple terms, that his very existence presented a puzzle to certain people. He pointed out that people liked to know where a man came from, especially once he had been publicised. "Ah," smiled Shawn, "yes, I come from the mountain."

"That's precisely the problem," said Young. "You come from the mountain but you don't come from the mountain as a baby, a little child, you understand? Babies are born on a mountain sometimes, then they are brought down by their mothers to see a doctor, to be baptized, to go to Geneva. But ...."

"Yes," said Shawn, "to Geneva, I go to Geneva."

"So," Young continued, "you are *not* a baby. You are a man. You are a big man. You have lived for at least twenty years. Once you were a baby, yes, certainly. But now you are no longer a baby. This puzzles people."

Shawn said, " A big man does not come from the mountain?" Patrick could not help smiling back at him. "Look," he said, "Did you fly that plane, that Pampini?"

Shawn had been shown the Pampini, had been made to sit in it at the controls. He handled the controls very much like Monsieur Clivaz' pen, thoughtfully, absently, a little foolishly as an ape might have, but with greater delicacy, greater intelligence. He had not, however, handled them as if he had ever operated them before. He had apparently had not the foggiest idea what it was all about.

"On the mountain?" Shawn now asked guilelessly.

Young nodded, "Yes, on the mountain, the plane, you know?" Young began to gesture as if he were at the controls of the Pampini. A conductor entered and asked to see their tickets. Young looked up, frozen in the middle of a particularly vigorous demonstration. He fumbled for the tickets. The conductor thanked him, punched them, returned them to him and exited. Young tried to get back into the spirit of the conversation, but couldn't quite.

"Plane," said Shawn thoughtfully, his sharp eyes unfocused through the window toward the alien landscape.

"Yes, plane!" cried Young jubilantly.

Shawn turned to him. "Show me," he said. "Show me, baby!"

Young hastily began to leaf through the magazines he had bought at the station. He found a diaper ad and held it up. "There," he said, "that's a baby. Cute, isn't it? That's what you looked like once. Now if that's how you had been found on the mountain, then people wouldn't ask so many questions. They'd think you survived because your bones were so soft, and babies often survive disaster when grown-ups don't. Or they'd say that you were dumped by nasty parents and it was a miracle."

Shawn listened, nodded. He seemed to like the idea. He was playing with a pen, holding it stiffly, like a child. He took the magazine with the ad from Young and began to draw something on the body of the baby, marking each line slowly and carefully into the pink, glossy paper. Young watched in amazement as a picture emerged, unmistakably, a lion and a lamb. When it was finished, Shawn handed the magazine back to him, pointing at the lamb, saying, "Baby, baby, yes?"

"Yes, baby sheep," said Young. "Lamb. That's a lamb! And this is a lion. Where did you learn to draw like this?"

So this man had seen a lion! Or at least a picture of a lion. And a lamb. There was something religious about the juxtaposition, wasn't there? Confusing, very confusing ....

The door to their compartment was pulled open, admitting a short, fat, sweaty man who dabbed his face with a yellow handkerchief. He looked quickly from Shawn to Patrick, and with a sigh let himself fall into the upholstery. Young informed him that all the seats in this compartment were reserved. The sweaty visitor was unimpressed. He handed a calling card to Young, who examined it. It was an expensive card in silver and black lettering. It said *Jan van Schmul Enterprises, Jan van Schmul, Directeur*. "I am Jan van Schmul," said the fat man, "and this is the young man who was found on the Durstli?"

Patrick Young nodded.

"In that case I shall speak directly to him."

He talked rapidly, first in German, then in French, and when neither of these languages had the desired effect he tried his English, which was less accomplished. For a short while Shawn stared back at the intruder with some amusement but then, slowly, he turned, his eyes slid away to the landscape which was broadening to receive the great Lake *Léman*. His face bore again that absent expression. Already he missed the crystal planet and the sister who had come to sweeten the bitter drink of his ordeal. He felt heavy and lost.

"Pardon me, monsieur," said van Schmul now to Young, "but your friend does not listen. Could you help?"

"Be glad to," said Young, "if I can. But you must tell me what you want from him."

"Very simple, I want a contract. I want to make him rich and famous. I want to manage him. He is interesting. I know I can make plenty money for him, good-looking boy like him, you understand?

You speak French?"

Young told him that he preferred English to French, and that Shawn did not need a manager at this time, thank you.

The fat man gave no sign of taking the hint. He sat squarely on the first-class upholstery, looking breathlessly from the unconcerned Shawn to the friendly, adamant Patrick and back again to Shawn. Sweat was running freely down his face but he did not bother to wipe it with his handkerchief. Instead he produced a large orange from a bulging pocket. He displayed it on the palm of his hand.

"Nice orange, isn't it?" he said. Young shrugged. Shawn continued looking out of the window.

"Peels good, too," said the fat man. As he began to peel the orange he slid back into the far corner of the compartment by the door, sweating and grinning at the same time.

What emerged was not the interior pulp of an orange but the bumpy, jagged metal of a hand grenade. Van Schmul held it up and shook off the last of the orange peels. He expertly crooked one thumb into the ring.

"No move," he said, almost conversationally.

With the free hand he disengaged the door and pushed it open a bit. Then he pulled a sheet from the inside breast pocket and extended it toward Young, who caught it.

"A contract," said van Schmul. "You will sign, both. Or you will both blow up now!"

Young stared, hypnotised. Even Shawn had turned his gaze back into the compartment, looking at the orange peels, the contract in Young's hand, the hand grenade in van Schmul's.

"Yes," said van Schmul, "good wood and metal in this train, Swiss made. I will go out now and watch the signing. If not I will throw the grenade."

He got up and stepped into the corridor, keeping the hand grenade low, ready to pull the pin.

Shawn was about to get up, but Young leaned forward and restrained him. "No, Shawn, don't! Let me explain."

He began to try to explain the situation. It was difficult. Shawn didn't understand, or pretended not to understand. Perhaps the elementary concept of death was foreign to him. Total amnesia sometimes produced even such a phenomenon. Young struggled in vain, talking simultaneously to Shawn and to van Schmul.

"Look, van Schmul, he doesn't understand me, so put away that silly thing ...."

"Orange," reminded van Schmul.

".... yes, whatever you like, orange, grenade, we can come to some understanding. I'll get him to sign the paper but first he has to understand ...."

"Now," said van Schmul. "He has the pen. He signs now."

Shawn irresistibly got up. Young flung himself forward at van Schmul. Van Schmul pulled the ring and tossed the grenade. Shawn caught it with the grace of a cat pawing at a ball of wool.

"No!" screamed Young, pulling himself up, going for the window. Van Schmul had pulled and thrown. He could get .... to .... the window .... and .... not enough ... time ....!

Shawn stood with a careless smile, weighing the grenade in his hand, paying no attention to Young's frantic efforts. He held the thing cupped like a ball of dough, rolling it from one hand into the other playfully. Then, as it exploded, as indeed it meant to explode, his hands clamped shut over it. There was no strain. The explosion was caught at the moment of its inception but just far enough into itself to allow the phenomenon of sound to occur. The tearing, bursting thunder shook the compartment but Shawn's hands remained firmly clasped.

Young, by the half-open window, his shoulders drawn up in the reflex of expecting deadly metal, turned. Now the man who had crashed in an unflyable airplane slowly opened his hands. Young winced - there should be nothing but stumps. Yes, blood dripped, he saw. Still, it was a miracle that only blood dripped, not gushed, that they were both standing there, Young staring at Shawn's hands. It was not blood that dripped, but juice - from Florida, from Spain? There was no trace of metal, no trace of death.

"Orange?" the miracle man smiled. "Grenade?"

5

BABY

Van Schmul was found cowering in the toilet by the two National Security Policemen travelling discreetly on the train. He was handcuffed to the bars provided for steadying travellers on the toilet seat if the ride got bumpy, which it rarely ever did in these well-made carriages on these carefully maintained tracks.

When one of the security men returned to the compartment to find out what had happened, Patrick was still straightening his tie and jacket. A neat pile of fragmented metal was heaped on the baby picture with Shawn's drawing of a lion and a lamb. Mixed in with the grenade fragments was the dripping mush of an orange. Shawn playfully held up his hands, which he had carelessly dried on his après-ski outfit. Patrick slowly began to explain what had happened. The officer was speechless, fondling the bomb fragments, still hot, inspecting Shawn's hands that showed no marks, let alone wounds. Finally, he shook his head, shrugged his shoulders, would not understand, could not believe.

After a long tortured pantomime expressing conflicting emotions the security man finally said, "Under the circumstances, Mr. Young, I would advise you to apply for a permit to carry arms. I shall try to find out who this man is and in Geneva you will be required to repeat your statement to a stenographer. It looks like a hysterical act to me, nothing organised."

He tossed a piece of the grenade hard up and down in his palm, shaking his head. "It seems," he said to Shawn, "that you stir up strong emotions in people. I'm no psychologist but why would a man want to kill you like this? Did you know this man?"

Shawn looked at the security officer with a look of innocent surprise. "Know? The man?"

"Yes," said the security man. "A man just tried to kill you, *that* man. Did you know him?"

"No," said Shawn, "no know, I do not."

The security man nodded as if what Shawn said confirmed his own speculation. He pointed out, still puzzled by the pile of grenade splinters, that while Shawn's nationality remained undetermined, and he would be issued a temporary identification card, his safety remained the concern of the Swiss authorities while he was on Swiss territory. No unnecessary chances could be taken from now on and, therefore, he was sure they would appreciate and understand why he himself would stay with them, at least until suitable lodgings could be found, perhaps on the premises at the Neuropsychological Institute.

Thirty minutes later they arrived in Geneva, and the fat man was immediately taken to an office of the Bahnhofspolizei for his version of the story. He kept repeating in German that he did not believe, averting his eyes from Shawn with signs of extreme fear. His eyelids fluttering, his brow perspiring, his hands trembling, he babbled hysterically that it was a case of mistaken identity.

Shawn, in his rapidly improving English, showed great unconcern with the incident. "Grenade can't kill me," he said. "I kill it first."

He was asked to explain, with Patrick's coaxing, how that could be. He did his best. He was well protected he said, he was here to do work. He was asked what kind of work, how long it would take to do this work.

"I do not know," he said. "I show the lion and the lamb, I will teach how not to use what I have."

He was asked again and again where he came from. With that disarmingly intelligent smile of his, he pointed up. The mountain? No, much higher. The sky? What was sky? Sky was what was above the mountain, above everything, higher than anything on earth.

"Yes," he told them, "the sky!"

But he pointed down, too, which was confusing. Was he trying to say that he came out of the earth? He said, "No, higher!" No doubt he meant deeper. "Yes, deeper than the earth, sky!" he smiled. "Sky, the highest. I come from the highest to show you why the lion does not kill the lamb."

These were intriguing and mysterious words, much puzzled over. They had the ring of Eastern mysticism, a touch of Zen, a bit of the sufi parable, but the man who distributed them so casually had just smothered an exploding hand grenade with his bare hands and apparently, in the process, produced the flesh of an orange which had not been there. That was the fabulous stuff of living legends.

The reporters had what they wanted - a perfect human specimen who claimed that he had descended from the sky to do work on earth. A human being stronger than an exploding hand grenade. Strong enough that days in glacial snows had not damaged his body. Now some of them began to accuse Patrick Young, their colleague, of foul play. In their revised scenario, van Schmul became a hired stooge and the grenade pieces, which were now being tested at a government laboratory, were part of a dummy prepared for just this occasion. Shawn himself had been planted on the mountain for publicity purposes, and the whole thing was a hoax through and through.

Young tried to explain to them that, in many ways he himself would prefer a hoax to the reality. He had come close to being killed by a maniac on the train and no one could tell what lay ahead. In any case, where was the profit?

"So far" he said, "I haven't made a penny off this man. I've been helping him get around, that's all. He seems to be suffering from amnesia, and the tests he will undergo at the Neuropsychological Institute are designed to uncover the roots of this problem. I'm no expert but I've been told that delusions of mysterious origin often go along with symptoms of total amnesia. I wish someone would recognize him - his parents, his relatives, some friend or girlfriend. We're trying to keep girls away from him as much as possible after what happened up in Durstlimas."

Young should have known better. His colleagues no longer felt the slightest loyalty toward him. The latest stories on the foundling included allusions to the peculiar sexual magnetism he exuded, which was so powerful that he had now been placed in isolation to prevent pathological rituals of seduction such as had taken place in Durstlimas. The foundling Shawn was quickly turning into a public embarrassment and the moment could not be far off when his case would be brought to the floor of the Swiss National Assembly. And then, when that happened, unquestionably someone or some group of politicians would demand his ousting from Switzerland unless he could present proof of Swiss citizenship. Young tried to explain the situation to Shawn. Shawn seemed to understand but was unconcerned. He was taking a bath in a hotel near the Institut International de Neuropsychologie. He had got hold of some bubble bath lotion and was having a great time in the tub.

"Nowadays," Patrick told him, "there is no-one with a history like yours. People don't just drop from the sky and walk into the world as you did. And it won't do you any good to tell them you come from outer space."

"Outer space," bubbled Shawn, "where is this, outer space?" Patrick told him that sky and outer space were the same, more or less. It meant far away, very far away. But people liked other people to come from close by. They didn't like anything that was too strange. Then he had to explain what strange meant.

Shawn showed a surprisingly immediate grasp of this new term, telling Patrick that it could not be strange to come from far away. It was strange that people thought far away strange. Here, right here where they were now, that was strange, he said. Right here was far away, too. This was, what? Outer space? Outer space was everywhere!

Young lost his patience. He told Shawn that he preferred to think of him as a human being, since he looked like one and acted like one. Shawn nodded and got lost in the bubbles, playing like a child.

Young called his editor. His editor was an alcoholic by the name of Kirkley Evans who hated Paris but nevertheless was stationed there. Evans hated Young as well, for no particular reason, but if one had to be found he could easily start with Young's red hair and washed-out-looking skin. Evans' skin was even uglier than Young's. It was pockmarked and dry, despite his heavy drinking. Because of all this, Evans had become mean. But because Young had been providing sensational news which was bringing in money he held himself back, at least for a minute. He said, "Young, you have news, really new news?"

Young told him that he was quitting. Evans told him to stop joking.

Young said, "I'm sending out my last two thousand words of copy on Shawn and you know what you can do with it!"

"Your contract calls for one month's notice," Evans said. "If you break your contract, we keep the money, vacation pay, accumulated insurance, everything." Young told him that he sounded as if he owned the paper. Evans told him to bug off.

Then Coalwaller came on the line. Coalwaller, nominally, was publisher of *Inter-Europe News* and he loved Paris. So even if the

Head Office was in London, Coalwaller was always in Paris, looking in on things. Like many common men, he affected cultured tones. His language was shot through with cliches.

"Now, my dear boy," he said sweetly, "what is all this talk of abandoning ship? Just now when the old gusher is gushing, eh? Oh, look now, let bygones be bygones, I've been meaning to talk to you about a raise in any case. I feel there should be a little more of the good stuff down there in the boiler room, ha-ha, or whatever you call it, a little bonus. How does an extra hundred pounds strike you, my boy?"

Momentarily off balance, Patrick conceded that, yes, a hundred pounds a week more would be considerable. The connection was so good that he could hear Coalwaller swallow. What it meant was that Coalwaller had swallowed his pride and his greed. Coalwaller did not point out that he had meant a month, not a week. Slowly their conversation deteriorated. Patrick began to realize that actually he was not that determined to quit. He was getting tired of Shawn. He felt like a babysitter for a giant baby. "Very well, then," he finally said to his employer, "I'll call you."

When Young got off the phone, his charge was unabashedly towelling off in plain view. Young was not particularly interested in the male anatomy, but the foundling was built like Michelangelo's David. Patrick could not take his eyes off this perfect creation. Shawn made a diaper out of the towel. "Baby," he said, "cute baby." The telephone rang and Shawn picked it up. He was still saying "Baby, baby," then he hung up. Turning to Patrick he said, "We need money."

Patrick told him that he agreed and asked how would they get the money. Shawn said, "Baby will make the money."

As if on cue, there was a determined little knock on the door, Shawn opened it and Suzanne, the Zip-Ski photographer, came in. She was instantly transfixed by the picture of the nude foundling.

"Money," said Shawn, "Suzanne and I will make money together."

A blissful, distant expression had come over Suzanne's face. She was beginning to unzip her clothes, getting out of everything with great speed. Patrick discreetly tried to leave, but Shawn stopped him saying, "Money is important. Time is important. Name is important. I will have money. I will have time. I will have name!"

"Sure," said Patrick Young, "you will have money, you will have time, you will have name, but this girl is out to have you first, so if you'll let me I'll retire and try to start thinking about my career!"

And the man who claimed to have come down from the sky to teach the world about lions and lambs smiled and paid no more attention to his terrestrial friend, Young.

6

BUREAUCRATS

Morris "Mike" Duffinger had become an important man in the United States of America, though his name was not bandied about too loosely in public. He had managed, during his ascent to second-in-command of the newly formed Bureau for Psychic Research and Development, to stay away from unfavourable publicity. He was married, had three - not two or four - children, and he kept his extramarital affairs tightly under wraps. Over him was only one man to whom he was answerable. That man, George Debussy, reported directly to the President. Debussy was at this moment forking some more french fries onto his plate at the Speedy-Mac where they liked to go for fast food and privacy.

"Tell me, Mike," Debussy was saying with his mouth full, "how would you like to hop over there for a week of fun and frolic in Geneva, Switzerland?"

The question didn't surprise Duffinger. For a few days now something had been brewing. His boss had acted strangely. Duffinger's paranoia had made him suspect some kind of shake-up. But Geneva made a lot more sense. Duffinger plucked a piece of hamburger from a newly forming cavity and swallowed it, shuddering. In fact, he'd been wondering when his boss would get around to the mystery man of the Alps.

"Somebody," said Debussy, "ought to take a look at the kid. It's been kind of dull lately in the psychic world, and what with appropriation time coming around in a couple of months we could use something or somebody to pull us through. That kid over there might just be the one."

Debussy poured ketchup liberally over his french fries. Duffinger watched him silently. He knew the boss well enough not to interrupt at this point.

"Probably just some prank, though," said Debussy, savouring a particularly juicy slice. "I mean a kid drops from the skies, goes in the deep freeze, is thawed out, squashes a hand grenade with his bare hands and turns up in the continental porno magazines as a superstud. We've got the lab report on the grenade, though. Totally uncharacteristic. Like nothing they ever saw before. So how would you like to go over there and take a look at this kid? And take some money along. He seems to be looking for a job."

"Well," said Duffinger, "what would we do with him?"

"Do with him? Hell, we'll put him through a little bit of the old mill, give him the acid test. Now that they let Dobzhov out of the bag, I mean what choice do we have? Before Dobzhov we could have just cooled it. We could have just let everybody believe that we've got the big guns, but not no more."

Dobzhov was a middle-aged Russian who hated to shave and whose fingernails were cracked and dirty. For years the Russians kept him out of the news because essentially he was not presentable. But then - who knew what made them change their mind? - they played off their card. They put Dobzhov on public display and agreed to allow a team of Westerners to set up strict laboratory-controlled conditions that ruled out fraud. With all that, Dobzhov levitated for three minutes and thirty-seven seconds. There was no way to get around it, the Russians were ahead in the race for paranormal supremacy.

"Dobzhov! Dobzhov!" Duffinger laughed a little. "So Dobzhov's got you rattled!"

George Debussy burped. He deliberately tried to fart but failed. He was the kind of superior who liked to pretend that he believed in equality. He said, "I don't give a good goddamn about Dobzhov. Dobzhov's just another clown. So he levitates, so what! I've seen guys levitate, remember Olson?

Of course Duffinger remembered Olson.

"Olson could levitate your ass off but his problem was he couldn't do it under pressure," said Debussy. "If you left him alone, if you went in the kitchen and had a cup of coffee, zappo, Olson would levitate and he'd stay up, too, when you came back in. But put him out there with the folks from the rotary presses and he'd levitate like a goddamn lead duck. It's not levitation that gets them. It's *tailor-made* levitation! Dobzhov produces. And we haven't got a single guy who produces like Dobzhov. So this porno kid over there, maybe he wants to join us. Maybe we can get a little mileage out of him."

"Why'd they come out with Dobzhov, anyway?" asked Duffinger, because he knew his boss loved to throw out an occasional tidbit of inside information to impress himself and the world. "I don't know, we had an agreement that they wouldn't," said Debussy. "They broke it. So they owe us one."

For a minute or two the two men sat, finishing their hamburgers and french fries. They drank their coffee then, Duffinger with cream and lots of sugar, piling the little sugar bags into a soggy ashtray, and Debussy black and bitter as it came from the urn.

"What about Martino?" Duffinger wanted to know.

"Goddamn spaghetti-eater," said Debussy. "He don't produce, neither. The telepathic messages Martino receives you can pick out of a garbage can. Listen, Martino is so dumb he starts every sentence with: 'I see - I see a burly, heavy-set man behind a big oak desk under a portrait of another burly, heavy set man. He's an important man. He is not a good man. I see a lot of tears. I see a lot of blood. I see a flag.' He'll go on like that. You spend a day with Martino and when he finally comes out with it, it's Stalin he's seeing all this time. Stalin! He lives in the *past*, Martino. Jeezus! They're gonna have to justify our expenses. With who? With Martino? Yeah!"

George Debussy liked to paint all situations a shade of grey. It made it easier all around. In fact, the Bureau for Psychic Research and Development was well and solidly funded. There would be no problem with appropriations, not even for special projects, which was where all the money lay. If there was a problem, it was with thinking up special projects. George Debussy was a bachelor. His sexual preferences were well known on the inside; he liked boys. It had not always been easy to tolerate George's tastes, but he was a reliable company man and, within the limitations imposed on him by necessity, he was brilliant. In fact, without Debussy there would be no BPRD.

George Debussy had come to Psychic Research in a roundabout way. During the late sixties, when parapsychology began to make a comeback in the U.S., he was wasting away in a minor post in the Department of Justice. But he took books home. He read up on Edgar Cayce, the Sleeping Prophet. He delved into Lobsang Rampa's colourful yarns of mystical adventure. He acquainted himself with the many journeys of Carlos Castaneda. In desperation he smoked a little marijuana, took a little LSD, and then one day, as he himself was fond of saying - zappo - it all came together.

He was not surprised to find that an organization such as he proposed already existed in fragmentary form. But it had no direction, no thrust, an uncertain future. He laboured for months, many, many nights, until finally a detailed proposal of almost ninety pages was ready for presentation. It made his reputation and landed him the job of director. And it was turning into George Debussy's life's work.

There were still the boys, of course. But if once this aberration had threatened to ruin his career, he now found himself genuinely enthusiastic about his job, not so reckless, taking fewer chances. George paid well for his pleasure. He had a reliable network of minor scouts who kept their ears and eyes open for new prospects. The young men were carefully screened.

"Don't react now," Debussy said to Duffinger, "but you notice that character over there, the hippie type, the one with the earring, filthy beard and the scar?"

Duffinger lifted up his cup and nodded.

"Well, how come he's always here when we're here?" Debussy whined. "Have you noticed?"

"No," said Duffinger. "I haven't."

"It doesn't take one hell of a lot of goddamn ESP to notice a character like that, Mike. Jeez, sometimes I wonder what a guy like you is doing in the Bureau. *You're* supposed to be the expert on psychic phenomena. Now take a good look at that guy, tell me, isn't he a suspicious-looking individual? Tell me, is he or isn't he?"

"He sure is, sir," Duffinger said quickly.

"Goddamn hippies," muttered Debussy, "they spoil everything! Now they're coming out with their own psychic magazine, too. *Saucer News*. Holier-than-thou type of people is what they are with their dope and their sex and their saucers. Bunch of goddamn squares is what they are. Eight little green men from outer space floating in a vat at Jackson Airforce Base, that's what they're after, that's what they want to believe in. Ought to throw them in there, too, and keep 'em pickled for posterity. They just want to be different. They're not satisfied to be like everybody else. They don't want to be like you and me, right, Mike?"

"Right, sir," Mike Duffinger said deferentially.

"Anyway, I want you to go over to Geneva and take a look at that kid, and if there's anything to him. I want you to bring him back here for the old red-white-and-blue, and it'll be a feather in your cap if you do."

"Believe me, sir," said Mike Duffinger, "if there's anything at all to him, I'll bring him back here with me."

They got up and started looking for a taxi to take them back to the office.

7

COMMUNISTS

George Debussy's opposite number in the USSR, head of the Psychkultura Section of the Advanced Studies Ministry, Dimitri Nihilev, was looking out over the gloom of Moscow, cursing the central-heating breakdown which had afflicted, again, the brand new Psychkultura Headquarters, to say nothing of the toilet plumbing. In his office it was cold and in the corridor it stank. Still, Nihilev managed to keep his thoughts focused on a man named Slavo Stentorian whom he wanted to send to Geneva to approach the Durstli crash survivor.

I know Slavo, Nihilev was thinking. If I send him to Geneva he will defect. On the other hand, they will not let me go. They think if they let me go, I will defect. They think I will ask for political asylum. What do they know! How would I live? Switzerland is expensive. I don't know anyone there. I might have to go to Washington and tell *them* what I know. And they may know what I know already. The question is simply this: What is my price, and do I dare find out?

He picked up the receiver and dialled a number. When the inter-office connection had been made he asked, in his even, official voice, which sounded gruff and unpleasant, to see Comrade Stentorian. He did not even ask if Comrade Stentorian was in the office. It wasn't necessary. Comrade Stentorian was never in the office, and he always had a perfect alibi. It was no use trying to trap him. Oh, thought Nihilev, you are a clever little fish, my little Slavovich, but one day, one day you are going to bite and then I shall pull you in and put you in my basket and let you gasp for air until you tell me what you've been up to all these years.

Strictly speaking, Nihilev was not old enough to be secure in his position. He had not even served in the Red Army during World War II. He was only forty-nine years old but he tried to make up for this deficiency of age by becoming stout. He ate a great deal of pork and drank beer and even for the standards that prevailed in the Advanced Studies Ministry, he cut his hair uncommonly short which showed his fat neck supporting a cube-shaped head. Dimitri Nihilev looked like a butcher who had come down in the world and was now selling potatoes. But all that was only a facade. Inside that hunk of unattractive flesh lived a clever man. A clever man indeed!

Slavo Stentorian, by contrast, looked like the slim, clever man inside Nihilev. He presented no facade whatever. He had lively brown eyes and a thick, black moustache which gave him something Romanesque in appearance. His gestures, too, were lively and he walked briskly and somewhat insolently into his superior's office, without knocking. Nihilev had long ago devised a strategy of overlooking Stentorian's perpetual breaches of etiquette. He was storing it all up, filing it away for the day of reckoning. It would do no good to catch this little fish with a mouthful of water, he kept thinking. When I hook him it will be with everything!

"That is a nice suit you are wearing," Nihilev began. "Fine cloth, isn't it?"

He reached out and touched Stentorian's sleeve, shaking his head. He said, "Is that made on the glorious looms of the Socialist worker's paradise, Comrade Stentorian?"

As usual Nihilev's voice was heavy with irony, and as usual Stentorian did not swallow the bait.

"Oh," he said casually, "I believe there is a factory in Ulan-Bator well known for the beauty of its girls and if I'm not mistaken that is where the cloth for this suit comes from. I was fortunate, a stroke of luck, Comrade, no more."

"At heart you are a capitalist pig," Nihilev told Stentorian, "and you know it! Don't think I don't know your tastes in music: Benny Goodman, Lionel Hampton, Elton John, all American capitalists, are they not? What is there in those negrified rhythms that our own State Orchestra for Lively Dance Music cannot produce?"

"Elton John is British," Stentorian said calmly, "and Lionel Hampton is a black man in an exploitive capitalist society. He has suffered a lot, but his music has been the cry of the oppressed, the joyous chant of those who struggle for freedom wherever they may be in the world. Benny Goodman? I admit, Benny Goodman is a capitalist pig but he is old now, a blind chicken that long ago by accident discovered the pearl of swing. Just as in our musical ensembles, in our State Orchestras from time to time there is a rotten apple, so in the rotten apple of Western music from time to time there is a clean revolutionary worm that will eat the rotten apple."

"Well," said Dimitri Nihilev, "I have never been able to follow your lofty expositions in the field of music. Many of your views strike me as tendentious and counter-revolutionary but I do not have the time to follow up on this. What I want to talk to you about is something with which we ought to be a little more concerned than we are, I mean the work in this Section. I have been thinking of sending you to Geneva to look at this man who survived that crash, this man who claims to have descended from the sky to teach the world about lions and lambs, what is his name? They call him Shawn, do they?"

"Yes," said Stentorian, "No one seems to know his real name."

"Yes," Nihilev went on, "but I know you, Slavo Slavovich, I know you well. If I send you to Geneva, you will give in to your pig nature and you will defect. Tushhh!" Dimitri Nihilev sealed his lips with his right index finger. "Don't say anything just now, Comrade! Let me tell you what I think. I think you are playing a very dangerous game, Comrade. And you are too young to know just how dangerous the game you are playing is in truth. Do you think that millions of our brothers had to be starved to death in the thirties only so you can defect in Geneva? Do you believe, can you be so naive to believe ...."

There was a gushing hiss from the radiator. A thin stream of filthy hot water leapt forward, over Nihilev's shoulder onto his desk. Nihilev stared as the stream subsided. Now there was another hiss and this time Nihilev threw himself to the side on the floor. The water splashed down where he had been only an instant earlier.

Nihilev jumped up, almost upsetting Stentorian in his chair. He circumvented the gushing fountain, approached the radiator from the left side and turned it off. Again the water subsided. Nihilev walked back to the desk, cautiously dipped a finger in the puddle, brought it to his nose and grimaced.

"Sewerage," he roared, "a brilliant idea right out of the Peoples' Idea Pool, and what a pool, a cesspool of ideas! Why not recycle sewerage into radiators, kill two birds with one stone, what, Comrade Stentorian, why not? And what is the result of this brilliant combination of ecological principles? Clogging and stinking! They clog up and they stink! Do you know what is needed in the Ministry of Building, Slavovich, do you? A revolution! Yes, Comrade, don't think that we can sit back now on our soft behinds and reap the fruits of the revolution idly. No, the revolution continues! It continues each and every day, right here, believe it or not! It takes courage and we must take risks, yes! And so, Comrade Stentorian, I am sending you to Geneva. I am letting you go, I am giving you your papers. Go to Geneva, defect and see if you can live with your conscience in decadent Switzerland, in the West. See what will become of you! You speak a little German, do you not? And a little English? You have a little money saved up, have you not? Well, go and find out how long you can live with that! They will laugh at you, Comrade, that is what they will do, laugh at you!"

Nihilev was furiously wiping his chair. He took his overcoat from the hanger and put it on, breathing heavily from the exertion of lecturing Slavo Stentorian.

"Comrade Nihilev," said Stentorian at last, "I have no intention of defecting. I love our glorious republics and all they have accomplished since the Great Sacrifice. I am fully aware of the blood that was shed to make it possible for me to even go to Geneva and expose myself to the temptations of capitalism. But isn't it in such fires that we are tempered like steel, Comrade? I shall return strengthened in my convictions, a better brick in the great red edifice of socialism which will remain forever the strongest bastion against Western decadence, and ...."

Nihilev stopped his subordinate with a gesture. He said, "Fine then, Slavo, let's get down to the situation as it confronts us, then. Dobzhov is indisposed. If you ask me, Dobzhov has been indisposed a little too often recently. Dobzhov is losing his powers, I think. He put his all into that demonstration of levitation and now he has nothing left. I don't know how he did it anyway, do you? But he doesn't look like the sort of man to me who can lift up a cup without breaking it, let alone lift himself unaided into the air and hover there. The world will want another demonstration from him, I know. We can postpone that for one year, maybe two years, but after that, what? I say let us not build on Dobzhov, do you agree?"

"Yes, Comrade Director," said Stentorian using Nihilev's official title deliberately at this point of apparent harmony between them, "let's not build on Dobzhov, I agree."

"We have Dumbatse, that's all. At least she still ignites those matches with the power of her will alone. But it looks too much like a parlour trick and we have all seen it often enough. The world, Comrade Stentorian, is moving on and we must move with it. The world wants to see more spectacular phenomena."

"Yes, Comrade," said Stentorian, and quoted audaciously: "If ye had but a thimbleful of faith, ye could move mountains!"

"That is true," Nihilev said, pensively hugging himself against the dampness and the cold. "Don't you ever get cold, Slavo, in your fine clothes?"

He had apparently exhausted the subject of psychic phenomena and was prepared now to let the meeting end with the familiar pleasantries, inquiries after Stentorian's fiancée, Vera, whom he met twice a year at the spring and fall Section picnics in the country.

"Thank you, Comrade Nihilev," Slavo smiled. "She is fine indeed. We are still waiting for our flat. We have been told that nothing now lies between us and the luxury of that privacy but a handful of months, certainly in the spring of next year, and that is when we plan to marry."

"Now, Slavo," Nihilev said, dispensing with the rigorous mode of addressing each other with Comrade, "you will be a good son of the revolution and you will not leave your touchingly, achingly young and beautiful Vera all alone in this ugly great city of Moscow to which we owe so much, will you?"

He got up, came around the desk and put an arm around Stentorian's shoulder, squeezing the lean flesh with dangerous affection.

"Defection is not a nice thing, Slavo," he said. "You are not a ballet star, after all. You are humble Slavo Stentorian, a good reliable son of the revolution, and you will accomplish your mission and bring back that young man who can hold exploding grenades together as if they were oranges."

"What if he declines the invitation?" Slavo Stentorian asked, squinting cleverly toward the door.

"Then we have to find our way back to the marrow of socialism, Comrade," said Nihilev with determination. "Then we must not shirk from our responsibilities. If we allow him to sink back into the slime of capitalistic enticements which are ensnaring him already,then we are no longer true to the great heritage of socialist thought to which we owe so much."

"If I can't bring him back," Stentorian asked pointedly, "do you want me to kill him?"

Nihilev beamed and let go of the smaller man. "That is why I'm sending you to Geneva, Slavo Slavovich," he laughed. "You have a way with words!"

8

LUST

Nanita, the wealthiest whore in Japan, squatted voluptuously on her bidet. The bidet had once belonged to the Marquis de Sade and had been converted to modern plumbing. It had been transparently enamelled over the original ornamentation. All around its upper rim a fine hand had drawn bucolic scenes featuring fauns, nymphs, satyrs and pudgy love gods in delicate pinks, greens and yellows. Nanita washed her genital and anal area with a hand now devoid of the influence of her will. She had done this many times, in fact it was the third time she had done it today, and this time, splashing dreamily, she was doing it for the *Generalsekretär* of the German Trade Mission which had its permanent seat here in Kyoto and received, from time to time, visitors from the homeland.

Nanita loved her body more than anybody or anything in the world. She had fallen in love with it when she was a girl of nine or ten, just entering puberty. She had become aware of its extraordinary tightly textured skin, its exquisite pallor that took and transmuted even sunlight to a subtler, cooler hue. She had discovered the startling contrast between that skin and the three darkening shades of aureole rings that surrounded her nipples which themselves were almost black. Soon she developed a habit of kissing herself in mirrors, feeling the cool glass touch her broad, flat lips which had a bluish hue that she covered with bright red lipstick and revealed only to a chosen handful of men for whom she allowed her passion to rule without restraint.

Into the bottom of the bidet the legendary Marquis had had inserted an oval mirror which had cracked during the French Revolution and been replaced toward the middle of the 19th century. Over a hundred years old, it now showed signs of dimming and Nanita had been thinking of having it replaced again. The decision was not an easy one. The old mirror made up for what it lacked in clarity with its superior dimensional depth. Nanita turned off the flow and allowed the water to calm itself. She raised herself slightly, using both hands to spread her labia for full display. It seems, she thought, as if suddenly there at the bottom of a crystalline spring a dark and crimson flower sprouts and cleaves.

The flesh in the interior of her vagina was shiny and dark but broad streaks of bright-red ran through it like veins through marble. Black, red-veined marble! She slowly dipped her right middle finger into the pond and began to tease her clitoris which responded immediately by extending into the lukewarm, accommodating water. She withdrew her fingers and took a long last look at the exotic tableau she had created there in duplicate in the bidet. It was that with which she was most of all in love, and she had learned early to serve herself in the yogic position known as The Snail; but more even than losing herself, she loved *looking* at it as she did now.

Then, resolutely, she raised herself to a towel and dried thighs and pubis, treating her skin at once with great delicacy and roughness. There was little about her body Nanita did not know and love. She paid particular attention to her pubic hair now, hair that had no curl and glistened in the deepest Mars black. She walked to a wide mirror that extended from floor to ceiling. She shook her hair, stretched slowly, yawned, took a comb and began to comb her pubic hair. She combed it so it fell on either side of its natural centre toward the hollows of the groin. She slicked it down with the tips of three fingers, then combed it again, advancing a little more closely to the mirror until she almost touched it. Finally, she appeared satisfied.

With another comb she began to comb the hair of her head which was cut gamin fashion. When this was done she lifted up her breasts, which were small, and kissed her nipples here and there. Then she placed her mouth on the cool mirror image of itself and kissed that, too.

When she was through with her toilette, she slipped into a kimono of pure black silk, put on black silk slippers and sat down in her favourite room, which was sparsely furnished in red silks and velvets. It was certain that the Herr *Generalsekretär* Huber - whose best German, she happened to know, was tinged with a southern inflection which made him not strictly speaking acceptable in the polite high German society which he thought he had penetrated - would be on time. She did not yet know what she wanted from Huber.

Certainly it was not money. Not that she did not need money. She could always use money. But she had learned long ago in the early years of her professional service to men that friendship and favours were more important than money. She liked to place men not only in her affection but in her debt.

Huber was announced a shade too early even for the customary diplomatic punctuality that prevailed in his circles. Huber was naturally eager. She thought of him as a brute, an ambitious man who had his eyes on the Chancellorship of Germany and might succeed one day, but if he did, it would be only because of his tremendous self-discipline. "Huber," she had told him, "you wait as a cat waits for a mouse. But that isn't patience. Patience is waiting which has no goal."

Huber had told her that he disliked waiting aimlessly and in this way they had drawn their lines which permitted them to communicate on a physical level without questioning each other's motives. Just as it was true that Huber was ambitious, it was also true that he loved sex. He confided that there had been a time in his life when he had seriously considered beginning to involve himself with males simply because he had begun to suspect that women were sexually inadequate. Nanita had shown him otherwise. This had freed him to admit that perhaps the truth was that he did not care with whom he had sex so long as it was the best, and sex with her was certainly the best.

Nanita was used to compliments from men who were tongue-tied as well as from men who knew how to turn a phrase. She had been complimented sincerely, insincerely, deviously, innocently - in any manner that was thinkable. None of that meant anything to her compared to her own adoration of her body. She liked Huber. She liked all men with appetite and Huber had a huge appetite which he presented undisguised as soon as their privacy was assured. No, she thought now, as she kept him waiting just a minute or two, Huber likes my body a great deal, and so I like him. Huber will always be a little rough because finally he cannot love his body as I love mine. This is natural. God has given him a body that is short and too powerful to be beautiful. And God has given me a body which is perfect, therefore, Huber adores me but what can he give me? So thinking, she at last consented to have the Herr *Generalsekretär* admitted into her presence.

Huber was impeccably dressed in dark-grey silks and he wore

the traditional Japanese attire without ostentation. He had learned some phrases in Japanese, and he now greeted her in the traditional manner. The ceremony lasted perhaps a minute. Then he went to her, took her in his powerful arms, lifted her off her feet and planted a kiss directly on her forehead as he sat her down.

"My conquering hero in his home of the middle," she said without affection. Huber twisted his face into a grin and told her to drop the formalities along with whatever else she chose to drop, for he was ready. "Tea?" she asked and clapped her hands so that tea would be brought and placed between them. When this was done, she questioned him severely. "Huber," she said, "what have you brought me from Europe?"

Huber turned his head slightly to the right and down so that his glance was slanted sideways at her. "Gossip, my lady," he said, "food to fill the remote and empty belly of Japan. I'm ready to betray all confidences, spill all secrets, make an ass of myself before you. Push the button and this ageing computer will reel out the tapes whose length will astound you, to say nothing of the information they contain, once deciphered."

She did not smile. She said, "Would it be clumsy of me to tell you how clumsy you are, Huber?"

He didn't stop grinning. He drank his tea slowly, having obtained permission from her eyes to do so. He set down the cup but did not withdraw his powerful hands from it as if he needed it for warmth.

"In Japan," he said, "I'm always cold. Perhaps distance makes me cold. Or the cold Pacific around us. I've come to see if your fires are still burning. Are they?"

"Huber, you may be cold and you are certainly a clumsy player but your enthusiasm charms me. Look!"

She had shrugged one shoulder out of the kimono, fully aware of the perfect setting created for her skin by the black silk and the red-velvet walls. Huber sighed but held back. He felt like reaching out and touching, but he did not.

"I'll tell you the deepest secret of Europe for a brush of your skin," he said, and did not wait for a reply but continued, "Europe is doomed and dull, chivalry is dead, politics is dead, alcohol and drugs reign, not that I mind or care and I'm aware that this news won't be enough. I have brought you gold, almost thirty ounces and I have handed the box, which itself is mahogany, to your valet."

It occurred to Nanita that gold might be precisely what Huber could give her, as he had in the past, and it was not always good to expect too much. Still, gold could not be thought of as enough, not in her present mood. But then, also, it would not be professional of her to play around with such a generous gift. Nanita had certain doubts about her own intelligence. She had seen many times in her life how her mind had played tricks on her, had led her into difficult and compromising situations from which only her magnificent body and its power had rescued her. perhaps Huber was cleverer than she herself. She took three minutes to end the tea ceremony, then she rose.

"If you are cold," she said, "a bath will warm you." Huber, too, maintained decorum as he got up, but it was the decorum of a coil in a watch restrained by a master watchmaker. They went along a narrow passage of natural wooden walls and muted top light to the bathhouse where Nanita left Huber with two female attendants who helped him disrobe and led him to the first of the three tubs, its water lukewarm. Huber slipped into the water and closed his eyes. From his pointed English, he drifted into German thoughts. These gradually dissolved and he did nothing to keep them together. In his memory, he saw Nanita as he had last seen her. He saw that she had stepped onto that gentle plateau which only the greatest physical beauty can reach, and that she would live there for a time, till the first frost of autumn.

"Verdammt" Huber caught himself, "this always happens to me when I'm in Japan. I get lyrical. I feel like a poet. I have to stop this."

He opened his eyes and saw that he was alone with Nanita, who might have been standing nude before him for some time. "This," she said, running her hands slowly over her breasts, her abdomen, her pubis, her thighs - "this is the great gift I'm bringing you to acknowledge the courtesy of your gold. Now let me sponge you."

She slipped into the tub with him and began to soap and sponge him. Secretly she marvelled at Huber's power. This was regrettably the 20th century and all that power was going to waste in the service of argument. Huber was a strong boy who wanted to play in the parlour of the grown-ups where he was not welcome. But here, here in these tubs, in this her palace, she would drink from the flush of his face and anoint herself in the shine of his adoring eyes.

She made him stand on a stool in the tub and soaped his legs and genitals but without special attention, treating his penis and testes no differently than his knees. And Huber, too, restrained himself, did not react. Then she allowed him to soap and sponge her, and after that they slipped into the cold tub to rinse off, and from there finally to another warm tub in which for the first time she reclined and allowed her spread legs to float the flower of her incomparable pussy to the surface for the Herr *Generalsekretär's* direct inspection.

9

SUICIDE

The Durstli Crash affair was beginning to snowball in Switzerland, threatening to produce an avalanche that would prove to be all the more devastating for being made of unknown substances.

The newly surfaced village of Morgendurst had become the mecca of the international psychic phenomena set. And the ancient Pampini, mysteriously resurrected from the ashes of its production mates, was prominently displayed in the town square of Durstlimas. With a payment of 25 Swiss francs anyone could inspect it and sit at the controls.

Officially, the Swiss Government vacillated between declaring the entire Morgendurst area off limits to the public and supporting the touristic efforts of Durstlimas, putting up a lift to transport visitors to the extraordinary site. The Swiss National Assembly voted almost unanimously to create a commission for the Investigation of the Morgendurst Phenomenon, but the problem was that there were no experts to send there. A hastily assembled gaggle of people at least suspected of being able to shed light on the affair spent a week in Durstlimas and at the crash site. They returned to write a predictably hasty report in which the newly found village of Morgendurst was described as a "*vexing puzzle in which, though every stone seems perfectly placed, and every item of furniture authentic, the main piece is missing and the question remains: Where Does This Village Come From?*"

Of course there were other questions, such as: Who or what made this village? How was it transported to where it appeared, or how was it built there overnight? And, of course, the entire Pampini puzzle remained entirely impenetrable. All these questions might have resulted in a certain amount of public frustration but strangely enough, the people accepted everything with nary a whimper or cry.

There was a solid class of citizens who shrugged their shoulders and declared it all a hoax but they were far outnumbered by those who enthusiastically invested their hard-earned money to go and see what it was all about. And, to eclipse even this great local attraction, the man whom Patrick Young had named Shawn made headlines in Geneva.

For two weeks, leaks of the tests he was undergoing at the Neuropsychological Institute trickled out but finally it was learned, somewhat disappointingly, that he was, organically, thoroughly human. However, he did suffer from a rather strange form of amnesia which was complicated by a delusion in which the subject thought himself a member or descendant of a highly developed race or civilization of intelligent beings in some other world, who sent him to Earth to do some still only vaguely defined work having to do with lions and lambs. While, in a guarded bulletin, the neuropsychologists at the institute pronounced him "marginally psychotic but peaceful in his attitudes, while still hampered by linguistic inadequacies," Shawn and Patrick Young walked into the main branch of the Banque Centrale du Lac in Geneva to cash a cheque for a photography session with a softcore women's magazine in Paris and the house almost literally came down.

In an instant, simultaneously, all the heavy plate-glass windows around the horseshoe-shaped tellers' counter fell. If it hadn't been for the ear-shattering, piercing noise accompanying the phenomenon one might have thought the bullet proof glass had turned to water. It disintegrated. In the process, it was later determined, it melted. The chandelier also melted. But all of it melted cold, forming artistically shaped globs on the counters and stalactitic icicles from the counters to the floor. Nobody was hurt.

There was also, though it was either not noticed or, if noticed, not commented upon, a gust of wind that swept through the hall. Perhaps it was not an objectively verifiable wind, but Shawn felt it. It was wind from the exile planet, and since the wind preceded the melting glass it might well have been that the Council had sent it to remind him of his mission. As if he needed it! There had been nothing in the women he had met on earth that could soothe the memory of his merger with the messenger of the female principle. One of the guards at the bank appeared on TV that night telling the world, "Two men came in. One was the young man from the Durstli crash. I've seen his picture and, this may not belong here but my daughter has been trying to get his autograph for weeks. So I thought to myself what a stroke of luck it was that he should walk in here. I mean, he could have picked the Swiss Bank Society or some other bank, but no, there he was, so I started to walk toward him and then there was a sound such as I've never heard before and hope never to hear again. It was a high-pitched *pinnnggh*. No, let me see if I can do it again. It was like: *psiannnggh,* only higher. It went to the marrow of my bones. I instinctively raised my arms to protect my face but I told myself at the same time that I had to look at whatever it was that was happening, and I did.

"I saw a curtain of cascading glass, that's what I saw. And that tinkling curtain went down, but smoothly - no shards, no splinters. It was all over in a moment but we all stood transfixed for half a minute perhaps. Only he didn't. He was smiling. Yes, that is as clear as day in my mind. He smiled and walked over to one of the tellers and then the other man handed over a piece of paper, a cheque. Then a really strange thing happened. The other man, the tall man with the curly red hair - his shoe, one of his shoes got stuck in the soft glass on the floor. It was cool, the glass, you know, but he couldn't get the shoe out, so when they left, he left it behind. It occurred to me only much later that I should have detained them."

A meeting of the Board of Directors of the Banque Centrale du Lac was immediately called and there were heated arguments around the table. The damage caused was estimated in the neighbourhood of one hundred thousand Swiss francs, and it was at first the overwhelming opinion of those assembled that the young man who had caused it should be held responsible, if necessary in court. There was only one dissident in this gathering, a slim young man with quick gestures who had joined the bank only five months earlier and whose concern had been public relations. He had been asked to attend the meeting in an advisory capacity, and he now made an impassioned plea against prosecution and against trying to collect damages.

He said: "Gentlemen, I'm trying to look at this through the glasses of my professional expertise. I'm asking myself, how will this affect the image of Banque Centrale du Lac? How will it look if we pull this admittedly popular man into court? But think for a moment a little further. How, for example, can anyone prove - I mean *prove* - that it was this Shawn who caused the glass to shatter ...."

"Melt," someone injected.

".... shatter, melt, whatever - how can this be proved? We can bring witnesses who will testify that the man was not stunned, that he was the only man who was not stunned, that he did not seem surprised, that he continued acting normally, unconcerned in the middle of a catastrophic emergency. But is that proof? Still, let us assume that the court will find in our favour, which is highly - I mean highly unlikely. We will be awarded one hundred thousand, fine! But how do we know he has that much money, how will we collect it if he has not? And then let's admit that there is something disturbing, something mysterious about thirteen tellers' windows ...."

"Twelve," injected the same not unfriendly heckler. "If it were thirteen, we ...."

There was just a slight, quickly passing breeze of laughter. The gentlemen were amused.

The young public relations man continued, "Twelve, fine, thank you. In any case I've been thinking how can the Banque du Lac profit? So, with the help of some of the talented staff in my department, I've made a few sketches and here they are."

With a flourish he produced a number of poster-size drawings which he propped up one by one so that everyone there could see them. They were crudely executed, but conveyed their message with vigour. A week later the first of the famous Durstli Man Series of Banque du Lac Posters began to appear in prominent places around Geneva. Following in the wake of the sensational melting of the windows, they caused an equal stir in the staid and conservative domes of banking around the lake.

The first poster, and perhaps the best, showed Shawn in front of the main branch of Banque Centrale du Lac, being handed a fistful of bills by a man who looked like a teller and carried an old-fashioned wooden lottery suspended from two shoulder straps at the height of his waist. This box, too, was packed tight with bills. The caption said in French, German, Italian and English: THIS IS THE ONLY MAN WE DON'T MIND SERVING IN THE STREET. The amount Shawn had received for posing, if any, was not disclosed.

When people looked at it, they smiled. And the people who did business in the bank developed overnight a new feeling of belonging to a privileged group, though there were some who expressed shock at this Americanised approach to business.

The second poster showed a close-up of Patrick Young's huge

battered British brown shoe sitting in melting glass like a big ugly fly caught in resin destined to become ornamental amber. The caption was the young P.R. man's personal favourite: WHEN OUR WINDOWS MELTED, CINDERELLA WENT HOME. He had laughed and laughed and laughed this somewhat obtuse slogan right onto the poster, though many Genevans were frankly puzzled by it.

Patrick Young's shoe, incidentally, became somewhat of a religious artifact. He had graciously consented to letting the Banque Centrale du Lac display it in a glass case in the hall of their main branch, soon famous the world over and many of those who came to look at it decided to do business, little or large.

The third and last in this series, and the one that got the widest circulation outside Switzerland, was an enormous close-up of Shawn, smiling his careless, intelligent smile, saying, in bold black letters, IF I DID IT, I'M SORRY, BANQUE CENTRALE DU LAC!

The fact was that he had received the sum of 300,000 Swiss francs for his services. It had not only made him at least temporarily independent but elevated him to the position of the most sought-after face in Europe.

"Look," Patrick explained to him in the sitting room of their five hundred and fifty francs-a-day suite at the Royal Palace Hotel overlooking the wealthiest lake in the world, "now we must be cautious. You're famous. We mustn't over-expose your face. Let's lie low for a while, six months, go to Greece or the Bahamas."

Naturally, he had finally quit his job but was still making notes for a book on his protégé who was really no longer in need of anyone's protection. Shawn had had what seemed like a partial breakthrough with the English language, or at least a sudden, unexpected acceleration in his grasp of it, and with this had come a great deal of independent thought. But the term "over-exposure" was still relatively new to him.

Lounging on a late 19th century chaise lounge in mauve and pale blues, dressed in a pink, skin-tight après-ski outfit, he asked Patrick what "over-expose" meant.

Patrick grinned cheerfully. "Well, you know," he said, "it's like food, like eating. The public is hungry for fame, but naturally they can never have it. Fame and youth is what they want - and money, of course. But there are too many, they can never have it. Sometimes they try to get it as a mass, Germany did, and that's bloody terrible.

Millions die in obscurity. So, since they can as individuals and as a group never be famous, or rich, or even young for any length of time, they feed on symbols. Now you, for instance, you are young, and you are getting rich - they think and hope you are - and certainly you are famous. You are just their cup of tea, just their meat. They have developed an appetite for you and so they want you for breakfast, for lunch, for a snack in the afternoon and for dinner, too. You are their croissant, their filet mignon, their steak tartare, even their wine, their beer. They want to devour you in your entirety, but being unable to become famous, rich and stay young, they are immodest in their desire to compensate. They know no restraint. The public is a voracious beast which feeds on the life-blood of its own fantasies. Now the trick here, my friend, is to keep up their appetite. If you let them eat you up every day, they'll get tired of your taste. No matter what you are - soup, sausage or soufflé - you are only one thing, and they will tire of you if they overeat, which invariably they will. Do you see? So let's say they've just had breakfast. Now let's starve them a little. Let's wait for lunchtime. We'll let lunchtime pass, right? They'll be hungry. In the afternoon they'll start screaming for you. And around four-thirty we let them have ...."

"Tea," supplied Shawn. "tea and cookies!"

Patrick Young could not help himself. He jumped up and pounded him on the shoulder. "Yes!" he shouted. "Tea and cookies in the afternoon."

"And," said Shawn, smiling and getting up to stretch his magnificent self before the tall, narrow window, "for dinner a sausage. Little sausage. A little sausage and ...."

"A glass of water," Patrick coughed and sputtered with laughter, "and a slice of bread, just one. That will be their dinner. They will spend a restless night, don't you know. Their stomachs will be rumbling and churning. And in the morning, why not, a truly sumptuous breakfast!"

The telephone rang and Patrick picked it up. He listened intently as his face grew serious. He said, "Are you absolutely in earnest about this? This is not a hoax, a stupid joke?"

He listened again, his lips compressed, ruffling his obstinate red hair with one hand. Then he hung up and turned to the Durstli Man and said: "That was the police. Suzanne has committed suicide. Emma, too. Both took an overdose of sleeping tablets. They are both dead."

The smile never left Shawn's face. He came over to stand directly in front of the tall Englishman. He looked him directly in the eye and for a moment it was as if his whole face disappeared and there remained only two brightly lit passages, two beams which led apparently nowhere.

"They did not like their bodies?" said the Durstli Man.

10

FLESH

Emma Gerber and Suzanne Mathieu were buried in adjoining graves in the Valais country, high above the valley of the Rhone, where Emma was born. This had been specified in a suicide note written by Suzanne:

Emma and Suzanne are going to prepare a place for him. We wish to be buried side by side in the Randogne Cemetery.

Against Patrick's advice, Shawn attended the funeral, so Patrick went along, too.

Fortunately for them, there were few others present apart from the distraught parents, close family and a few friends of the dead women. Such a slice of good luck - if, indeed, so inappropriate a phrase could be employed on such a sombre occasion - was due in no small part to the efforts of Young himself, who had called into play his still-considerable influence with the Swiss police and security authorities. Pointedly reminding them how he had co-operated with the initial bogus story about the origins of the Durstli Man, Young had managed to persuade them to suppress issuing news of the double suicide deaths, at least until after the funeral was over. There were, of course, dark mutterings and protests from the official side, but reluctantly the authorities had yielded to Patrick Young's entreaties, as they realised that the veteran newsman remained their vital link in keeping the mysterious Shawn both friendly and accessible.

Shawn, resplendent in a yellow après-ski outfit, his blond hair outshining the snow that sparkled in the sun, stuck out like a sore thumb. Patrick had tried to get him to wear something more subdued, something dark, but he failed to persuade his friend.

"These people are grieving," he had said, "and your colours are going to offend their eyes. If you wear something dark you will show that you are with them in their grief, do you understand?"

Shawn had smiled, "I'm not grieving," he had said. "If they do not like my colour, their grief is not as strong as they say, or as you say. And, what is grief?"

Patrick had got used to strange twists of conversations with Shawn. Here the foundling had been using a word as if he knew precisely what it meant, had used it properly, in the right context, and then asked to have it explained. Like so much about him, this made no sense at all.

"Grief is a human emotion," Patrick Young explained, "the sorrow a mother feels for her lost child, the tears of a father for his daughter. These are the tears you'll see at the funeral."

Shawn had simply walked out and they had taken the train to Sierre, and from there the old cable car up the mountain to a town called Bluche from where it was a short walk to the cemetery. Shawn's arrival caused a stir. The funeral service in the little church by the cemetery had not yet begun, and they stood off to the side, away from the dark group of people. Finally Shawn walked over to them, smiling. Patrick stayed behind, watching the scene.

Shawn had picked up a few words of French, and immediately misplaced his polite "*Bonjour!*" There was no response. They stared at him as if they could not believe their eyes which showed them this gaudy apparition. Certainly they would have tried to turn away from him, turn their backs to the offence but they seemed hypnotised. Then one of the fathers attacked Shawn. It was Emma's father, a sturdily built man in his fifties, with a thick moustache and weather-beaten face. He threw his arms around Shawn and tried to wrestle him to the ground but the Durstli Man paid no attention to him, continuing to apply another French phrase he had mastered: "*Comment ça va tout le monde*?"

Patrick found it amazing to see that a broad-shouldered man, fully mature, could not so much as budge his friend by an inch. In fact, it seemed as if Shawn was not aware that someone was trying to dislodge him from his position. That moment the man gave up and stepped back, his face ashen. There was the sound of his trying to gather saliva up from the depths of his stomach and then a thick blob of spit flew out at Shawn. It missed. Then the man turned and walked the three, four steps back to his wife and the others. And now, as if on cue, the church-bells began to ring and everybody slowly walked into the chapel.

The service was brief and, Patrick thought, the priest extremely ill at ease, taking his refuge in what must have been an appropriate Latin text of which Patrick understood words like: *gloria, excelsior, requiescat, pace, deus, filius* and such. The coffins stood side by side and, mercifully, they were closed.

After the service, for which Shawn and Patrick sat in one of the rear pews, the mourners filed out and walked to the cemetery, many of them weeping without restraint. Without much ado, the coffins were lowered in their places into the cold late-winter earth and in a short while it was over and the two men left along the narrow road down to the cable-car station at Bluche, where they sat down to wait. Foggy mists had come up from the valley and the sun was veiled. It was getting appreciably cooler. Then, as they sat there on a cold, red bench, snow began to fall.

"So this is human grief," said Shawn. Patrick said nothing.

When they got into the cable car and began to move slowly down the mountainside, Shawn was smiling. In fact he seemed in a buoyant mood, several notches above his customary energetic elation. His manner was infectious. Patrick suddenly felt hungry and he told Shawn. They decided to have a big lunch in Sierre and to walk into the first restaurant they saw.

"Grief makes you hungry?" Shawn asked.

Patrick said, "Can you explain to me what they meant by 'preparing a place' for you?" After a while Shawn replied that there already was a place for him.

They found a restaurant and ordered more than they could eat - salads, cheeses, three varieties of meat, a bottle of red wine, cold cuts, snails, mineral water, ice cream, coffee, and strange little pies of which pictures had been printed on the menu - the speciality of the house. As they ate, Shawn's high spirits began to settle down.

Finishing off the last escargot, he said, "Why do they put these bodies in the earth, Patrick?"

Patrick elucidated that it was an ancient custom, though in times past even in these then wild regions, corpses were burned or left for the birds of prey, but that the Christian doctrine was essentially ashes to ashes and dust to dust in accordance with the idea that God fashioned Adam out of clay, or earth, out of dust, did he understand? Shawn only nodded, savouring the Italian ice cream.

When they had finished eating, Shawn leaned back and said,

"Patrick, it's cold where these bodies are now. Emma, Suzanne, I warmed them and they warmed me, now they are much too cold!"

"Yes," said Patrick. "Well, there isn't a damn thing...." He broke off in mid-sentence, staring at his mysterious friend. Something had hit him. As if he had been on the dark beach of some darker ocean and a wave had struck him in the forehead and stopped him before he could finish what he had meant to say which was, there isn't a damn thing you can do about it.

"Come," said the Durstli Man, "let's go back up to them."

So they left the restaurant, went back to the cable car and found one that was about to begin the ascent. They rode up in the ominous silence of Shawn's bright smile. They got off again at Bluche Station and walked through the densely falling snow back to the cemetery and there, before entering, they saw the figure of a woman in black, huddled by the fresh graves.

"One of the mothers," Patrick whispered. Shawn went in and walked up to the woman, who either did not notice him or did not show that she noticed him. She was kneeling. She had been kneeling for some time, perhaps since it started snowing, for around her the snow had piled up. She was praying, but her face was hidden in the folds of her coat and gloves. She wore a black kerchief.

Shawn stood for a while off to the side, slightly behind her, totally composed. Patrick, too, was waiting but without patience. He found the scene unbearably tense and finally cleared his throat unnecessarily. The woman looked up, and saw Shawn. She made a sound, a deep throaty sound. It was not necessarily a sound of grief or pain; on the contrary, there was something deeply sensual about it, but also it was primitive and terrifying in its lack of restraint.

For a long time she looked up at Shawn from this kneeling position in the snow. Then she began to crawl toward him, never taking her eyes off his face. Shawn did not move. When she had reached him, she clasped one of his ankles with both hands and bent her face to his boot in a gesture of kissing it. In French she began muttering at first, raising her voice slowly, gathering force. She said. "I kiss the foot of the monster, I prostrate myself before the devil incarnate, I pray to the seducer of man and I offer myself as sacrifice. Here is my cold flesh. Take it, warm it, melt it, boil it!"

Her voice was very loud now and she had begun to pull herself up on Shawn, kissing him all the way upward and calling out between kisses, "This for the flame of your lust, devil! And this for the death of your seed, monster! And this as a challenge!"

So kissing out of a tear-streaked face, she worked her way up until she stood, her eyes at the height of his chin. Then at last she stepped back and took off her kerchief. Then she took off her gloves. Shawn did nothing. Patrick watched incredulously. The woman began to unbutton her coat and took off a grey sweater and then, deliberately and with apparent calm, the woollen skirt beneath. She had large breasts and when she unhooked her brassiere these fell, with the weight of an ageing mother. There was something so wild, so reckless about this - her bare torso above the long black skirt, in the falling snow - that Patrick Young felt a pang in his abdomen, something more primordial even than an erection. This, he thought, is how a mother feels! He tried to walk forward but could not. So he merely stood and watched, as did Shawn who had begun smiling again. It was a friendly, open, innocent smile of singular intensity.

The woman now silently completed her bizarre undressing, stepping out of her skirt and undoing another, thicker one beneath so that finally she stood naked in the snow, except for socks and shoes, and these she took off too. Patrick closed his eyes but only for a moment. He reminded himself of an execution he had witnessed in North Africa, and how he had forced himself to look. Was this worse? And so, looking, he saw a woman of perhaps forty-five in a curtain of snow which enveloped her, filtering her image. This was a woman of great strength, with powerful thighs and pubic hair of thick, curly black in which now dozens of tiny crystal snow stars alighted, melting to be replaced by new ones, until the black pubis glistened silver-white.

The woman had spread her arms and closed her eyes. Neither snow nor cold seemed to bother her. Though she was only six feet away from the Durstli Man she called with her powerful voice, "Love me then, Monster! Take me, too, so that I may know what my daughter knew! So that I may judge you, judge myself, judge her! Take me so that I may judge God Himself in His Holy Heaven!"

Her eyes still closed, she began turning, calling into the swirling snow, "And am I not attractive? Is this not the flesh of her flesh? When you drink the water, you must know the source! I am the spring of my daughter, Monster, drink me, drink me dry if you can."

She completed two, three turns, then stopped abruptly and

flung her arms at Shawn, her eyes suddenly wide open, rolling wildly. She screamed. "Devil, I challenge you! A mother challenges you, Devil! Come, come now, you coward! Come, founder on these loins."

Then she collapsed in the snow, Patrick leapt to catch her but was too late. They carried her to the shelter of the chapel and quickly dressed her while she half regained consciousness. When she could recognize them and hear them, Patrick asked her where the others were, where her husband was and she told him, docile as a wept-out child, that she was a widow and that Suzanne's father had died when Suzanne was nine. She had asked the others to leave her behind. They were in Bluche, waiting. Patrick offered to accompany her, but she seemed not to hear him.

For a while she stood, leaning against the wall of the church, her lips moving wordlessly, her face pale. Then slowly she began to walk away. Patrick started to follow her but Shawn motioned him to stay. She walked over to the road, turned and began to walk up the incline, slowly passing them again without looking down at them. In a moment the snow had obscured her.

11

PHENOMENA

The suicide of the two women had shocked Shawn into the reality of the world to which he had been sent. It was, he found, a world full of humour that was mistaken for tragedy by its inhabitants. This was natural, since apparently even the most elementary lessons of velocity and the vibrational structure of the universe had not yet been learned. Human grief had touched him. They wept for crude bodies such as the one he himself had been given! The cause of their grief was comical, but the grief itself was real. He nodded at Patrick Young as they were escorted into the main courtroom of the regional court in Geneva. Both had been summoned as witnesses in the trial of van Schmul, whose true name turned out to be Fritz Lewin. And, since it was convenient, the court had called in as expert witness Mr Jack Baldwin, President of the American Society for the Investigation of Extraterrestrial Phenomena who, by his own admission, had a doctorate in physics and had once been a professional magician.

For the occasion, Mr Baldwin wore a conservative suit. Between the hem of its trousers and the shoe-tops could be seen a strip of yellow nylon sock three inches wide. The suit itself seemed to have been cut by a second-rate tailor in Des Moines, Iowa. It was green and it hung. With this, perhaps to accentuate the full mop of grey hair and neatly trimmed beard that gave him a distinguished, professorial appearance, he wore a tie of shiny silver rayon speckled with what looked, at least from where Shawn was sitting, like a dozen large, black flies. Since, however, throughout Mr Baldwin's testimony these creatures never stirred, they were no doubt part and parcel of his extravagant neckpiece.

Mr Baldwin's manner was authoritative and thoroughly professional. He had been an expert for quite some time. Asked by the prosecutor to comment on the apparently erratic behaviour of a hand grenade that had come out of an orange and not quite exploded in Shawn's hands, he settled back comfortably in his chair, lifted his glasses to the height of his chin, and shook his head.

"I don't like the word 'erratic,'' he said thoughtfully, "I like 'typical' better. But of course an orange can't be a hand grenade and vice versa. People behave atypically often but oranges and hand grenades rarely. Certainly there is no such thing as an exploding orange that hasn't been tampered with, dummied up, if you know what I mean. Let's face it, it's a pretty cheap trick. If it was done on a stage, for entertainment, where it's understood that it's a trick, then it's okay. But for somebody to come along and claim that this actually happened - that's ridiculous."

Since Mr Baldwin spoke English, his testimony was translated via earphones into French and German. A little was lost in the translation. What remained was the impression that Mr Baldwin knew what he was talking about. The grey hair, green suit and fly-specked silver tie served to solidify the impression of an eccentric American professional: colourful but clean, outspoken but honest. That, in fact, was very much what Mr Baldwin thought of himself.

"If the court would allow me," he was saying, "I've rigged up a little demonstration which might save considerable time." He waved to a rotund young man who had done his best to look like Mr Baldwin, and by means of a bright-yellow shirt and electric-green tie, was succeeding to a certain extent. The young man carried forward a medium-sized picnic basket and deposited it on the prosecutor's table. Mr Baldwin explained that the basket contained an orange very much like the one he thought Jan van Schmul - that is, Fritz Lewin - had used to get Shawn into the papers. In fact, Mr Baldwin surmised, he would show that any trained magician could perform the same trick without the slightest difficulty or risk.

Patrick Young was as surprised as anyone in the courtroom. He had spoken with Baldwin only briefly up in Durstlimas and there had been no indication that Baldwin did not believe in the authenticity of what had happened up there. Well, apparently he had changed his tack. Shawn was smiling benevolently at the judges, prosecutor, and witness.

Having been given permission for his demonstration, Mr Baldwin now produced from the basket a spherical object wrapped in a colourful handkerchief. Unwrapped, it turned out to be an ordinary orange. To prove this, Mr Baldwin cut it in half with a kitchen knife and held up both halves, juice dripping. He then pressed the two halves together and, with a strip of adhesive tape, taped them so that the orange was restored to its original fullness.

Baldwin now began to peel the orange. Something metallic emerged. Exclamations of astonishment could be heard in the spectator section and even from the judges' rostrum. The peels fell away and Baldwin held up what looked like an ordinary hand grenade, perhaps a little rounder than the army-issued one.

Mr Jack Baldwin allowed a fine, practiced smile to play around his bearded face as he said: "Now, for the explosion. Please, everybody, there's no need to seek cover or to be afraid. It's a perfectly harmless procedure. Or else I wouldn't be doing it." Carelessly he yanked at a ring that dangled from the grenade by a short chain. He counted dramatically .... one .... two .... three .... four .... all the while holding the contraption in his cupped hands. The explosion proved anticlimactic, however. It was no more than a loud crack.

Mr Baldwin held up his hands, still cupping the grenade. Juice was dripping. The juice was a bit too red, but could have passed for blood at a distance. Now, dramatically, Baldwin uncupped his hands and, to the ooh and ahh of the gallery, there was a pile of what looked like metal fragments heaped in his hand, mixed in with the remains of an orange. Baldwin quickly dropped all this in the picnic basket but kept a few grenade fragments, which he passed around to the prosecutor and the judges.

It would have been against the nature of the predominantly Swiss audience to show enthusiasm in such an austere setting, but they got as close as they could with a brief smattering of light applause. The judges, too, were evidently impressed. Patrick pulled up his shoulders and frowned at Shawn.

When the courtroom had returned to a calmer, expectant state, Mr Baldwin was back in his chair. The basket had been removed by the yellow-shirted young man and Baldwin spoke in a low, persuasive voice.

"As you can see," he said, "certain phenomena can be easily .... uh .... produced. It would be unscientific and unprofessional of me to attribute the alleged incident on the train to anything but stage magic and showmanship. I don't know who this young man is and I don't know anything about Mr Lewin here, but I would say that the chances of his killing anybody with a hand grenade that came out of an orange were very much like me killing anybody in this courtroom with the gadget I just demonstrated." Shawn was called next. The first question to him concerned his name, his nationality, place of origin, current status.

Shawn, resplendent in Italian silks from a shop he had discovered near the Banque Centrale du Lac, said: "My friend Patrick Young calls me Shawn, but my real name is Nonomine. I come from above and I go to below, which is above too. I have no nationality."

He smiled at the judges who did not smile back.

"Since I come from above Switzerland, I may be Swiss."

Fritz Lewin's attorney now appealed for immediate dismissal of the case on the grounds that the alleged victim could not establish his identity and that, therefore, in the strictest sense, there could be no victim - potential, alleged or otherwise. The judges rejected the argument and Shawn's testimony.

He was asked if he believed that Lewin, alias van Schmul, had tried to kill him. He replied that this could be answered only by the accused himself but, generally, from what he had heard and seen of the world since he had come to it, yes, it was possible.

Shawn was looking at the prosecutor who did most of the questioning. He was a youngish man, powerfully built with black hair and green eyes that shone evenly and coldly. Shawn had recognized him immediately: Oba, the Councillor. Or at least that of Oba which had permeated a respectable Swiss bureaucrat of impeccable credentials, appointed many years ago to this court. That which was Oba in the prosecutor shone malevolently at Shawn, and could do so only because malice had long been eliminated on the home planet. Evidently it could easily be resurrected here in this far-flung place!

It would have been too much to expect them to leave him alone, of course. Here was Oba, watching, registering, supervising him. That which was Nonomine in the newly formed human Shawn, however, remained fixed, focusing on the prosecutor. Oba's role on the council had been, as far as Nonomine knew, to demonstrate imperfection in all its subtle aspects and keep the members of the council informed. No doubt, Oba had accomplished this by easing himself into this court, like a demented professor who imagines himself to be a student who sneaks into school and squeezes himself into a narrow seat built for slim youngsters.

"It seems," the prosecutor was saying, "that a great deal here depends on Mr Shawn's credibility. If that can be established, or as it were, disallowed, then Mr Lewin's behaviour might be seen in perspective." The court agreed with this and the prosecutor addressed himself directly to Shawn.

"Sir," he said, "we have heard and read statements you have made concerning your mission on Earth, and these in themselves have provoked in many of us a crisis of faith - a minor crisis I might say. We recognise that, for the purpose of this inquiry, we must act in good faith if we are to make any progress at all. Will you, therefore, again tell us where you come from and what your mission is, so that this may be recorded officially and incontestably?"

Of what had Nonomine's rebellion consisted? Shawn sat entranced in thought. Why was the rebel exiled? To teach him a lesson, a very important lesson. To make him less rebellious? Did not his rebellion distinguish him further from, for example, Oba? Now was the time to demonstrate this, here on neutral ground, in this primitive culture of backward creatures.

"My world has not yet been mapped here," Shawn said. "It doesn't even have a number."

"Well," said the prosecutor, "if that is so, you might draw a map for us and show us. Would you?"

Shawn rose from the witness chair and walked to the blackboard. He picked up a piece of chalk, raised it, then half-turned and spoke to the judges.

"I will draw twenty-three bodies of the All, seen from the approach in a direct line between my home and Terra, Earth." He began quickly to sketch stars and planets, emphasizing some, merely dotting others. When he was finished with his work, a simple but effective star map graced the board.

"One of these is the body you call sun," Shawn said. "If anyone here can see it, please!"

Shawn was not looking at Councillor Oba in the form of a prosecutor. Naturally the Terrestrians could find the sun, clearly shown on his map, only by accident and could never be certain, for they had never seen their part of their galaxy from this perspective. But naturally Oba knew. It would have to be Oba or no one. And even if Oba pointed it out, he risked exposure. Shawn returned to his chair, satisfied. The silence grew.

“It does not seem,” said one of the judges, “that we can identify the sun.”

“This means nothing,” the prosecutor said. “I could draw a jumble of dots on this blackboard and ask you to pick out one to represent the sun. This may or may not be a true chart of a certain part of the universe.”

“Yes,” said Shawn, “I show you that I cannot show you where I come from. Unless ....” Now staring down on the prosecutor, he allowed his voice to break off abruptly. Oba had been bested, as was fitting. It could not be in the Council’s interest to have Nonomine give a revelatory performance for the Terrans. Oba would, could do nothing now but sit and stare at Shawn, squinting, smoothing his Swiss hair with both palms.

Then, suddenly, Shawn began to trill and warble - at first in the high-pitched chatter of routine business communication. Then in a quickly descending scale to the slow, sweet fluting tones of intimacy. Everyone present was caught by surprise and before they knew it they were entranced, their pupils dilated, their ears, unaccustomed to such caresses, wide open, drinking in the sound, addicted in the space of thirty seconds to such heavenly harmonies.

“That is my home language,” Shawn smiled. Even Oba, in his coldly terrestrian cloak, had leaned back to listen. It was that instant that the message flashed between them: “Missionexile missionexile,” and Shawn understood that the roles were reversed now. Terra was Nonomine’s mission and Oba’s exile.

12

PRELIMINARIES

Even though van Schmul alias Fritz Lewin was released and the charges against him dropped for lack of evidence, Shawn instantly again became the Number One topic in Europe. In the U.S., the story was underplayed. The press concentrated largely on Jack Baldwin's appearance and Baldwin received numerous offers to appear for lectures at colleges and universities. Implied in these invitations was the understanding that he would do his orange-grenade trick on the stage. Mr Baldwin was flattered by these invitations. If it had been up to him only, he would have accepted at least those that came from the larger, more prestigious institutions with fees to match the prestige. But there was the matter of acting responsibly as president of the American Society for the Investigation of Extraterrestrial Phenomena. Mr Baldwin spent an agonizing afternoon in his Durstlimas hotel room, pondering how to combine the sensational aspects of stage magic in this context, with the serious role of the investigative scientist. At last he decided that what was good for Baldwin had to be good for ASIEP, had it not? After all, he reasoned: "I'm its founder, ASIEP is I!"

And Mike Duffinger called George Debussy from the Four Seasons Hotel in Geneva.

Debussy did not like Duffinger's tone of voice. How cocky the sonofabitch sounds these days! Debussy thought. Swiftly, Debussy set about dismantling his subordinate's inflated posture. "Tell me something I don't know," he rasped, "I'm not asking for a diplomatic communiqué and I don't want to hear about the hookers of Geneva. I know they dropped the charges against van Schmul, or whatever. We got television over here, remember. And I heard about the bird-song our boy delivered that had everybody cooing and crying. What I want to know is - yes, right! Now remember we're on an open line."

"Well, sir," Duffinger said in his most servile tone of voice, "he looks like the real article to me. He drew this star map ...."

"Fuck," said Debussy, "are you in your hotel?"

"That's right, sir."

"Go out and call me collect from a pay phone!"

"Yes, sir. As you like."

"And cut out the continental schmaltz, will ya."

Twenty minutes later Duffinger was in a phone booth overlooking the lake. There was a warm, damp wind blowing in from France, ruffling the waters of the majestic Léman. A trio of swans that had weathered the winter breasted the breeze, treading water, their black masks pointed in the direction of the Banque Centrale du Lac edifice that rose, squat and reliable, just beyond the Tell Bridge. Debussy accepted the call.

"Okay," he said instantly, "what gives?"

"Well," said Duffinger, "there's quite a group of people here, as far as I can make out, all after him. It's like an international crap shoot. Everybody wants a piece of the action."

"Yeah, like what?"

"Well, I've put my feelers out a little. There are Russians, Germans, even Japanese. But nobody seems to want to make the first move. If I jump in there now with an offer, I'll have to establish a floor price. It'll certainly mean that we'll have to pay more. On the other hand, if we let one of the others start the bidding, they might come in with a lower base and we can bag him maybe even for less than we planned. We can probably save ourselves some money that way. That's why I haven't done anything yet. If you ask me, the Germans are tight, always have been and the Russians are cheap, I doubt they've got a fortune for a budget. The Japs are my only concern, they just bought a van Gogh for 22 million. God knows how much they'll offer the mountain man. They might outbid everyone!"

There was two, three dollars' worth of pause on the transatlantic line, then Debussy said, "What about this star map and this weird twittering?"

"The map looked damn real," said Duffinger. "If this guy is faking it he's got more confidence than a hatful of rattlesnakes. And as far as his singing is concerned, it was like nothing I've ever heard. You know me, I don't scare easy but he had me back there with the dandelions when I was a kid, dreaming. There wasn't a dry eye in the house. Whatever he's got, we can sure use it, that's what I think."

There was a sudden, long, screeching sound through the phone. Duffinger held it away from his ear. When he listened again, Debussy was saying, ".... what do you mean he's dangerous?"

"I didn't say he was dangerous, sir."

"I clearly heard you say he's dangerous."

"That's funny, but I didn't say anything like that."

"Well, is he dangerous?"

"I guess he could be, if he wanted to be. I mean, look at his record. Survives a crash, freezes totally, is thawed out, and lives. Claims to come from another planet. Learns to speak English in weeks. Smothers a hand grenade with his hands, melts glass, draws a star map, trills a weird tune that has everybody weeping in the courtroom. I don't know, maybe he could do something bad, sure. Hell, if he can do it with a hand grenade, he can maybe do it with an artillery shell, and if he can do it ...."

"Okay, fine, listen," Debussy said. "Something tells me this guy's a soft touch. He's not going to attack you for offering him money. Now I want you to go in there with twenty five thousand dollars a month, expenses extra, no questions asked, okay?"

Morris Duffinger assured his superior that he would go in and do his best. Debussy told him that his best would not be good enough. He didn't want him to go in and do his best, but to march in and do it, tie the man up, get him to sign a preliminary agreement, bring him back and do it all without fuss or fanfare. Duffinger assured him again that he would try and they broke the connection.

By a quirk of circumstance, just as Mike Duffinger stepped out of the phone booth onto the wet sidewalk by the lake, a little lost in this foreign environment, undecided which way to turn, gazing without curiosity at the swans that were still dipping in the wind, another long-distance telephone conversation - this one from Geneva in the opposite direction, to Moscow - had just then ended. Slavo Stentorian sighed in Geneva, the receiver still in his hand, shaking his head.

And now in Moscow Dimitri Nihilev managed to let out a satisfactory fart. He got up and beat his arms about his chest to warm his fingertips. He kicked the radiator. It responded with a death rattle that made Nihilev jump aside, though no filthy jet was forthcoming on this occasion.

Nihilev proceeded to the window, crossed his arms, noting that his fingertips were still cold. He quoted an old Russian proverb to himself:

"A long winter shortens spring!"

He squinted, thinking of Stentorian, his little fox. Then he thought of Stentorian's *fiancée*. On impulse he picked up the phone and dialled her extension. Vera Verovna answered brightly, prettily, as was her nature.

"I just want you to know that Slavo is well and sends you his love," said Nihilev.

"Oh, thank you, Comrade Nihilev," said Vera.

"He misses you and wants you to know that he thinks of you every day."

"Oh, Comrade Nihilev, you are kind to relay this information to me."

"My pleasure is mixed with pain in this case, Vera Verovna," Nihilev said.

"Pain," Vera asked, "why pain? He is well, isn't he?"

"Yes, my sweet," said Nihilev, "your Slavo is well. So long."

Nihilev replaced the receiver and stood still. It was already dark outside. Dark and somewhat lonely. It was cold in this room and though not quite so chilly in his apartment, there was nothing there. A few slices of cheese in the refrigerator, half a bottle of vodka, some bread. He could close up shop and go home now! But the great shop of the revolution never closed up. It was always supposed to be open, was it not? What was the revolution, he asked himself, without war to fuel it? And there hasn't been a war in a long time! All we have is the internal struggle, the little department wrestling matches, the big department fights and subtle purges, the Section Picnic with .... uh .... Vera. Yes, the stage is set, Dimitri Nihilev told himself. Stentorian is in Geneva. Let him defect, all the better! The dog has gone away and left his bone behind. And what a delicious bone it was, that Vera Verovna, what a fair bone packed with the finest, most succulent fresh meat!

13

ROCK

Dimitri Nihilev handled his best overcoat very carefully. It had obviously been tailor-made, of a gabardine-like material, but warp and weft so closely resembled one another that it presented a surface that was both slick and dull. It had been cut at a time when there was still something called "Russian style," in the year 1946 with the Red Army in the heavy flush of victory and Soviet leaders, like particularly weighty chessmen, posing, sitting, listening, leaning heavy chins on cupped hands, wearing heavy gold rings with Chinese stones in them. Lavrentij Beriya, for whom this coat had been made, had possessed ostentation of a different kind. He looked like the book-keeper of a small enterprise that had been failing slowly over thirty years, an enterprise which began by killing three million people a year and was now down to four hundred thousand. Nevertheless, Beriya had insisted on the best his tailor could provide and when Chief of the Secret Police Beriya died "of natural causes," Nihilev, then a young man, had audaciously "inherited" the masterpiece. Death of natural causes had not been uncommon during that period of Soviet history. A particularly natural cause was that of political expediency. Just before he died, Lavrentij had told the youngster Nihilev in icy jest that whenever he, Beriya, caught a cold, all of Siberia sneezed. It did not matter now. Lavrentij was gone. Only his coat walked on.

True, it was a touch too tight for Dimitri Nihilev, a bit too narrow in the shoulders, but still he liked to wear it on special occasions such as this one - a rendezvous with Vera Verovna in the May Café just across Potemkin Park, two good stones' throws from the new headquarters of the Advanced Studies Ministry.

Nihilev trotted down the three floors. In keeping with his status he shunned elevators, emphasizing physical fitness. More often than not a group of young comrades gathered perchance by the elevator would follow him, either up or down, to impress him. But today he skipped down alone, a little heavy, a little clumsy, but not that bad for a man of almost fifty. He paid no attention to the black Volga limousines at the entrance, barely acknowledged the doorman's salute, and trotted across the road, entering the park.

Already a gloomy twilight had descended on Moscow and by the time he got to the *May Café*, it would certainly be dark. Nihilev thought it was no good trying to beat the fading light. Furthermore, no one was watching now, so he slowed down to a leisurely stroll. His mind was in Geneva with Stentorian. If Stentorian succeeded, it would be another egg in Nihilev's basket and what an egg - he thought. A nice, big, round egg in the world of psychic phenomena which had suddenly bloomed for everyone. I am, Dimitri said to himself, in the right department! Things have worked out in my favour. The world has turned and Dimitri Dimitrivich had profited handsomely. Five years ago, only a handful of people listened to the babble of the new frontier in the Socialist arsenal: psychic exploration. Today a General Dvat can toss down a large glass of vodka and declare, as he did two weeks ago: "Socialist Russia, in her historic struggle with revisionist and counter-revolutionary forces everywhere, needs the psychic world as much as she needs rockets!"

Nihilev heard music, soft music, a guitar. A young man was singing a sentimental ballad, then abruptly changed to harsh chords. Dimitri hastened his steps. Not far ahead he made out the silhouettes of a group of youngsters, or, he told himself, a group of irresponsible loafers, to be more precise. Cowboys, he called them disdainfully. They were all singing now, and ugly though it was he thought he recognized the tune.

He had almost reached them now when he realized that it was a song Stentorian had once played for him, a silly, crazy American thing. It was too much for Dimitri Nihilev to pass by. He stopped and looked at them, trying not to hear what they were singing in a Russian translation that could not be an improvement on the original. He made out snatches of the refrain: "I remember when stones were young, me and Tanya had so much fun ...."

He took two, three steps toward the group, stopped again. In the quickly gathering darkness he lit a cigarette and waited. When they were through, as if by common impulse, they burst out laughing. No doubt they had seen him, but they paid no attention. He took another step, and another. Vera Verovna was probably already at the Café. He would not let these wastrels ignore him.

"Don't think I haven't heard of Elton John," he said. There was more laughter. Nihilev winced. "Yes," he said, "how could you know this music if you had not bought the record on the Black Market, and how could you buy the record on the Black Market without breaking the law and hurting the common Socialist cause of the people?"

"Ah," said a voice that seemed to drift out of the gloom without connection to the speaker, "what have we here - a revolutionary?"

"What I despise," said Dimitri Nihilev coldly, "is that you don't care to sing the song in the original, that you must put it into Russian, that you must befoul the language of the revolution."

"Ah," said the same voice, "Comrades, let us give our friend a sample of the culture we have acquired via Black Market records! Ready?"

They started up again, more vigorously than before, singing pointedly directly at him: ".... I remember when rock was yu-hu-hung, me and Suzy had so much fu-fu-hun ...."

Dimitri turned and started to walk away. Behind him the chorus swung neatly into: "Yaaaaah ya-ya-ya-ya-yaaah, ya-ya-ya-ya-yaah ya-ya-yaaaaaaaaaah; yaaaaah ya-ya-ya-ya-yaaah ...."

Slowly their voices ebbed. He had almost reached the other side of the park now, but still some phrases drifted after him, tugging at his irritated ears: "....did a thing.... called the.... Crocodile.... Rock...."

He crossed another road and briskly walked toward the yellow lights of the *May Café*. Even before he reached it, he saw Vera Verovna sitting by a window, wispy strands from her straw-yellow hair like a halo against the light above the silhouette of her face. Without being entirely conscious of this, his bearing changed. When he stepped through the door which led to a small space that served as a buffer against the cold and was separated from the interior of the café by a heavy blanket-curtain, the metamorphosis was complete. It was indeed Dimitri Nihilev, Head of the Psychkultura Section of the Advanced Studies Ministry of the Union of Soviet Socialist Republics, who walked into the *May Café*. And he was indeed wearing the overcoat made to measure for Lavrentij Beriya.

14

CARDS

For Dimitri Nihilev, the conquest of Vera Verovna, he knew, required work. It would be, already had been, at best, excruciatingly laborious. And he had already played most of his high cards. For Nihilev only power, his power over Slavo Stentorian for example, could accomplish his goal. For Hermann Huber, on the other hand, things were simpler, at least for the moment. If all Kyoto had been deserted at this hour, if the temples had stood yawning and nary a birdsong heard, the *generalsekretär's* entry into Nanita - one last time, without haste - would not have offended the silence that reigned.

Nanita for her part had finally decided to ask him a question that had developed in her mind during the seven or eight visits he had paid her. News from Geneva had been frustrating. So far, the girls she had sent to make contact with Shawn had not succeeded. So it was time to be evasive, she would simply have to trust Huber.

As he paused inside her, allowing himself the pleasure of growth inside the most expensive whore of the East, his eyes closed to savour the moment, Nanita's hand slid over and touched the pack of postcards he had brought her on this parting occasion.

There were fifteen of them, identical, and they were touching in their simplicity. Each one had a sky-blue background and, slightly off centre to the right of the viewer, two thick bamboo poles that stood parallel with each other, just close enough to permit a beautiful girl to rest her shoulder against them. The girl was dressed in the traditional kimono and obi. Her left shoulder was turned toward the camera, her left arm and hand hidden in the sleeve. Her right hand, slightly raised, held a fan. Her black hair was combed upward to form a crown held by a mother-of-pearl comb on top of her head. The kimono was of very light-blue silk with red and blue flowers on delicate stems. The broad waistband, held by a slim white belt, was ruby-red silk. To balance the picture a blue vase had been placed on a small blue table to the left. In the vase were white and yellow tulips.

The girl's face was as perfect as a traditional Japanese painting. She might have stepped out of a past century with her straight, delicately bridged nose, dark-lipped mouth and tiny shells of ears. Her head was inclined sideways at a perfect angle and she was smiling.

The girl on the postcard was Nanita, and when you tilted the card or changed your angle of view, she was suddenly naked, leaning against the bamboo.

So seen, in the nude, the subtle artifice of the traditional Japanese attire became apparent. The waistband and backpack hid a startlingly small waist. And by contrast her posterior was provocatively prominent, marvelously round. It could now be seen that the left arm, previously hidden, led to a small hand which rested lightly, a dove with wings folded, just on the inside of her thigh, touching her hipbone at the wrist. The fan, having disappeared, had permitted her right hand to delicately touch her small left breast in classic fashion: four fingers on the heart, the thumb squeezing ever so lightly from the other side. It was a portrait of such erotic impact that the postcards had become collector's items. Their appeal was both overt and subliminal at the same time. Unquestionably they had been, when they were manufactured, a masterpiece of kitsch.

Nanita had spent a fortune buying them back from the general public. A total of ten thousand were printed originally and for the sum of $25,000 she had managed to persuade the manufacturer to turn over the plates to her and to enter into a contractual agreement releasing her for ninety-nine years from the waiver she had so foolishly signed before she began making money.

Luckily, she had done this early in her career. But, still, as unavoidable word-of-mouth carried her praise through the Orient to the West, many of those who had carelessly picked up the trick cards at some news-stand or tourist shop in Paris, New York, Munich or London, began to realize their value and hoarded them. The tiny ads which appeared in the newspapers of all the major cities in themselves cost a small fortune but they immediately drew out most of the cards. Through agents, Nanita bought them back for an average of $5.00 apiece. Within two years she had acquired almost nine thousand. It was a guess that approximately ten percent had been lost, thrown away, mutilated or otherwise disappeared. But, certainly, there were still a hundred, two hundred, perhaps as many as five hundred postcards out there and almost every week she received offers to return one, two, three of these to her at outrageous prices. She had settled into a very businesslike attitude. Yes, she would pay, she would pay dearly, but there was a limit to her vanity. She realized, of course, that even the price she was willing to pay, which now hovered about £500 per card would have to go up. For now, the stack Huber had handed her was worth £7,500 to say nothing of the work involved in getting them. Moreover, Huber had probably been forced to pay even more, so it was, she thought, a ten-thousand-dollar fuck plus Huber's courtesy effort in gold. A man like this, she decided, had to be trusted simply by the dictates of common sense.

Her hand returned from the feel of the little postcard treasure to Huber's right shoulder. Gently she pushed him up and began to suck his nipples, here .... and there. Huber's eyes were still closed and he felt himself growing inside of her to vast proportions. It was no longer only her expensive vestibule and chamber he possessed, but he was filling a vast, pulsating hall with his treasure. He was all of the forty thieves and Ali Baba in one. *Verdammt*, he could not help thinking, Japan will make a poet out of me!"

Slowly now, involuntarily, he began to move, searching with that blind, slimy head down there for the only passage out of the treasured cave, Nanita's cervix, which itself had become elongated and distended at the tip to meet the German's probing snout.

"Huber," said Nanita against his hairy chest, "what do you know about that boy in Geneva?"

The Herr *Generalsekretär* was not startled by the question, he had expected something extraordinary from her. Without slackening in his exploration of the cave he said, "Officially we are not interested in him, but actually I believe he's causing a stir, quite a stir ...."

It occurred to him that the word "stir" in this context had a quality of existential humour to it, enough of it to remind him of his Munich student days. He began to laugh. This caused larger more erratic thrusts of his penis inside Nanita. It made contact with the mouth of her cervix, which attached itself to him with infallible expertise. This in turn created a suction effect at the very tip whose particular character had become nothing less than Nanita's trademark. She had him now and they both knew it.

"I will tell you something that has been a secret for a little while," Nanita said as she began to lead him toward that inevitable plunge of her famous orgasms, "and I shall tell you while your ears are open and while your mind is on vacation. I want that man! I have two servants in Geneva now whom I myself have trained, and they will persuade him to come to me. But you will do me a favour, won't you?"

The Herr *Generalsekretär* did not have to reply. His whole body was giving the answer. He had thrust forward now as deep and far as he could and there he had been stopped. In there a toothless snake with many tongues seemed slowly to be devouring him. It was a snake stuffed with fire, a dragon in the cave. He had brought the forty thieves and Ali Baba into the dragon's cave.

"Go to Geneva," she told him. "Call my servants and let them serve you! Find out what progress they have made! Then call me! Tell me! I am dying for good news!"

Was it good for Huber's flaming blind prince in the depths of Nanita's cave to be so devoured? Was it fear that made Huber groan? And were these not the spasms of death that made him expire to the tune of a chunk of gold, many gifts, and fifteen postcards that had never been mailed?

15

KISSES

This was the third glass of Krim wine Dimitri Nihilev raised to Vera Verovna, who smiled her sweet smile at him and brushed some of those golden, late-summer straw hair clouds away from her forehead. The Krim wine sun was shining in the cloudless, azure sky of her eyes. Dimitri had not yet dared to approach those tiny craters of her pupils in that peaceful landscape.

He gazed into her face, looked around her eyes. And he said, "Vera Natalia Natalina ...." And she said, "How do you know I was called Natalia?"

He tried to smile mysteriously, but on his face it came out as a drunken pull to one side. It was not pretty, would not have been attractive to an unbiased observer. "In our files," he grinned, "in our files .... well, I have taken an interest in you, Vera Verovna, and now that Slavo Slavovich has defected, or shall we say is on an important mission in the land of money, watches, cheese, chocolate and mountains, I want you to feel safe under the great big, feathery wings of Old Dimitri."

Vera laughed a little and took a sip from her glass. It was still her first glass out of the bottle standing between them. She thought Dimitri Nihilev was funny. She had always thought he was funny. Once Slavo had told her that Nihilev was the kind of a man who could kill another man if he thought it expedient and Vera had laughed and said that he, Slavo, was funny too, even funnier than Dimitri, because this was precisely the kind of remark she might have expected from Nihilev, not from her own dear fiancé. Then they had kissed and held each other.

At one of the Section picnics, Nihilev got drunk and tried to kiss Vera. He had held her around her waist with one arm and hand, and pushed her head forward at the neck with the other. He had been acting more drunk than he was and much clumsier, too. she had laughed and easily turned out of his grip and danced away from him. She had made him look like the Russian bear, but she had not told Slavo about it.

When Nihilev got drunk, which did not happen often, his face began to droop and sweat. He began to look like a soggy old melon. Vera could imagine that he liked to weep when he got really drunk. Weeping and music, the Old Music, that was Dimitri Nihilev when vodka and beer stripped him of inhibitions. Strictly speaking, it was quite an honour, a social advance, to be seen drinking wine with this man. Every girl in her office would envy her when the word got out, which it would. She had already smiled at a number of familiar faces in the café.

It was precisely because he got drunk so easily that Nihilev rarely drank. On the other hand it was difficult for him to get really drunk. So he had developed a habit of pretending to be intoxicated when he reached the plateau which for him meant being drunk. In his fourth glass of the heavy wine, he now began to slip into this role.

"My dear Vera," he said, reaching for the hand which she let him have, "the dangers of the West are not exaggerated, did you know? Our good Slavo is out there now .... in the jungle. Yes, I mean it. In the jungle of capitalist indifference. You know that he's lonely and in danger, I tell you."

She asked him how he meant that: "Slavo, in danger?" Dimitri pretended not to be able to quite focus as he looked at her. He pretended to be speaking the truth contained in the wine. He said, "Vera Verovna, my dearest Natalia, you are too young .... how old are you now, twenty? .... or nineteen, are you nineteen? No, you couldn't be, you could not have passed the examination, so you must be even older than twenty ...."

"Oh, much older," said Vera Natalia, "twenty-three."

Nihilev grinned, nodded vigorously, squeezing her broad, short-fingered little paw of a hand that felt so warm and limp in his. He said, "Yes, yes, and soon you will be married to our good Slavo, if .... I mean *when* he returns from his vacation .... eh .... I mean *mission*. Which may be just some little while, because, well, there are many knots to be tied before the ship can sail."

Despite the label of secrecy under which the entire Geneva trip had been planned, Slavo Stentorian had told his fiancée. And Vera

Verovna was acutely aware that Nihilev was trying to find out if and what she knew. She smiled at him and said, "There is nothing to confess, Comrade Nihilev. Slavo told me nothing. And, if you would like to know, I'll tell you why he tells me nothing. It's for my own safety, he explained to me. It's better this way. What I don't know can't hurt me."

"Ah - ah," Nihilev brought up a heavy index finger from his free hand and wagged it at her, "how can ignorance be such a good thing?"

He pulled her hand just a little closer. It was a move much too precise for his drunken facade. Instead of picking up her glass with her right, as she had been doing, she now pulled her left away from him. She lifted the glass and drank without paying Nihilev the courtesy of touching glasses or at least dipping hers at him before drinking.

She was wearing a tightly knit yellow turtleneck pullover, which showed off the full, firm roundness of her breasts further accentuated by a broad, blue belt with a golden buckle. Nihilev kept his eyes on this marvellous vision of youth and health.

"Vera Natalia Carolina ...." he began in a slurred voice.

"No, no, no," Vera protested, "now you are going too far. My name is not Carolina, I ...."

"What's wrong with Carolina?" Dimitri grinned. "That's my little sister's name."

"In that case," she smiled, "I'm honoured."

Now at last Vera Verovna knew what she felt like: the mouse before the cat, the bee before the bear, the frog before the snake, the child before the dinosaur, the leaf before the wind, the beauty before the beast. She suddenly and at last sensed that Dimitri Nihilev was determined to make love to her, this evening, tonight, in a short while.

"My sweet little Vera Carolina," he was saying, "I melt before your innocence and beauty. Don't think of me as the man who tells your *fiancé* what to do. Don't think of me as an important figure, think of me as a young man, a boy who adores you and who wants only to be near you."

"Thank you," she tried, "I'm happy to hear that Slavo is well. Do you have any idea when he will be back?"

"Ah," said Dimitri with a flushed, sweaty face, eyeing what remained in the bottle, "now there, you know, I want to tell you this, Vera Verovna, I do not determine when Slavo comes back, it's...well, it's you. You yourself!"

That, Vera thought, is the cat's paw, the first tentative, playful swipe at the mouse. Now is the time to run!

She got up, or rather she tried to get up. But Nihilev had anticipated her move, catching her by the wrist and keeping her down.

"It's important you realise that you determine Slavo's future," he said in a low, steady voice. "As I told you, he is out there in enemy territory and anything can happen to him. Now, Slavo is an intelligent man with good reflexes, but a man has only two eyes and two hands. I have been thinking of sending two men after him to protect him, Vera. I've been thinking this but I'm undecided, I'm waiting for something to make up my mind."

He pulled her hand toward himself, bringing his face slowly down to the table, his moist lips ready. He kissed the back of her hand with a loose open mouth. Then, without looking up, he said "Something or *somebody*, Vera Natalia!"

"And," he continued, "let's stop playing games. I want you. Vera, for this night and as many future nights as I please. Think of it as lending me your body, think of it as pawning something valuable. In return I guarantee your good Slavo's safety. I will bring him back to you. You know that I don't have to make such guarantees. And if I don't, who knows what will happen. Would I grieve if I lost a smart man like Slavo? Yes, of course. But there are a dozen eager young men waiting. Parapsychology is the newest, freshest, most sparkling of the sciences. General Dvat..."

"Damn General Dvat!" said Vera loudly, finishing off her glass of wine. She reached for the bottle and poured herself another one. She had planned it all in seconds. No doubt Nihilev would kiss her hand again, would bend to it and then she would hit him with the bottle.

"Ah, but what is all this business talk?" Nihilev said, lifting his face from her hand and looking at her now, seeking those tempting black craters in her eyes with his own. "I'm your friend, Vera," he said, "and you can count on my discretion. The sight of your wonderful breasts is bound to rouse the man in any man. Forgive me for speaking so frankly. No, no, I don't want you to give yourself to me in anger, Vera Verovna, in fact I don't insist you give yourself to me. I want you simply not to resist so that I can take you without force. The rest will come by and of itself, believe me. I am an experienced man and in the war of the bed I have fought many battles. Far be it from me to pretend that I won them all, but conquest isn't everything. Surrender to me, Vera Verovna. You will not regret it!"

Predictably he bent to her hand. At this angle his mouth disappeared from Vera's view, but at the last moment before it did she noticed a thick filament of saliva, almost a froth, connecting his parted lips. She could feel goose bumps appearing on her arms. Dimitri kissed her hand again, with a wet and soulful and seemingly interminable kiss. Then, when his mouth and her skin parted company, he said distinctly, but in a voice calculated to reach only her ears, "Tell me, Vera, is the hair on your..."

Her free right hand had hovered by the bottle. Just before he started talking she had gripped it firmly by the neck. Now it came down on the back of his head, interrupting his question. Blood gushed and sprayed over the finely laundered tablecloth as Nihilev brought up his head, his eyes wide in disbelief. The bottle had broken but Vera still held it by the neck. And Nihiliev still had her hand. Slowly now, with blood running down the sides of his face and a small rhythmic fountain gushing from his head, he pulled her across the table with his iron grip. Vera did not resist. She drew back the jagged bottle, readying it for a direct thrust. She said, "Let me go, Dimitri Dimitrivich! Let me go or lose the sight of your damn eyes!"

Dimity Nihilev let her go. She swept her coat off a hanger and strode out, her magnificent bosom heaving with the breath of pride.

Nihilev, too, staggered to his feet, just as the most courageous among the young waiters began to wake from his wide-eyed trance.

Nihilev walked unsteadily to the coat rack, one hand at the back of his head, trying to cut off the flow of blood. The waiter got there before him, took the coat Nihilev pointed at and draped it around his shoulders. Through Nihilev's fingers a steady stream of blood seeped, dripping to his neck and shoulders. Nihilev shrugged off the coat, caught it with his left hand and got into a sleeve. Then he exchanged hands, to cover the wound, and slipped his other arm through. The waiter helped him belt it. Blood flowed freely onto the historic garment once worn by Lavrentij Beriya, the bespectacled accountant of death.

16

DEATH

Dimitri Nihilev's head wound was deep and dangerous,but it was nothing in comparison to Patrick Young's. The red-haired journalist had made the mistake of flying to London. This was an error that could have been rectified by immediately flying back to Geneva. Instead he ventured inside a pub, put ten pence in a public telephone, dialled, or at least began to dial, and was blown to kingdom come.

While Dimitri Nihilev was still recognizably himself, though slightly disfigured by blood, Patrick Young could be identified only by the one hand which was found. It still had a ring on it with his initials and the mark of the jeweller who had sold it to him. This fact, and that the bartender knew him, while it could not save his life, at least allowed the world to preserve the appropriate memory. So little could, in fact, be found of him that, had it not been for the hand, he would have been declared missing altogether.

Credit for the bombing was claimed (in a note to *The Daily Mail*) by lunatic fringers who called themselves Humans Against Enslavement by Extraterrestrials. Expert sources speculated that HAEBE was no less than a front for Global Eliminations, Inc., a private hit organization which contracted with governments. Global Eliminations was known to specialise in so-called "common-goal" jobs in which two or more governments separately contracted for the elimination of the same individual. According to these sources, Shawn was next on the hit list.

It was a heavy blast and it made front-page headlines in all the British national newspapers. *Inter-Europe News* published a kind and maudlin editorial in which the departed journalist was posthumously recommended for the Prix Dardentor, the cherished Continental honour for special achievement in the field of journalism.

Shawn, in the safety of his suite in the Royal Palace Hotel, smiled when he heard the news. The doors were now guarded by burly gentlemen in what, no doubt, they thought of as inconspicuous attire. Shawn was reading the paper, looking at the pictures including one of Jan van Schmul, who, on the advice of his solicitor had placed himself in psychiatric care. It was pointed out that nowhere in van Schmul's history could be found the slightest motive for trying or wanting to kill Shawn, a perfect stranger to him.

Shawn continued smiling. For a moment he closed his eyes, allowing his mind to spin back home, gaining perspective on this world of low-vibratory frequency to which he had been sent. Patrick Young had encountered sudden contact with a high-frequency vibratory device and, naturally, he had been torn to pieces. But it had happened only eighteen hours ago and so it would be easy to reassemble him. His vibratory pattern, established in more than three decades of living, would take much longer to disintegrate than his physical body. It still functioned almost normally. Shawn, through closed lids, could actually see it in the large green-velvet armchair where Patrick the entire man had been fond of sitting. Working on Terra was like being exiled on a lava planet, or a body of stinking mud. One did not want to abandon one's form to the dominant mass, and soon had to slosh through it step by step. Even so, Nonomine admitted to himself, the dominant mass on Terra is flesh, and flesh is not so bad.

It was a thought that served well enough for a point around which to rally the resurrection of Patrick Young. Shawn, eyes still closed, lowered the newspaper.

"You see, my boy," he began to speak as though Patrick were actually sitting in the armchair, "it's all a matter of acting as if. If Terrestrians learned how to act as if they would soon begin to control all their diseases, their ageing, their flesh in general and particular. Still, it makes a difference who it is that acts as if. Take me as an example. I am talking to you even though you are not here, I am acting as if you are here. I do not have to believe that you are here in the flesh, because it is becoming true even as I talk. There is no need... to... believe... that which...is...self evident...!"

These last words were spoken slowly, with terrifying emphasis, and when Shawn opened his eyes, Patrick Young was sitting pale and exhausted in the velvet chair.

Patrick raised his left arm minus the hand. He said: "Look - if you resurrect the dead, will you please give me my hand, too!"

Shawn put away the paper, smiling at his friend. He said: "Patrick, officially you are dead. We can't let you walk around without a hand. Getting your hand is not easy, because it's still intact, I understand they're keeping it as evidence of your death. It's much harder to grow *new* flesh when the old flesh is still around, do you understand? If you had been shot, for example, it would have been almost impossible for me to make a new, living man out of you - without bringing your corpse to life. And making a corpse live again cannot be a desirable thing to do. So, be patient for now. I need you, Pat. When I have to talk to you, I'll bring you back. Now relax, think of this as a va...ca...tion!" At this last word, Young faded in his chair. Shawn got up, walked to the window and looked out at the lake. Groups of swans were gracefully competing with boats in the yacht harbour. Shawn went to the telephone, called the desk and gave instructions to send up the two Japanese women who were waiting in the lobby.

Shawn walked to the door, opened it and told the guard that, in a few moments, two Japanese ladies would arrive, and to let them in. He closed the door and stood silently, waiting. He was thinking of Oba, the Councillor. No doubt he would turn up in some other disguise soon, to provoke him. Oba had a thankless task for a Great One. On the Home Council he could allow his wisdom to reign undefined, uncluttered, shapeless, almost absolute. But here, in the dimension of time, flesh and money, he was obliged to work through a hundred restrictions. Perhaps, Shawn smiled inwardly, it will at last make a rebel out of him!

When the girls were admitted to his suite, they stood smiling by the door of the sumptuous room. Shawn walked up to them, touched them on their shoulders and led them to a couch. As they sat down, he picked up the phone and ordered tea. Then he sat down across from them and said:

"You've come a long way, but I have come a much longer way. She who sent you is beautiful indeed but she is not my sister and I am more beautiful than she is. I am the light, she is the insect. I am the insect, she is the dust!" The women, still smiling, said nothing.

"Now take off your robes!"

They got up and began to take off their pastel-coloured robes. They did this slowly, as if in a trance, revealing their soft, small breasts, turning to show off the delicate napes of their white necks set off by perfectly combed black hair. They let their robes fall to the waist and then they sat down again.

"I shall devour you," said Shawn smiling, "and then you will be free to return and tell your mistress of the flame!"

There was a knocking on the door. Shawn opened it to let in a young waitress in a blue and red dress, who carried a tray to the coffee table, set it down, turned and walked out as if she had seen nothing of what she saw. Now they shared the tea. Shawn asked them to tell him of their mistress and they did. They said that she was more beautiful than the morning sun and more distant than the farthest star and paler than the moon, to which Shawn replied that such beauty could not be matched by wealth in time. They continued describing her to him. They told him that as moon, as sun, as the farthest star she called to him to join her in Kyoto.

When they were finished with tea and talk, they rose and took off the rest of their clothes. Their pubic hair kept the promise of their necks, and their nipples complemented their cherry lips. They stood, turning at the waist, smiling, showing off the ridges of their hips, creating the traditional lines of Japanese pen drawings. Then they sat back on the couch and spread their legs. With nimble fingers they spread all available lips and used small, mother-of-pearl combs to arrange their pubic hair attractively while Shawn watched them.

Finally they rose and began to dress again, with Shawn smiling. When they were neatly clothed again, Shawn said, "I have this message for your queen. Memorise it well for I will say it only once. The moon, the sun, and the farthest star are contained in mystery, and all the mystery is contained in me, and I am here now."

They repeated the message to him. Then one of them said, "But, sir, we were sent to invite you to Japan and if possible to bring you with us. Our lady will be disappointed if we return without you!"

"I have devoured you," said Shawn, "you now know the flame!"

The girls looked at each other as if to say they did not understand him, that they did not feel devoured, that they didn't know the flame he was talking about.

Shawn said: "You know the flame by its light, not by its heat. I have devoured you by the light of the flame. Don't ask to be devoured by the heat. You want to return to Japan, and you want to be alive. Go now!"

As one they rose and walked to the door. When the door had closed, Patrick Young appeared in his armchair, heaving a deep sigh, saying: "Shawn, I had a beautiful dream of swans."

"Good," said Shawn, "you will go back to your dream soon enough but listen to me first."

"My hand," Patrick exclaimed, "where is my hand! Please?"

"Stop talking about your hand," Shawn smiled. "In your dream of swans you do not talk of your hand, why talk of it here? There are a number of people here in Geneva with a great deal of money at their disposal and they want to trap me. I need your advice. These men are Americans, Russians, Germans. They want to use me and they are prepared to buy me, to hire me, but also to kill me. I can send them away, I can bring them back. I can make them disappear or send them home. But I want money. What shall I do?"

"You," Patrick marvelled, "*you* are asking *me* what to do?"

"Yes, Patrick, I need your advice. As you say, look! Look! You died for me, you lost your hand, perhaps forever. There are events even out of my reach. I grace you with my question."

"I was blown up in a pub in London," Patrick said, "To be blown up in London is not such a great event. It's a regular occurence in Ireland. If I did it for you, I assure you that such a generous act of sacrifice was far from my mind."

"Dreaming of swans is doing you good." Shawn smiled. "I need your advice."

"All right, then," said Patrick, "if you like. My advice is talk to them. Talk to them all. Get them all together and talk to them."

"Very good," said Shawn. "Thank you. That was exactly what I thought I should do. Talk to them, show them something. Convince them. It is better to negotiate. The lion will talk to the lambs."

"Lambs!" Patrick exclaimed. "Is that how you think of us, as lambs?"

"To become lambs, that is your destiny. Didn't you tell me that there was once a man who walked on water and likened himself to a lamb? Well, where I come from there was also such a one. And the lion is the closest there is on Terra to describe his spirit. Go back to your dream, Patrick Young!"

Slowly the man who had been blown to bits in London faded, except for his left hand which, far away, sealed in a container filled with fluid, was not alive and therefore could not fade.

17

SURVIVORS

Patrick Young was not the only one who had suffered an untimely accident. The Herr *Generalsekretär* Hermann Huber was worse off, not being a friend of Shawn's. He was dead, and dead essentially without recourse.

He had been found at the end of the Quay-du-Paradis on his back, naked. To the police it looked like random violence, a spontaneous mugging, even though such incidents occurred very rarely indeed in Geneva.

The matter of the man who was found in the mountains did not concern his department but it had not been hard to convince his superiors that he, Huber, was the right man to take a closer look. The two German negotiators were ordered back to Bonn and the matter placed in Huber's hands.

Not long after his appointment to the task of negotiating with Shawn, he received an invitation to attend a conference which was cautiously called "preparatory" and at which Shawn would be present. Huber did not bother to ponder how the phenomenal young man could have known all the facts of Huber's trip from Kyoto to Geneva, his jockeying for the spot as negotiator, his hotel. Huber did not care much for the occult, for parapsychology, for phenomena of ghosts, reincarnation, bent spoons, telepathy or astrology, for that matter. He was a realistic man with a penchant for whores and his eyes on the Chancellorship of the Federal Republic of Germany. Everything seemed to be coming together harmoniously, and this Shawn might be just the colourful little trophy he needed on his shelf as *entree* into the conversational circles that had admitted him only so reluctantly these past years. *Verdammt,* thought Huber, I don't care if this kid talks through antennae that grow out of his head!

It would be one more occasion to kill two elephants with a single blowgun! This was an expression coined by Huber himself, and he was very proud of it since it never failed either to pique or to provoke laughter. Huber had asked himself many times what exactly might the elephant be doing in any given situation and how one could possibly kill two elephants with a single blowgun. He had finally decided that the very charm of this little nonsense aphorism - if indeed it might be thought of as an aphorism - was that it made no sense whatsoever. A poison dart from a blowgun might nick an elephant and glance off and hit yet another elephant. But in practice it wouldn't work. "Elephant skin is thick," Huber chuckled to himself. If the dart penetrated deeply enough for the poison to be effective it would not have enough momentum to continue into another elephant. Well, he had been in his cups when he came up with it. It had a certain surprise value. Huber grinned ruefully at himself in the bathroom mirror.

The entire evening, it had appeared, still lay before him. Huber called the number Nanita had given him and told the two geishas that he had news from Kyoto, and that he would be over in one hour precisely. While he showered he examined his penis - a habit he had acquired as a young man, when he carelessly went into whatever woman he came across without thought of possible consequences. How stupid he had been. Huber pulled back the foreskin, twisted the shaft and glans and bent forward to look for anything out of the ordinary. It was a purely ritualistic gesture and he passed quickly through it, satisfied that everything was all right. There was no burning, no itching, and in order to assume that he had contracted syphilis in Japan he would have had to be not merely suspicious but paranoid.

Well! The Herr *Generalsekretär* began to soap the entire genital appendage. Well, he had *never* had syphilis! Nanita was clean - the cleanest! By his standards the cleanest and the most corrupt woman in all of Asia. But then, he had not had time to explore Asia thoroughly.

Huber thought also: How curious! When I'm there, when I'm with her, she turns me into a sensual poet, not only that, she makes a meek lover out of me. As soon as I put some distance between us I see her for what she really is: a beast, a piggish vampire in human form, a bloodsucker! Huber was hooked and he knew it.

He asked himself finally, still soaping away under the arms, around the neck, what was truly the addictive ingredient in their relationship. Sex, of course, the orgasm. It had to do with his being allowed by her to abandon himself, to rut, yes, she lets me rut, she makes a pig out of me. The big German pig and the little Japanese bird!

Some water had entered his nose and he had a coughing fit. When it passed, Huber turned off the water, got out and began to towel off. His thoughts drifted to the forthcoming rendezvous with Nanita's servants. Looking down, he noticed that he had an erection. Hermann Huber roared with laughter. He had begun talking to his penis, saying aloud: "*Na, mein Kleiner* (which was in itself plainly an understatement) are you looking forward to the evening's entertainment? Can you sniff those perfumed little purses, those tight little cunts, my good boy, can you taste them already?"

Not much later, death had taken Hermann Huber out of the bidding for the services of Shawn, leaving only Slavo Stentorian and Morris "Mike" Duffinger in the running.

Duffinger had moved from the Four Seasons Hotel to a small guesthouse on the Route-de-Chêne to be less conspicuous. He had registered under an assumed name backed by a perfectly made passport, letting it be known that he was a wine merchant from California, travelling on business. Inwardly Mike Duffinger cursed the department for saddling him with such a profession. He hated wine. Now, with every meal at the guesthouse, he was obliged to drink a small bottle of the stuff, French at that. He finally solved the problem by pretending business engagements and eating out.

At this time, just before the discovery of Huber's body, Duffinger had still not solved the problem of contacting Shawn. In his opinion it was a delicate situation. Duffinger thought that you couldn't just call up and say: Hello, Duffinger's the name and hiring-you-away-from-under-the Russkies' noses is the game. Or: Hello there, I represent a branch of the United States Government called the U.S. Bureau of Psychic Research and Development, and I want to buy you.

No, of course, one couldn't do that. You couldn't even call up and say: Good afternoon, sir, I'm Morris Duffinger. My friends, among whom I should soon like to count you, call me Mike. Won't you call me Mike, too? Could we meet? Oh, I almost forgot, I work for the U.S. Bureau of Psychic Research and Development and I'm authorized by my government to offer you - ahem - one million, yes, sir, that's right - one million bucks in .... what am I saying, not quite that much, but certainly a great deal of cash for your paranormal services, whatever they turn out to be.

No good that, either! Duffinger had been sitting in an excellent fish restaurant into which he had happened and from which he had not been able to extricate himself for fear of making a scene. He was ladling a thick soup and there wasn't a chance of ordering a stiff shot of bourbon with it unless he wanted everybody to notice. As he ran mentally through the various speeches he might try, he managed to case the place for broads. There were a good dozen or two and some appeared unaccompanied, but that was Europe; they might be hookers, they might not. It would take him weeks to get used to the local customs. But he was horny now, dammit!

Good day, sir, Duffinger started another silent monologue. My name's Duffinger, Morris Duffinger. I work for the U.S. Bureau of Psychic Research and Development and I happen to be passing through Geneva. Yes, sir, I'll come directly to the point. I understand that two girls, I mean ladies - and may God give them the rest they deserve - took their lives out of love for you. Well, the U.S. Government would like, for a change, to see why these women thought you so lovable. I mean - pardon me - you can melt glass and snuff out exploding hand grenades with your bare hands and I just wanna tellya that's mighty impressive and we're not disinterested in that kind of thing back home in the U.S., neither. In fact, we've got a cute programme at the Bureau, and some of the top people in the business are with us, man by the name of Martino, Vitrio Martino, for example, helluva telepath and clairvoyant! It wouldn't surprise me if he is aware of this conversation at this very moment which is impressive, even you must admit.

Duffinger swallowed a little too much soup and coughed. He tried to stifle convulsive movements of his hands but succeeded only in aggravating his predicament. An Italian waiter hurried over and expertly slapped his back. Some of the soup gushed back out into the bowl and onto the table. Tears were running down Duffinger's face. The waiter was dabbing at it with a large, white napkin. Duffinger tried inconspicuously to fend him off but even though no one appeared to pay attention, he knew he was being noticed. It was a good excuse to leave. He overpaid handsomely and left a large tip, but was nevertheless followed by the waiter, who insisted on more money. It was then that Duffinger realized he had miscalculated and paid only half of what he owed.

When he got home he found a note on his bed. It was written in terrible English, informing him that Mr. Shawn would like him to attend a meeting in the morning in the small conference room at the Royal Palace Hotel.

"I'll be damned," Mike Duffinger murmured, "now how could he have known where I was, who I am and what I want?"

He walked over to the sink where he kept a small bottle of precious bourbon from the duty-free shop at Washington airport and poured himself a stiff three thumbs' into a glass. No more than two kilometres approximately to the north as the crow flew, at about this same time, Slavo Stentorian, too, was pouring himself a stiff drink. It was vodka. He downed it and then pressed the play button on his battery operated Novotny Portable Cassette, setting in motion the entire instant electronic marvel.

Even as he flung himself on his bed, even before he had stopped bouncing, the intoxicating strains of Woody Herman's "Apple Honey" swung into the room. Slavo closed his eyes. His right foot started tapping the air. Yes, he told himself, all is going well. The little fish is biting. I shall not defect. Not this time. This time I shall enjoy myself here as a lepidopterist. I shall catch this rare little butterfly I've been sent here to catch. I shall bring him home with me to Moscow. And then ...."

Slavo propped himself up on his elbows and jerked his chin up and down to mark the wild and divine beat of the incomparable Woody Herman.

....Yes, he informed himself, I'll bring him back to Moscow. I'll pick up my precious bundle, Vera. And *then* I shall defect!

18

CONFERENCE

The chairs in the little conference room of the hotel were Louis-Quinze imitations, upholstered in green velvet. The table was heavy mahogany. The drapes too, were heavy green velvet and since the sun was shining on this rare occasion, they had been drawn back, bunched, tied and tassled.

Shawn, too, was dressed entirely in green silks. His hair shone like spun gold as he told Slavo Stentorian and Morris Duffinger that the third participant in these talks, a representative of the Federal Republic of Germany, had died last night.

Mike Duffinger had not yet learned of this switch in personnel and found the information slightly confusing. He said, "Far be it from me, sir, to gloat over this unfortunate event but the way I understood it there were two boys from Germany in on this. Correct me if I'm wrong."

The Durstli Man said nothing and Slavo Stentorian wisely withheld comment. He, too, had thought there were two German competitors and he, too, was surprised. But at heart he was a deeply religious man and he felt that one was a fool to question or argue with fate. Whoever that fellow had been, he was out of the way.

Duffinger looked at Shawn, then at Slavo Stentorian, then back at Shawn. He said, "Sir, if you'll pardon me, do you think it's wise to have an open session like this? I mean we're always prepared to meet a potential friend half way, but if I could just have a few words in private with you ...."

Shawn raised his right hand, cutting him off. He smiled

disarmingly at both men and said, "This is not a business meeting, my friends, this is a classroom! Let me say first that I am not for sale. I am for hire. But my price is going up even as we're talking. Before you start bidding, and before we discuss particulars of money, I want to show you something."

Occasionally he still hesitated, but in general his English had become fluent and firm. Now, as he said "particulars" or rather - just before he said "particulars," there was a slight hesitation, something akin to a tournament equestrian approaching a difficult jump. But he went over it smoothly and finished the sentence.

He got up and walked to one of the heavily draped windows and he motioned the two men to follow him. They noticed now, as they moved to the window, that the light had subtly changed in the room. It was no longer the pale sunlight of a wishy-washy Geneva spring day, but a tint of turquoise so evenly distributed that one could not have imagined the sun to be its sole source. Yes, Mike Duffinger had to admit to himself, it's an eerie light, an eerie day! An eerie feeling!

Shawn now opened the window. He leaned out and looked down. When he straightened, his great smile had deepened. But it was not his smile that disturbed Slavo Stentorian, it was his eyes. They were enormous and appeared to be spinning, eddying, creating a vortex of dazzling blue. This man, Slavo Stentorian decided, is crazy! And in the head of his rival, in the head of Morris Duffinger a similar resolution began to form itself, culminating in the word "nuts."

Nevertheless both men followed Shawn's invitation to look out and see for themselves. What they saw was a full view of planet Earth, from space. It was the traditional poster picture that had made the U.S. space programme famous, the great misty blue ball with its parched brown continents and prim skirts of white clouds. A beautiful vision under other circumstances but at this moment it was fit to inspire terror - nothing else.

"Is that ....?" Duffinger mumbled, trying to withdraw his head, but he could not. It was held in position by a force very much like a hand of steel gripping his neck from behind, though Shawn stood three feet back and had not lifted a finger.

"Yes," said Shawn, "that is where you live."

"It is .... b-b-beautiful," Slavo Stentorian actually stuttered. "I can't believe this - I must be going mad!"

Duffinger felt the steel grip being released. Both men pulled their faces back into the room and, in a reflex of panic, Duffinger slammed the window shut and tried with trembling hands to untie the knots and bows of tassled cords that held the curtains. But then Shawn told them to sit down at the table. They obeyed like schoolboys.

They sat there, Duffinger's face pale, Stentorian's flushed, breathing heavily. That was all the sound that could be heard in this room for some time. Then Duffinger spoke. He said: "That, sir, must have been an illusion. That couldn't have been real!"

Stentorian nodded. A similar thought had been on his mind. Shawn shrugged.

"My friends," he said, "that is the Earth, really the Earth. And you are really up in space. And nobody really misses the little conference room in the Royal Palace Hotel or Geneva, or Switzerland. You are not missed. There is a hole in the hotel and nobody cares. People cannot see that hole. Why not? Because it is too terrifying for them to see. They might see it, but they cannot acknowledge what they see. So they see the door inside, the door to the little conference room. And nobody will dare disturb us. What do you call it, a phenomenon?"

Again there was that moment's hesitation in the tournament rider's approach to the word. Again he vaulted the hurdle smoothly.

"Patrick," said the Durstli Man to Patrick Young, who was beginning to solidify at the other end of the conference table, the luminous stump of his left arm resting before him on the smooth and shiny mahogany surface. "Patrick, what shall I do with these men?"

Patrick blinked, shook his head. When he spoke his voice came out as a chant, a hoarse chant but nonetheless melodious. "Send them away," he chanted. "Send them home!"

"Thank you, Patrick," said Shawn. "So long!"

Barely materialized, Patrick Young disappeared before the staring eyes of the two negotiators.

"Yes, my friends," Shawn went on, "that was Patrick Young whom a bomb tore apart in London. You knew that, didn't you?"

Duffinger tried to get up. He was trembling violently. His teeth were chattering. "Sir," he clacked away, "sir, please l-l-let me g-go, let us go, I want t-to get out of here, please! I want OUT!"

"Sit down," Shawn said. Duffinger sat down. Stentorian, too, had tried to rise but had not been able to move. Finally, his military training gained the upper hand over blind panic. He even managed to force a smile.

"My friend Patrick Young has just advised me to send you home," Shawn said. "Do you know what that means?"

"No," Duffinger stammered, "Springfield, Illinois?" Shawn shook his head in amazement. "So you think you come from Springfield?" he smiled. "Springfield, Illinois? Shall I truly show you where you come from? Do you wish to visit your true home? Do you want to dream of swans?"

"Swans?" Duffinger inquired in a quavering voice.

"And you, Slavo Slavovich Stentorian," Shawn went on, "do *you* wish to see *your* home?"

"No, sir," Slavo Stentorian managed to get out. "No, thank you very much, sir, I have no homesickness, no desire for the land of my forefathers. I just want to get ....! Please let me go! I beg of you .... Please!"

"Good," said Shawn, still smiling. "In that case, let the bidding begin!"

The word "bidding" hit them like a slap in the face. They had forgotten all about bidding, especially Duffinger. But yes, he now thought, that's right, little turquoise conference room, now we're getting down to business!

Aloud he said, "The U.S. Bureau of Psychic Research and Development is prepared to offer you a minimum of twenty five thousand dollars per month, all expenses paid, if you'll just come over and kind of mosey around, look around, sir, and answer a couple of questions or two."

"Sixty thousand," said Slavo Stentorian. Shawn asked him if he meant rubles.

"U.S. dollars, sir," Stentorian replied.

"Well, said the Durstli Man, "that makes eighty-five thousand dollars per month, or over a million dollars per year. Not bad, not bad at all. Good, my friends, very good. Very good and very cheap!"

Suddenly his eyes were whirring, dizzying discs again. They thought they saw two hollow beams of light that led inward into and through his face and away into endless space and they felt themselves drawn to that journey, but could not go. It was their great sadness and pain, and their great terror, that they could not follow that two-lane highway into space.

Shawn's voice filled the room as he told them in simple words that they were no-good men, cheaters, who tried to buy the safety of their countries for a lousy million dollars.

"I have shown you," the Durstli Man thundered, "I have shown you what I can do and you offer me an amount so small, so insignificant (again he hurdled the word smoothly) that I laugh. This is my laughter and listen well. This is the laughter to which the Union of Socialist Soviet Republics and the United States of America must dance!" The two would-be negotiators felt themselves drawn by an irresistible force back to the window, which opened for them. Below them, closer than before but still far away, the globe turned slowly, majestically. There was an acceleration, a sudden compression of distance and they had an even closer view: cities were collapsing in the U.S.A. and in the USSR. Great dark clouds hung ominously over the countryside, flashing green lightning. Both men stared, horrified.

"Take a good look," said Shawn evenly, but his voice sounded strangely hollow and disembodied behind them.

They tried but could not close their eyes. Lightning still flashed through the black clouds, cities still fell. Rivers welled up and became swollen, poisonous serpents lashing the land. Oceans frothed greedily, devouring coasts.

"That is not *my* work," Shawn intoned. "That is the work of man. It is already etched into the cosmic book. I am showing it to you so you cannot doubt."

They felt the pressure subside. They slunk back to the conference table and slumped in their chairs, deflated, exhausted, trembling. Shawn told them to go home - go to their terrestrial home and tell their superiors what they had seen.

"Tell them," he said calmly, "I want fifty million dollars deposited in my account with the Banque Centrale du Lac. Fifty million from each of you, immediately. You have a week to get it."

Stentorian managed to pull himself together. Though his voice shook, he asked: "But .... for what shall I say .... this money, for what shall I say ....?"

Shawn stood up. He looked down on the two demolished men. He knew that, had he been thoroughly human, he might now have felt sympathy with their grief, empathy with their fate, pity for their situation. But being human was not a prescribed part of his stay on Terra, at least none that had been specified. He chose to remain aloof. His face showed a cool, incalculable, alien distance.

"Tell them the money is for services rendered!"

Then he raised his left hand and in that moment Slavo Stentorian found his feet groping for the dull linoleum of the corridor approaching Nihilev's office in Moscow. And Morris Duffinger stood on shaky legs, trying to steady his failing knees across the street from Speedy-Mac in Washington where he could discern Debussy's profile, munching energetically on a mouthful of junk food.

Both men needed minutes to orient themselves. Both thought they might be in a dream, a nightmare, and so they waited for reality to fray, but it did not. On the contrary, it became self-assertive. Stentorian was discovered by Nihilev when the latter came out of his office on his way to the toilet, and Duffinger had the willpower to cross the street and feebly reach his boss just as he got up.

"I'll be fucked!" Debussy allowed.

"Coffee!" croaked Duffinger.

And in Moscow, Dimitri Nihilev was obliged to catch the swooning Stentorian in his arms.

19

ENCOUNTER

While Shawn was "negotiating" so dramatically in Geneva, Mr. Baldwin had been no less busy and performed, within the limitations of his more modest talents, no less spectacularly. After a show at the Palais Urban in Paris, a great, somewhat draughty hall that had seen better days, he presented himself for a question-and-answer period which, as usual, was stormy.

"Mr. Baldwin, please!"

Frowning slightly, Jack Baldwin pointed at the questioner whom he had been trying to avoid. The young man was dressed in the typical garb of the student know-it-all: rough boots, baggy grey work pants tightly belted, a worker's blue denim shirt relieved only by a blue and red bandanna at the neck. As if to mock the capitalist system, he wore over this outfit what must have once been a grey silk vest to go with a tuxedo. It now showed stains and other signs of careless wear. The questioner's face was thin, hollow-cheeked and pale. A great oily mop of curly hair topped his head. His hands gesticulated nervously.

"Mr. Baldwin, I cannot afford to go to Geneva to inform myself first-hand concerning the events there. On the other hand, we have your personal testimony and performance, which is negative. Naturally, I must be cautious. Will you tell us, why have you chosen to debunk that man?"

"Well ...." Jack Baldwin cleared his throat. It was necessarily a question he had expected and for which he was prepared. Still, he did not like it. "Well, let's say I'm doing it for all the gullible people, all the innocent, trusting young people in the world. They are being misled. The simplest way of putting it, maybe, is to say that I hate to see them build something in their lives on a lie."

"Ah, do you think all young people are gullible, innocent,

trusting?"

"No, not all, but most."

"But why should we believe you?"

"Because I don't lie about what I do. You saw my show. You saw the grenade explode ...."

"That was not a grenade," said the young man vehemently.

"Right. I made that clear. Nor was what exploded in Shawn's hand a grenade. It was a device very much like the one I'm using in my show."

"Are you saying that it could not have been a grenade?"

"Absolutely. Just think! Think how far we've all been brainwashed if we can even consider the idea that a man can contain the explosion from a hand grenade with his bare hands. It's impossible. It's against the laws of nature."

The young man let out a short, mocking laugh. Jack Baldwin tried to end the exchange by pointing at another questioner. It didn't work.

"Mr. Baldwin, please! Mr Baldwin! We are not far from the Sorbonne. There was a time when in the halls of learning right here in France a man contending that Earth was spherical would have been laughed at, dismissed, or forced into exile, or perhaps killed. Such a thing, in those days, was also considered impossible - against the laws of nature. Laws of nature are not fully known to us. If we knew them, we could truly command them. We wouldn't be in the mess we're in."

There was applause and encouraging calls from the audience. Mr. Baldwin looked around. He suddenly saw these youngsters for what they were - cynical, aggressive punks without respect for their elders! And to think that he had been trying to reform such as these! Well, he had received his guarantee and there was no need to expose himself to further ridicule. He turned to leave but couldn't quite bring himself to do it. Vanity, that great demon of those in the public eye, detained him. "You are wrong," he said loudly. "You are young, naive and wrong. You are looking for heroes and saints. You'll pick on anybody that comes along. That's what this guy's plan is. He knows this. He knows there's plenty of money to be made with people like you in the world."

"But how does he make this money, Mr Baldwin? Why isn't he doing what you're doing?"

It was a bad question and Baldwin knew it. There was nothing to do but shrug. It would have been a natural response. He should have shrugged and walked away. He missed his second opportunity to disengage himself from this unpleasant situation. He pretended to get impatient. Impatience to him was preferable to ignorance.

"We're dealing here with a very clever man," he shouted, "don't you understand that? He's a good magician, an illusionist, and he's modern in his clothes and his looks. His illusions aren't confined to the stage. He's understood that to be really successful you have to take your show into the streets, to the people. You can't let up for a minute. Wherever you are, that's where the show is. He is always performing, deceiving people. He doesn't just do it with tricks, but with ideas too. He perverts everything, he's a perverter of ideas and of people. He himself is a damn pervert!"

There, he had said it. No use pretending that he could take it back. The long silence told him that he had gone too far for this intelligent young audience. A young woman stood up, brushing the hair away from her forehead. She gazed at him levelly.

"Mr. Baldwin," she said, "is that why you are so against him - because you think he's a pervert?"

This time Baldwin forced himself to shrug. He shrugged with exaggerated casualness and turned away. His assistants followed him as he made his way to the exit. Nobody tried to follow them and they had no difficulty hiring a cab in front of the Palais Urbain. Baldwin sank back into the upholstery, heaving a sigh of exhaustion. Damn frogs! The French were treacherous. So were the Swiss. But at least the Swiss, he told himself, are stupid into the bargain. But the French are smart. They'll make a monkey out of you if you let them!

By the time they arrived at his hotel, Jack Baldwin had brushed off the frustrating events at the Palais. He took a shower, being reminded once again that showers are not the French fashion. The showerhead was so low that he had to stand hunched over and had trouble soaping his armpits. Afterward he slipped into a fresh pair of red and white striped pyjamas and turned on the TV, trying to find some news on Shawn. There was none. Even though his French was sketchy, he continued switching from channel to channel, which was easy - there were only three. Still nothing, though. Finally he switched it off and poured himself a drink, a petite glass of Cointreau. You had to hand it to the French in the liqueur department, no question about that!

Instead of drinking, he told himself, I should be eating. He would call room service, but was too exhausted even to get up to reach the telephone. He had not realized how exhausted he really was and so it was not surprising that Mr. Jack Baldwin nodded off. His mouth opened but his hand still held on to the little glass. Finally his fingers relaxed, too. The liqueur glass tilted sideways and fell over, spilling what was left of the Cointreau. It wetted his fingers and the sensation slowly crawled up to his sleepy brain. Mr. Baldwin's eyes opened, he slowly lifted his right hand and licked the liqueur off index and middle fingers. Still licking, his gaze unfocussed, he beheld a figure standing across the room, half in shadow. Mr. Baldwin sat up, suddenly. His hand had sought and found the liqueur glass. He held on to it as if it were his only link with security. He was scared.

"Mr. Baldwin," said a voice with a disturbingly hollow quality in it, "good evening. Don't be alarmed. If you co-operate you will not be harmed."

"Who are you? What do you want?"

"I am Oba. I need you to help us."

"Who is 'us' and what help, what can I do?"

"We need you to lend us your body for a time, Mr. Baldwin."

Now it was clear to Jack Baldwin that he was dealing with a lunatic. Probably a religious maniac, with which France abounded these days. People are nutsing out all over the world, but especially in France which had been, after all, always a hotbed for tourists and religious fanatics! On the other hand,the accent this man had was not French. Maybe he was Yugoslavian or Rumanian, something swarthy and untrustworthy, certainly. Why the hell had he ever come to Paris? Things were getting very unpleasant indeed!

Jack Baldwin might be slightly overweight now, and he had worked himself up in the world in order to carry his weight with dignity and even, he told himself occasionally, a certain amount of grace. But he came from the street, from a working-class family that had lived in a working-class neighbourhood and seen it turn into a ghetto. He reached all the way back there to those noisy nights of imminent muggings and hurled the liqueur glass through the room at the figure in the shadows. As it flew, the glass slowed and grew simultaneously. By the time it had reached the halfway point between himself and the intruder it was already the size of a balloon. Its progress toward the shadowy figure became negligible while it still grew, its sides thinning, the stem beginning to be absorbed until there was a large, thin-walled, glass sphere suspended in the middle of the room, a big bubble still turning slowly in the rotation caused by Baldwin's throwing hand. Now the figure stepped out of the shadow, but Baldwin could see him only through the floating bubble. He saw, therefore, a grotesquely bent creature with very long, curved legs, a short fat middle, and something that resembled a grossly disfigured melon for a head. The mouth looked like a slit and clapped open and shut as he spoke.

"Don't be afraid, Mr. Baldwin. Get up and step closer."

Baldwin wanted to resist, but couldn't. Anything to escape this nightmare, but nothing would do. He got up and walked to the former liqueur glass. He had an urge to touch its rubber-thin walls.

"Don't touch it," said the visitor, lips clapping open and shut. "Look at me!"

Baldwin looked. It was a sight that might, under other circumstances, have provoked a grin at least. Here somehow it was frightening. Now there were no longer spindly legs and a bulbous middle. There was only the melon-shaped head, but even that had changed. All had become more vaporous until only the clapping mouth remained.

"Now, Mr. Baldwin," said the mouth, "you will join me in the sphere. We will merge. Then, for a while, I will be you and you will be me. It won't hurt. On the contrary. It will be a convenience for us for some time. When we part company, you will have benefited greatly from our union. Do you understand?"

"No," Baldwin said desperately.

"Do you *wish* to understand, Mr Baldwin?" asked the clapping lips.

"No .... I mean, *yes*," Baldwin croaked.

"The man you know as Shawn is sent here for his own good and, of course, for the good of your world. In order to accomplish the maximum good he must be challenged. You are an earnest though perhaps somewhat ineffective challenger. I, Oba, shall reinforce you. To do this properly we must merge."

"But then .... then it's true ...." rasped Baldwin, who had developed an inexplicable splitting headache. He had never had headaches.

"What is true, Mr. Baldwin?"

"That this .... Shawn .... that he comes from somewhere else, not from this planet. It's not just a stunt, a gimmick."

"He is real," said the thing that called itself Oba, "and he is really not from Earth."

Jack Baldwin began to shake his head. He stood there shaking his head incredulously and this wagging of the head became the proper accompaniment to his entry into the bubble. He felt suddenly light and porous. So porous, in fact, that he entered the sphere without breaking the skin. It was amazing. It was a trick, certainly, but one he would not be able to duplicate. That he knew instantly. It was finally, after all these years, magic, true magic, real magic in the old sense of the word. It was that which had prompted the Great Houdini to admonish stage magicians.

"Beware," he had said, "of the borderlands of true magic. You will reach them. They are misty and soft underfoot. Turn back unless you wish to sink in quicksand."

Jack Baldwin had set one foot on a treacherous film of thin glass. It gave and broke. He was sinking. But somehow, as he sank, he was not afraid.

20

BATHS

Whenever there occurred in the life of the great whore a crucial event, she reacted by taking a bath. So now, having been informed by phone of Huber's death, Nanita was soaking luxuriously in her bath. The ventilation system in the bathhouse was designed to prevent clouding of the mirrors so that she would not be obliged to forgo her magnificent image even for a short while. Wherever she looked - up, sideways, even down - there was a mirror glass showing her what a hidden observer would have seen: Nanita soaking luxuriously, cat-eyes half open, thinking barely at all.

What was there to think about, in any case? That was one of the compensations of advancing years- that thinking became less and less necessary. Circumstances developed their own wonderful logic and that Huber had been murdered in Geneva was a stupid failure on his part, but it did not surprise her. It was no good to get involved with men who had ambition and who had not yet realised their ambition. Such men were a nuisance. Basically they were failures, because even if they did not fail in what they were after, once they had gained it, they would fail the woman who had helped them succeed.

Circumstances were clearly inviting her to go to Geneva and, very early on in her long bathing orgy, she understood that she would go. She had not been away from Japan for years, had become very comfortable here. Island life pleased her. She was well when she was surrounded by water. In certain places of the world, Paris for example, water was too distant. One could not feel it. Perhaps that is why she loved to bathe, it made her an island in the sea.

Huber was nothing now. Already they had probably taken that stout peasant body up to Germany to treat it with all the honours the state lavishes on its faithful servants. Now was the time to show what a great man Huber had really been. Was it not always like that? Was there not always the pomp of the relief of bad conscience, bad feelings when an important man was laid to rest? An important man could not fail to have enemies in important places, those that envied him. When such a man dies, Nanita mused, there is cause for rejoicing. One less competitor! One less stubbornness in the world.

She smiled. Yes, Huber had been a very stubborn man. For a Westerner a very sensible man. She could have done business with him, perhaps important business, who knew now? It was all over! Nanita inhaled deeply and watched her breasts break the surface, iridescent bubbles clinging to her nipples. What a primitive world men live in, she thought. How they fashion for themselves a clumsy, creaking order in which they move like robots this way and that, with stiff shoulders and stiff spines. It could not always have been this way. It must be, she decided, the nature of the male martial spirit in the modern age when killing had become mechanized. Men had tried to pass on their suppleness, their willowy martial nature - a nature that bends before the blow - had tried to pass it on to their machines. In the machines it had become stiffer than it had been in them. Much, much stiffer. So they pushed machine against machine, stiff, grating, creaking, cranking communication from machine to machine, from computers to computers. Even the swift arrows of their rockets were unbending. A dash and a flash, that was the way they worked. A smooth arc, contact, flash - oblivion. They had become very good at the in-and-out, advance and withdrawal, but all of it with a stiff back. They were as stiff as the rockets they had learned to launch, and as hollow as the silos their rockets left behind. Even Huber, even he, who was more primitive, more natural than most.

Nanita knew that not only circumstances had invited her to Geneva, but necessity. There had never been a man who loved her as she loved herself. And she could not imagine one who had loved her differently and more fully. But she could imagine that it was possible. It was something that was possible with Shawn, she felt it. She also felt that it was her last chance, for as men had their stiffness, so had women. She had begun to feel it. She liked bathing too much. It was something that covered up this inkling of stiffness she had begun to feel in herself - something that was not even physical. Not yet. It would be, though. It was old age. Men have always been old that way, at least in modern times, she thought. But women are born new and willowy in every generation. Men are born stiff no matter how they bend their bodies. Women stiffen with time.

Five hours after this bath she was being chauffeured to Tokyo to board a Japan Airlines jet bound for San Francisco via Hawaii. On the plane she paid no attention to anyone and as soon as she got to the Fairmount Hotel she took another long bath. Now, unfathomably, she was really getting angry with the dead man. Huber, she thought angrily in her perfumed bath, I sent you to Geneva not to become a corpse but to secure a lover for me. I am no longer entirely and unconditionally young. I need intermediaries. I can no longer place myself in environments where my glance can hope to be met. I sent you to Geneva and you get slaughtered!

Since there was no bidet in this elegant and lavishly appointed suite, she knelt and began lovingly to play with herself, her pubic hair. It was her way of compensating for the jet lag. Her anger softened away.

Ah, Huber, she was thinking, is there a great lover in Germany today? No! There can't be! The young men are too timid, and the older men are too greedy. And the old wise men need weeks to be provoked! Besides, they don't last. One cannot lose oneself in their eyes because their eyes are veiled. Nor do they have enough of the life force left, no more strength in their thighs. They cannot ride me out. I need a lover. Certainly I shall lose my charm, my magnetism, that which bristles about me! I shall lose my worth, my money, shan't I? What is my body but the tray on which I present *you,* she said, fondling herself.

Without *you,* she continued this conversation with that so faithfully cared-for part of herself, I would be nothing. But if the tray is brittle, who will trust the teapot? Who, my little pot of hot and scented tea, will trust one's tea if he doesn't trust the pot and he won't trust the pot if the tray is brittle!

She sat back, laughing, spreading her lithe legs, tensing her muscles in the large, sunken bathtub with a capacity for four. It was a little too large, a little too deep, obviously, but for continental conditions it was acceptable. She looked up at the mirrored ceiling, admiring the sight of her pubic promontory which thrust up out of the water. She pushed little waves over it.

My little island, my little refuge, she cooed, watch out - a high tide is coming and all who live there will be swept awayyyyy!

She thrust up her pelvis to avoid the onrushing wavelets she herself had created. Then, finally, she sank back and began, in a small, thin voice, to sing an aimless song, a narrow, meandering creek of meaningless words. It was about a lover and a twig who were both floating down a river, the lover looking for his lost other half and the twig looking for the shore to find a tree. Or perhaps it was about a river floating in an ocean looking for a riverbed, or about a twig and the breaking of a lover swimming in dreams under a tree. It was a song of boredom and despair and it bored her so much that her right hand again found her perfect little teapot. This time the hand had come to work. And this time the sleek black island of sealy hair began to heave and shake until the tea boiled over. Then for a long time, the Whore of Japan lay soaking mindlessly.

When at last she rose and reached for one of the profusion of heavy, pink towels, she felt refreshed and purposeful. She selected a black and red gown and sat down to dry and comb her hair. When she was through with that, she took a cigar box from one of her bags and extracted and lit a thinly rolled cigar. This cigar was made of the finest djah harvested in India, and she inhaled deeply.

For a while she lay on the large bed. She opened her robe and smoothed back the sides to make a perfect black and red frame for her body. She looked up at her reflection in the ceiling mirror. You are no longer young with the youth of youth, my dear, she told herself.

These were the only signs she could see. At the first, fifth, hundredth glance a man would still encounter too much perfection not to be overwhelmed, so dazzling was her beauty. The world is cheap, reflected Nanita, the world is shabby.

She got up, walked to a closet and took a gold-bound diary from one of her bags. She opened it to a page which had three names written on it. These were the names of men she had marked for death a long time ago.

Still smoking the djah cigar, she walked back to the bed, carrying her diary. She lay back and studied the names. She inhaled the djah fumes deeply. Now that she was here in the United States of America it was necessary to cleanse her mind of all superfluous matter, because these three men were Americans and it would be important to kill them in a way that could be thought of as American.

She would kill these men so that she could meet her lover cleanly.

She tried to read these names coldly, dispassionately. But the djah fumes made her world delicious. Under the mirrored ceiling she began to slither and writhe, seeing herself as the shiny serpent, the downed and downy angel, the small, lithe animal all slick in its skin. The animal to which the world would have to come and which, but by its volume of flesh in which it perfectly displaced all existing matter, would neither be noted nor missed.

Her tongue licked, her legs scissored like tentacles. She could kill these men or she could drive them crazy. She would make herself the perfect tabernacle for the great nothing, would let that for which there is neither yesterday nor tomorrow decide.

21

VIEWS

A clairvoyant, according to Vitrio Martino, was like a reporter, an observer, except that he himself produced what he saw and reported on it. By no means, and never, should a clairvoyant allow fiction in any of its forms to enter. Sure, he could make up a story as well as the next guy. And sure, he'd done it. But he had learned that such stories had no lasting effects. They were stopgaps. People soon found out. Even while they forgot and didn't take time to check one vision against the hard reality of facts on a certain date, those visions which were too far in the future or those that were refuted by circumstances tended to accumulate. "Not very good, that," mumbled Vitrio Martino and took his crystal ball into the kitchen where he held it under the running tap.

Better to keep the damn thing clean. Better to put in a little work. It would pay off in the long run. Yes, Vitrio Martino had cheated in the past. It had been necessary. If he hadn't cheated, he wouldn't be what he was today, which was plainly the only reliable clairvoyant with security clearance in the U.S. Sure, there were others in his league, of his calibre and reliability, but they were foreigners whom the U.S. Government would not employ. There was Jorge Manuel Bompha, the Brazilian. Ah, Vitrio smiled, scrubbing the crystal ball, what fire, what flamboyance, what style that man has! But could a man like Bompha be trusted in delicate matters of international intrigue as they related to the U.S.A.? No, most decidedly not! Vitrio had been born in Italiana, Wisconsin, and he'd come a long way to dry off the crystal ball here on the outskirts of Washington D.C. And how he hated the place! Even if the kids were trying to look like Sicilians nowadays. Even if the south side looked like Palermo or Genoa!

"So, now, let's see," Vitrio mumbled, as was his habit. The grapefruit-size sphere sparkled and shone and there wasn't a speck of dust on it. He placed it on its black alabaster base and lit a cigar. He took the sphere and the base and set it on the small, round table in front of his armchair. Then he took up what he liked to think of as his working position, that is, he sat down and made himself comfortable in the company of his crystal ball.

Ordinarily Vitrio Martino didn't need the ball. He could come up with at least one good, reliable vision a day - a vision that stood the test of everyday reality with the foreseeable future. Even now he could come up with a good vision more or less on command, and on some days, depending on the flow of energy, he could produce two or three good ones.

Vitrio shook his head. "Good and well, no use getting soft again," he reminded himself. His quota for the day still lay before him and he might as well get to work. He switched on the tape recorder with which he recorded each and every session of clairvoyance. He did this because, often, he fell into a trance-like state in which he talked, and he had found out early in the game that he couldn't remember what it was he talked about. These tapes were numbered and labelled, and he had accumulated a well-ordered library which filled two small rooms in his house and grew each day. They were government property and he had signed a contract in which he agreed to pass each and every new one on to the U.S. Bureau of Psychic Research and Development, fresh out of the oven.

Now Vitrio Martino looked into the crystal ball and delighted in its flawless clarity. It was like gazing into a lake of pure mountain water. It gave him a feeling of joy and of great strength, though this was mixed with the slightly nervous anticipation of images that were bound to appear and spoil the lucidity. For the moment though, there was nothing. No speck, no flaw, no shape that could be interpreted. Only the marvellous purity of the crystal in which a man, were he so inclined, might ponder the filth of humanity; might, by comparison in relative terms of course, understand what had happened to the world since the eternal smile of terrestrial nature had produced this marvellous crystal.

Vitrio's gaze began to lose itself in the limited vastnesses of the sphere. Then, with what inside of him was an almost audible soft plop-plop, he had passed through the separating membrane, had become part of the crystal. He was in the crystal and everywhere about him, below as well as above, a sweet, primordial clarity dominated the universe. Which did not mean that Vitrio had changed. He was old enough to have begun to develop a jaundiced eye and casual patter that wound its way between amusement and disgust! "So," he said to himself, "what else is new?"

In actuality, however, this: So, what else is new? had not been a thought. In the visionary trance he had actually mumbled these words and they were now recorded on tape later to be listened to and interpreted by the Bureau's staff of psychic experts, then to be submitted to George Debussy for the final word.

"Nice day, as usual," mumbled Martino to the tape and the tape recorded it faithfully. "Great to be in here," said Martino. "Sure wish I could stay. Well, let's see now, what kind of day is it going to be, apart from cloudiness and cheerful? Hello there!"

This last "Hello there," referred to a woman Vitrio saw and whom he thought he recognized. No, not merely recognized, not merely knew, it couldn't be, not again! Vitrio tried to pull himself out of the trance, because encounters with the great Nina Dumbatse of Russia were not, strictly speaking, visions. He counted them as dreams of fantasies and they were of no interest to anyone but himself, though lately they had begun to bother him somewhat. It was clear that sooner or later, since she was not going to come to see him, he would have to go to see her, though this might not be easy to arrange. Some sort of pretext would have to be made, some way have to be found, because this Nina Dumbatse of Soviet Russia was playing havoc with his emotions.

By anyone's standards, Nina was a big woman with breasts as large and round as pumpkins in the Autonomous Region of the Ukraine, if pumpkins grew there indeed, which Vitrio would not have doubted. And even whether or not the Ukraine, known to the world primarily for its wealth of grain, was autonomous was also a matter upon which Vitrio would not have liked to be questioned. But that Nina's breasts were large as pumpkins - any region's, anybody's pumpkins - that could not be doubted. Nor that she was here before him, with him, in the crystal ball. And Vitrio did not succeed in breaking his trance.

"Hello," heard the tape again, "hello, fancy meeting you here under these circumstances! Miss Dumbatse, isn't it?" Like her great namesake, the Soviet discus thrower, the psychic Nina Dumbatse had shoulders to match her pumpkins, and she now shrugged them, batting her eyes and cooing, "Hello, Vitrio, my dark little sparrow, when will you come to see me at last?"

"That's very kind of you," Vitrio Martino replied, "As soon as I can arrange it, I would really love to ...."

He broke off. It was not good to talk like this on a working tape. It would not be easy, later, in his daily report, to supply the proper context of visions in which to present such a treacherous conversation harmlessly to the Bureau of Psychic Research and Development. But he could not help himself. Nina's belly matched her shoulders and breasts. It was a convex armour plate in which even the navel played an important role, like the navels on the breast shields of the heroes of Greek and Roman antiquity. Hers was plainly delineated under the thin cotton dress which was much too short, revealing her massive legs which were marred by a cluster or nest of varicose veins at the inside of her left ankle - a mere trifle, a nothing. A big heavy woman like Nina was entitled to a few varicose veins. It gave her something human. If it hadn't been for this delta of bulging blue lines she would have appeared terrifying in her apparent invincibility.

"And it's not easy," Vitrio told Miss Dumbatse, "I'm not even sure I can swing it. They're a little uptight up there at the bureau, you understand?"

"Swing it, my handsome little one," lisped the large woman. "If *you're* possible, *it* is possible. Ah, you don't know how your Nina is pining away for you, for your delicate limbs your shadowed eye, and for your curly hair in which her little hand loves so to lose itself!"

She stretched out her paw and touched his hair. This occurred inside the crystal ball, as well as outside, where Vitrio Martino sat in objective, observable reality, staring into what for an amateur would have appeared to be an empty sphere of glass. Outside too, the real Vitrio felt his hair being ruffled and teased lovingly.

"You know, Nina," he confessed, "that I love you and have loved you for a long time, ever since I saw you light a handful of matches with your bare will."

"So, you too," Miss Dumbatse smiled, "you, too. I tell you, my sweet, forget the matches! They're nothing. The flame I will ignite in your loins will make that burst of nothing look like match fire exactly. Anybody can do it. Anybody with a little love can do it, Vitrio my darling. Now that you've declared yourself, you must come to visit me, will you, so that we can place our bodies in embrace and rock away deep into the sweet, wet earth, into the fields and roots, down there where it's cool and damp and fill our mouths with the taste of it, do you promise?"

"Oh, I promise, Nina, I promise," Vitrio moaned. "How could I not promise? How could I withhold a promise from *you*?"

"I'm offering you the fruits of my own field, shiny black crow of spring, my Vitrio, have a look at this!"

Still caught under the crystal skies above the crystal earth, Vitrio Martino could not take his eyes off the slow striptease Nina Dumbatse now performed for him, baring those pumpkins, those hips, those thighs, legs, her whole great physical self, to say nothing of the short, frizzy hair of undefinable colour which weekly assaults with cruel permanents had not managed to weaken. Through the thick, bright red-lipsticked mouth came Nina's voice: "Look at this, touch it, my chirpy little sparrow, my tweeting little bird, my little kitten, touch this."

She placed both palms under her breasts and lifted them up, for Vitrio's inspection. Then she let them drop. They did not drop far. Nina slapped her thighs. "And this!" she laughed. Then she slapped her armour-plated belly. "And this!" she cooed. And finally, as Vitrio's mouth fell open, she turned slowly and thrust out her rump, what a rump! No, it was not a rump. It was *rump*!

"That's not fair, Nina," called out Vitrio Martino with some presence of mind. "It just isn't. It may be nature, but it isn't fair! You know damn well that I can't touch, can't feel, can't really join you. So stop teasing me, darling, and wait until I come to join you with my body."

Nina did not withdraw her rump. She stood there, leaning forward, her hands supporting her thighs, leaving Vitrio to confront the facts. It was in a sense a despairing sight. But in another sense it was a visionary sight. What Nina showed Vitrio were two lumps .... clumps .... bumps, two great mounds of flesh, two camel humps stuffed to bursting with fat upholstery, or with packed flesh, stuffed so full that everywhere dimples had appeared, maybe two, three dozen dimples. A great landscape of two clumpy, bumpy hills full of dimples into which Vitrio wanted to dive and delve, dive forward, be received and lost and never come back. What was there in the world to compare with this?

Though, as a professional, he knew that this was not possible,

Vitrio Martino tried to march forward into the great psychic Nina Dumbatse. His legs appeared to move, his head was thrust forward along the line of extended arms and hands. He, Vitrio Martino, would be the first to break through the limitations of crystal ball gazing, and he would do it now.

"Let me feel it, Nina," he gasped as the tape continued to record, "let me get my hands on ...."

And then the phone rang, shocking him back into his body and driving Nina from the sphere. Naturally it was George Debussy who called, saying: "Did I interrupt you, Vitrio?"

"Yeah, you sure did," Vitrio moaned.

"Too bad," Debussy said coldly, "but we need you. We've got a problem. Drop everything and make a note of this and start working on it right now."

"I *am* working, I *was* working," Vitrio sighed.

"We've got a problem and it concerns Blue Friday," Debussy went on. "You look that up in the Days of the Week book. You've got last week's revisions, haven't you?"

"Yes," said Vitrio Martino, "I have, and I couldn't make heads or tails of it."

"Look under Blue Friday and see if you can get a line on the whole thing," said Debussy. "We want you to zoom in on it and explore it. And, Vitrio, we don't want a history lesson. We want pictures from the present and from the immediate future. We want to know all about Blue Friday. We want to find the .... well, the chink in the armour of Blue Friday. Incidentally, are you on green or red button on your phone?"

"Green," said Vitrio Martino.

"Damn," he was told, "switch the goddamn thing to red, will you?"

Martino switched to red. When he listened again, Debussy had hung up. Vitrio got up and started looking for the code book. When he found it, he began taking out the old Blue Friday sheets and replacing them with the latest revisions. Then he placed the old pages in a shredder and what was left in an infra-red burner and burned them, leaving only a thimbleful of white dust which he carefully scooped up with a spoon and flushed down the sink in the kitchen. He hadn't read them. It wasn't easy to keep up with all the paperwork. He was, after all, an artist, not a bureaucrat. He shouldn't be expected to keep files.

Again he sat down in his working armchair. He felt heavy and tired. He closed his eyes. "Nina," he mumbled. Only now did he realise that the tape recorder was still running. He sat up abruptly and switched it off. But it was too late. All the tapes were numbered and carefully marked. He had a choice only of erasing what was on them, thereby losing the valuable clues to his memory - and still having to provide an explanation of what it was he had erased - or leaving everything on the tape and facing the music later.

Trying to decide what to do, he sat there thinking that he did not have to make any decision right now, none at all. He was developing a slight headache. There were a lot of people in Washington who thought that Vitrio did not work, that he was a wastrel. Martino grimaced ruefully. "They should be in my boots," he moaned.

Impulsively he got up, went to the kitchen and shook three capsules out of a large, economy-size jar. "A harmless sedative," he mumbled, grimacing as he washed them down with water. Harmless they were indeed, but extremely potent. Vitrio Martino, in his illustrious career, had found that sometimes Mother Nature, in the form of sleep she so benevolently took from time to time, worked greater wonders than the finest crystal ball.

Pleasantly anticipating the effect of the tranquilisers, he slouched into the bedroom and sat down on his bed. With practiced movements he adjusted the electrode cap on his head and lay down, making sure that everything was in working order. He would sleep. He might dream! Let the *machines* sort out fantasy from reality!

22

VISIONS

From Vitrio Martino's brain sleep-impulses were relayed via electrodes to transformers and intensifiers which not only gave account of his dream-states, but also permitted audiovisual monitoring via a series of flashing lights and bell signals which were video-recorded and filmed to provide a complete record. Now, at a crucial moment, Vitrio Martino woke, bathed in sweat. For a moment he lay terrified in his bed unable to move or orientate himself, knowing only that he had escaped a terrible and incredibly real fate by a hair's breadth.

Yes, he was in his bed, in his home! But even so it took him long minutes to begin to feel safe and sound. What had Debussy once told him? Take it easy, Vitrio, even a psychic like you can have a nightmare once in a while! A nightmare? No, this had not been a nightmare. This was a dream of such shattering, apocalyptic impact that Vitrio had his hands clasped firmly to the edges of the bed, dared not move, dared not even close his eyes for fear of falling asleep again and being returned to the horror.

Fragment by smashed fragment, his true life, that of a distinguished government employee in an exciting new field, began to return to him. Though still shaky, he got up, went to the bathroom and ran some cold water over his chest and neck. There was a foul taste in his mouth, too. He brushed his teeth. And he blew his nose, which still held a sulfurous stench, the smell of his own fear. In that awful nightmare he had been afraid to inhale, he now recalled. But why? What had it been? Yes, he had been terrified of inhaling the odourless death, afraid of tasting the tasteless dissolution, the invisible end of his beloved country and the world!

At last Vitrio Martino returned to his bedroom and sat down on the edge of the bed, teeter-tottering on the brink of that abysmal stage where he had been so tormented. He began now to remember in full detail what the dream vision had been and he shook his head to deny it. "No, no," he told himself, "this can't be true, there's nothing we can have done to deserve such ...." Then the telephone rang, rang again, and rang a third time until Vitrio's heavy damp hand lifted the receiver. It was George Debussy.

"Vitrio," he said, "what the hell is going on with you? I got Peak Activity signals, clanging bells, the whole works. Woke me up, too. What time is it - four, five?"

Martino told Debussy that it was eleven minutes after five o'clock. "I had a vision, Mr. Debussy," Martino said formally, in the same instant realizing that he'd been caught off guard. Peak Activity, Red Zone Activity, now Debussy would want to know everything.

"I bet I know what it was," Debussy rasped. "It's about that freak in Geneva. You're gonna tell us what's going to happen, aren't you, Vitrio? Vitrio, are you there? I want to know about this vision of yours, what is it, speak up! I mean, I don't want to wait another minute."

"A real vision, sir," said Vitrio Martino, "as clear as day, undeniable, genuine - for the record."

He sat back on his bed, felt the pillow still wet with his sweat, and turned it over to the dry side as he said to Debussy, "America, sir, it concerned America. This was the clearest, most decisive picture I've had in years. It will rank with my finest prophecies, I'm sure. I was shown the future of our great nation as clear as if it were yesterday."

"Hold it," Debussy told him, "hold it! I'm gonna take this on the extension."

Martino had about a minute to ask himself what had got into him, why was he lying? Words kept pouring out of him. Words he did not mean to say. What did *he* care? Wasn't he just a simple clairvoyant doing his job? Wasn't it his duty as a patriot, as a good American, to pass onto the Washington administration what he had seen? Wasn't that what they paid him for, why they interviewed him, why they had called him one of the most important psychics in the U.S. today? Vitrio Martino understood that he had come up to that moment in the life of any man involved in the top-level decision-making process where he must weigh truth against the concept known as National Security, which includes a maze of agencies, the navy, the air force and the army, The Joint Chiefs of Staff, the Pentagon, the Central Intelligence

Agency, the Federal Bureau of Investigation, the Defence Intelligence Agency, the National Security Council and half a dozen special operation groups where effective co-ordination between them was almost impossible. Worse, in this case it was truth versus personal security. What if they didn't like what he had seen? He himself had been terrified by it! Was there not a limit to tolerance even in such essentially intangible spheres as clairvoyance? Was it possible for a clairvoyant's vision to be subversive? And, if so, could he ....

George Debussy was back on the line. "Okay," he said, "now I'm ready. Phew, this better be good, my boy!"

"Sir," said Vitrio Martino, "I cannot lie to you or to the world. I haven't had time to think about this, but already I can see that the content of my vision, if publicised, will cause great controversy among American Intelligence Services in the world. It's a two-edged sword. Our enemies will call it trashy propaganda and it may embarrass our friends."

"Lay it on the line," said Debussy. "Lay it on the line before you lose me!"

"Yes, Mr. Debussy," said Vitrio Martino, pressing the record-key of his tape recorder, "I will. I saw America in symbolic form, a giant frontiersman come home from the wilderness, bathed, shaved, hair cut, dressed in finery to take his place at the head of the table of nations. I heard America speak with a clear, strong voice telling stories, parables, yarns of adventure like a sailor come home to haven after a long voyage of discovery. And the world listened. I -"

"Jesus," he heard Debussy say, "this is great!"

"I saw and heard America weep, saw her tears of humility and watched as the nations of the world bowed their heads in shame and appreciation of the courage of the strongest among them. Then I saw her raise her face, cleansed by her tears, her eyes shining, a conqueror's smile on her lips, and I heard her speak of the world's destiny."

"Is this *it*, is this the real dope?" Debussy asked incredulously.

"I am relating it to you as I saw it," said Martino. "I'll try to give you everything word for word. This is what America said in my vision, sir: 'I have suffered, I have died a million deaths in the death of my poor, my soldiers, in the death of my children who died in martyred innocence. I have not slept in the thousands of nights of my torture, and every night of my life has been such torture. I have been divided against myself, I have torn myself apart and I have torn others apart and it has been no more than tearing apart a wink. Now my eyes are open and I see. I shall turn back and walk all the way along the path I came. I shall return to the first who fell along the road of the American Nation and there I shall stoop and help him to his feet, support him, feed him, give him drink, turn his eyes ahead and bid him take my hand. From that spot I shall walk forward and neglect not a single one of my children who are I and without whom I am not. One by one I shall gather them and lead them forward so that the past may be forgotten. I ...."

"Vitrio," Debussy called out, "are you getting this on tape?"

"Yes, sir," Martino said, ""I'm recording everything."

"That's fine," Debussy told him. "What the hell am I saying, fine! This isn't fine, this is great, Martino, this is grand! This is what we've all been waiting for, this is what we've known you're capable of. Don't you think we've known how hard it must have been for you to come up with a prophecy here, a prophecy there, some good, some very good, some so-so, and some, well, you yourself have said it - there's a lot of garbage in the world! But this, Vitrio, this, coming from you, this is dynamite. This ...."

Vitrio Martino's head was reeling. What am I saying? he thought, what am I doing? Why am I lying like this? I must be going crazy!

To Debussy he said: "Yes, sir, I myself am still stunned by it, I'm trying to collect my thoughts. Where was I? Oh, yes! 'So that the past may be forgotten.' And then America said, 'And I shall return to this juncture and show you my crowds, my masses, my families. I shall conceal nothing before you. I shall invite all of you in to share with us what we have learned along that road and then all of us, you and I and all the nations shall stride forward proudly, our faces into the balmy wind that blows whence we know not, toward countless sunrises and sunsets of suns we have yet to see, steadily, unerringly, all of us into the light of our human destiny which must be the everlasting light, the everlasting perfection and sweetness of everlasting creation!'"

Vitrio Martino had run out of things to say. He was silent and so was Debussy. Between them there was only breathing and the slightly audible vacuum of the telephone line. Then Debussy said: "Look, Vitrio, go back to bed! Sleep as long as you like! Later you come up here and we sit down and go over this thing together. Bring the tape. We'll fill in the detail, you'll come up with the rest of the picture. But I can tell you this already, this is a history-making vision. This is the greatest thing I've heard since the Gettysburg Address, and I'm not kidding you, either. Then, when we've done that, then you take yourself a vacation, my boy! You richly deserve it. And I want to apologize to you, too. Frankly, I didn't think you had it in you, Vitrio. I gave up hope, do you understand?"

"Yes, sir," said Vitrio Martino, "I understand."

"And listen," he was told, "about that vacation. It'll be all expenses paid. Just tell us where you want to go, and we'll take care of all the travel arrangements, first class."

"Russia," said Vitrio Martino. "I want to go to Russia."

"Russia?" Debussy laughed. "Russia? You must be .... wait, no, why not? And why not Russia? They've got a bunch of good clairvoyants over there, that Dobzhov, I bet you've been itching to meet him for years. And Dumbatse, too, haven't you? Will you accept my apologies again? It has to be hell for a clairvoyant like yourself to be isolated from his colleagues in other parts of the world, just so he can produce, produce, produce. Sure, you go to Russia. You come in here when you're ready and we'll get everything down. And then you go to Russia, how does that sound?"

"It sounds just fine, sir," said Vitrio Martino. "Thank you. And I'll do as you say, but I think I'll be in today. I don't think I'll be able to sleep much more. Not after this!"

They hung up. Vitrio Martino heaved a sigh, jumped out of bed, grabbed the pillow and threw it at the panel of discreetly flashing lights.

23

BEER

"So you see," said General Nicolai Constantin Dvat to Carl Dobzhov, who had been levitating without interruption for thirty-two hours and twenty-seven minutes now, "I have come to believe that psychic phenomena and military strategy are not mutually exclusive. They do not contradict one another. For example, the fact that you can levitate like this does not mean we cannot throw missiles wherever we like in the world, should that be necessary."

The levitating Dobzhov said nothing. He had started levitating like this involuntarily just after midnight, early Saturday morning, and now it was 8.00 a.m. Sunday. Dobzhov was not a religious man in any strict sense, but he didn't like this. He did not like not having control over his faculties, even if levitation was a remote faculty.

He lay ramrod-straight in the air, about eight feet above the hard oak floor, just below the ceiling. He had never spent this much time close to the ceiling, for in the public demonstration that had been so successful the ceiling had been far above in the vast hall and no closer for his having ascended a bit. And he was still in his linen night shirt, with red and black flower embroidery. It lay tight over chest and belly and hung slack below, at such an angle that a tall man could easily look up his legs to his behind - an embarrassing position to be caught in.

General Dvat was not a tall man. In fact, he resembled one of those small, squat tanks that were popular in World War I. His face betrayed none of the sensitivity that had made him the primary exponent of psychic warfare in the USSR. "Yes," he was now saying, "we always have the hard rocks to throw at them, if the soft ones don't do the job. But I prefer the soft ones. I'm thinking now, my dear Carl, how we can fit this levitation into our defence program. This is not an easy task. It may have to go into parachuting. What would be the practical applications? That's what I'd like to know!"

Nina Dumbatse, who had been called as soon as Carl started levitating, came in from the kitchen. She was not half as big and voluptuous as Vitrio Martino had seen her in his crystal sphere. In fact she was rather dainty of bone, and had wanted to be a prima ballerina before she discovered her ability to light matches purely by the force of her will. She still did not know what it was that did it. All she had to do was look at a match and think about it bursting into flame, and it would. She could do this with any match, domestic or foreign, or any number of matches. She had ridden roughshod over the accusation that she used trick matches in her demonstration, challenging one and all comers to bring their own matches. And she had lit them all. No question, Nina Dumbatse was the champion psychic match-igniter of the whole wide world.

"Levitation and psychic match-striking," said General Dvat, "aren't easy to accommodate in modern warfare. After all, it's the dynamite that blows up the munitions dump, not the match, even though the match lights the fuse. In other words, we still have to place the dynamite and string the fuse and put the matches there, and then you, Nina, can use your powers to ignite them at a distance. What it really means, my slow-eyed little bird, is that you personally are safe but everyone else still has to take the same risks as before."

He turned his large, flat face with the strongly delineated cheekbones toward her like a radar dish and smiled.

From his height Carl Dobzhov told them that he did not like this. That this was like nothing he had experienced before. That he wanted to come down.

"We'll have to think this through very carefully, my lad," said General Dvat calmly. "You see, ideally you are in a fine position for another public demonstration which we sorely need, I assure you. Nihilev and Stentorian should be here any moment and we can then discuss this further. But right now, it seems to me, in view of the fact that the presence of others doesn't seem to disturb your condition, we should call in the public. I'm sure we can direct you to a larger, more comfortable place ...."

"Comfortable?" Dobzhov said from above him.

"In any event a place airier, more accessible, and there you can be marvelled at by the international press, the bloodhounds."

"Ah," said the slim Nina Dumbatse, "General, why don't you

leave him alone? He must be tired. Carl?"

"Yes?" said Carl Dobzhov.

"Are you hungry, do you want more beer?"

"Not for now," Dobzhov replied.

There was a silence now which threatened to become too profound and too long, broken when the doorbell chimed and Nina went to admit Nihilev and Stentorian - Nihilev still with an ugly adhesive tape of green colour on a large, pale, bald spot on his head. They came in, shook hands, embraced, and General Dvat allowed himself two ceremonial kisses, bussing Nihilev slowly on either side, but not Stentorian.

The general explained to the newly arrived two what was really self-evident. He said: "We want to fit all this together, Dim, and we want you to try to fit in the man in Geneva and then we should come up with a working plan which we can submit to the Chairman and the others. I don't have to tell you that things are getting a bit desperate, especially if that astounding story Slavo here tells is true about this Englishman materializing out of thin air, sitting in a chair, with one hand missing."

"I'm satisfied that it's true," said Dimitri Nihilev.

"Who exactly is he?" asked the general.

"I believe that was a man named Patrick Young," Stentorian said casually. "Patrick Young is a former journalist for the decadent Western press who quit his job to work for the man in Geneva. He was recently killed in a bombing in a pub in London and only his hand was found. Apparently he is not entirely dead."

"Amazing, absolutely incredible!" exclaimed Dvat, scratching the top of his head.

Suddenly there was a small explosion and a simultaneous burst of flame at the edge of the table. A box of matches now burned in brightly diminishing flames. Nobody moved to put it out. Nina explained that she had felt the urge to express herself.

"Well," said the general, who quickly regained his calm, having been a seasoned and peppered frontline soldier and braved many an oncoming machine-gun burst, "no need to get nervous here. This is all within the realm of the newly developing psychic sciences. Do we not have good Carl Dobzhov levitating here before our very eyes? And has not Nina just ignited those matches? What we need is a readjustment, a new plan, a new strategy."

"Sir," Slavo Stentorian ventured, "if I may, I believe that the man in Geneva masters not only matter but the non-physical as well. There is nothing we can do that will surprise him. He knew that not only I had come to Geneva to make him an offer, but of all the others as well. His powers are so unique and frighteningly powerful that we have nothing to match them."

"No man is invincible," said the general comfortably, reaching for his pipe.

"If you'll forgive me .... " Slavo started, but the general cut him off with a controlled but vicious thrust of his pipe in the direction of Stentorian's Adam's apple.

"No man is invincible." he repeated. "There never was a man who could not be killed. Rasputin came perhaps closest, but then there was really no concerted effort in his case. No, friends, the man in Geneva is subject to death, even as all of us are. But killing him may not be what we want. He has demanded fifty million dollars from us. We still have five days to effect the transaction. I propose we deposit not fifty million, but eighty million in his account, not only to show our good will but also to trump the Americans. What do you say?" Nihilev waved his head from side to side. Dobzhov made a croaking noise from above.

"I don't think," continued General Dvat, "that eighty million dollars is such a high price to pay for the goodwill of a man who may well be capable of destroying the world. But that is not all. Let me see if I can go through this thoroughly with you, and perhaps that will give us some original and effective ideas. This man, this crash survivor who calls himself Shawn ...."

"Correction," Stentorian chimed in, "Shawn is the name given him by the late Patrick Young."

"Good, then," nodded Dvat, "we all know about whom we're talking. That man has powers which could give not only us, but the Americans as well a great deal of trouble. Now the first thing that comes to mind is naturally an alliance, a coalition with them, even with the Chinese if they got interested in this, which I doubt, they are too preoccupied with their domestic uprising. But what good would it do us? It seems to be a question of money for this young man. So let's give it to him. And surprise is an important element in any attack. Let's give him eighty million and tell him not to worry about money. The question is, what else does he want? What is he after?"

Within this short exposition General Dvat had established his true superiority of thought in the room. Even Nina Dumbatse had to admit to herself that she could have done no better and probably not as well. She began to look at Dvat's essentially ugly mug with renewed interest. This was a curious man. Not curious in the poetic way in which sweet Carl up there was curious, but in a dangerous way. This, she decided immediately, though she had known the general for some time, is a man who would never levitate! Strangely, that very fact seemed to make him suddenly and achingly attractive to her. Never before had she thought of Dvat as eloquent.

Since nobody could come up with an answer to Dvat's last question, the general himself continued by saying that this was a crucial question and upon answering it accurately depended all future actions in connection with this man Shawn.

Something flashed in Slavo's mind that moment. "Ah," he cried out. "Ah, I know, I remember - it's on the tip of my tongue .... yes, he did talk about time. He wanted time."

"Time?" said the general slowly, "is that what he wants, time?"

"Fetch me a beer, Nina," Carl Dobzhov made himself heard. "I want to talk."

Nina Dumbatse walked out to the kitchen and returned quickly with a beer which she handed up to Dobzhov. She could just barely reach his hand. With some difficulty, due to the peculiar muscular conditions that accompany this type of levitation, Carl brought the small, thick bottle to his lips and drank. It was important for him to talk now, he knew that. Here he was, levitating spectacularly and they were talking about a new boy in Geneva, a *Wunderkind* of sorts. Even Nina's attention, he could feel, was wandering.

He had a little trouble wiping his lips with the back of the other hand, but managed. Finally he drank up and handed the bottle back down. Yes, he would talk. He would give them something to think about.

"Don't think this is sour grapes," he began, "but I can feel that this boy in Geneva is bluffing. He's a flash in the pan. He's clever, I'll admit, but let's see him up here alongside the great Carl Dobzhov!"

He had not intended it as a joke but it caused a brief flurry of laughter.

"What's so funny about that?" Dobzhov went on. "I've worked a long time on this. Let's see you do it, any of you! You can't. But you've seen me do it so often that you've got used to it, you've, you've lost your respect. I remember when I first did it, the first five minutes of levitation and later the longer periods. With tears in your eyes you stood around, marvelling. If I hadn't stopped you, you would have been bug-eyed, sobbing on your knees, praying! You disgust me, the lot of you. What is this boy in Geneva, who is he, what good does he do us, what good can he possibly be to us? Even if he has all these powers, even if he can do all that, even if he can levitate like myself, he's not *Russian*. Nobody knows what he is or who he is. He isn't Swiss either, is he? He himself doesn't know who he is. He has no loyalty. Believe me, that boy is dangerous and I say let's get rid of him while we can. I don't believe in him. He is bluffing. Now, get me down from here so I can ...."

"Just a moment," said General Dvat earnestly, almost solemnly, "just a moment, my dear Carl. I consider you an artist, and as an artist you are entitled to your temper tantrums, but let us not forget that we are all comrades in the revolution here in this room. Nobody leaves without my permission. And whoever tries to interfere with the free exchange of ideas for the ultimate benefit of the great Soviet-Russian people, is a counter-revolutionary and as such subject to martial law. One more outburst like this and you'll be a levitating corpse, Dobzhov!"

To emphasise the point, the general pulled out of his holster his chrome plated service revolver of the old-fashioned type and placed it within easy reach on the table.

"I don't like the way this is going," he said. "I am offering all of you a socialist democratic forum in which to express your ideas, but I am not offering you the foolish freedom of veto or opposition. I want only creative contributions. Now let's go on!"

"Still," said Slavo Stentorian, "there is something in what Carl says. We must harness our own resources and see how we can best employ them. Eighty million dollars is an extremely great deal of money. I agree that it should be paid, but I feel that this man will destroy us if we do not destroy him first. How to destroy him I cannot now imagine, but destroy him we must. He's already shown that grenades don't hurt him. We probably couldn't shoot him with artillery. I just don't know. But if I sleep on it, perhaps I'll have an idea!"

"We should all sleep on it," said the general at last. He looked up at Dobzhov and added: "Even Carl, if he can. How do you feel, Carl?"

"I feel all right," said Carl Dobzhov. "I'm making history up here."

"Bring him a blanket, Nina," ordered General Dvat.

"I don't want a blanket," said Dobzhov, "I want down. In fact, I'm tired of making history. I'm tired of clairvoyance and teleportation. I don't care about mind over matter. I don't like telekinesis or extra-terrestrials. If you knew what I know, you wouldn't like levitation either. Nor would you like telepathy. Outer space and astral travelling is a pile of shit to me. I don't give a damn any more, I couldn't care less about the turn of a revolution. You can send me to Siberia. If you can get me down, that is. Yes, get me down and send me to Siberia. And then explain to the world about the great Carl Dobzhov, who was once a good comrade of the great Soviet Socialist Republics of Russia and who was ruined by levitation!"

Since there was no reply from his stunned audience, Dobzhov continued.

"When I first started levitating I thought it was fun. It was a great thing. It occupied my mind, my time, my days. When I wasn't practicing, I was thinking about practicing. Look where it's got me! Under the ceiling! And since you're all so amazingly attentive, I'll tell you what that ceiling looks like. It's made of oak beams and oak wood. It's dark and old and stinks. It's a stupid ceiling. I've been studying it. It's full of worm holes and there's patches of paint, blue paint, here and there. It doesn't need a paint job. It doesn't need to be examined from this close for this long. And when I shut my eyes I still see it. I feel bloated. My gut is full of shit, like the gut of the revolution, like the gut of Siberia and levitation. A man has to evacuate, wouldn't you say? So if you don't want to be sprayed and splattered you know what you must do. You don't need me! You don't need me anymore because you have a new boy in Geneva whom you're going to buy for the great Socialist Revolution that was going to sweep the world and hasn't, has it, General Dvat?"

General Dvat had risen. He playfully aimed his revolver at Dobzhov. Then he thrust it into his holster. On his way to the door, without turning, without breaking stride, he said: "Nina, get our baby another beer!"

24

MONEY

It was not the policy of the Government of the Union of Soviet Socialist Republics to send military officials on tour to foreign nations. The reasons for this were obvious, but bear repeating. Theoretically the military in the USSR was subordinated to the political faction of government, even though in practice military considerations frequently determined political action. It had happened in the past that a military man had become confused or over-zealous and done harm to the cause of Soviet socialism in the world, and at home. It was, therefore, something of a surprise for the Swiss Government to be informed of the imminent arrival of General Nicolai Dvat, who would come to Geneva not only to reaffirm the friendly ties which existed between the two countries, but to spend a number of days at the United Nations and at UNICEF headquarters as an observer in order to bring back information which might better equip the Soviet military to keep pace with the demands of the times.

In keeping with the rarity of the event, General Dvat was received at Geneva airport with all the military honours due to such a distinguished visitor and veteran. A two-hundred-man guard of honour in white and green parade uniforms were precisely placed on the runway, parallel to the sparkling Tupolev air force jet. The wind blew. The Swiss flag, the Soviet flag and the flag of the United Nations flew. An energetic band played enthusiastic renditions of both national anthems, through which the general stood at attention, saluting. He then briskly marched along the front line of the guard with an unsmiling face, every inch the warrior. When the ceremonial part of the dramatic arrival was over, Dvat shook hands with a number of minor officials and was then whisked away in an enormous limousine to the Soviet Embassy.

The USSR Government had made it clear that the general

would not be interested in visiting military installations or troops in Switzerland. It had been expressed, with uncommon diplomatic flair, that the USSR was well aware of Swiss fighting strength and that it respected the peace and neutrality and the great restraint with which Switzerland had conducted her affairs in the world. What this meant in practical terms was simply that General Dvat had plenty of time, which is what he had asked for.

Among his baggage which, as was customary on such diplomatic occasions, had not been inspected, were eight rather large suitcases of grey leather, not uncommonly strapped and locked, containing eighty million U.S. dollars. These were placed in the general's quarters at the embassy, even before he himself arrived there. When General Dvat walked through the door he immediately demanded coffee and a sandwich and asked not to be disturbed until he lifted the restriction himself. He then unbuttoned his uniform and the collar of his tunic, heaved a great sigh, stretched, and walked into the bathroom, where he turned on the light and examined himself in the mirror, saying: "Now then, Nicolai Nicolaiyevich, you will do what has to be done. You will do it for Russia!" Then he placed a telephone call to the man who had been named Shawn.

General Dvat was informed that his party did not answer the telephone and was presumed out; would he care to leave a message? The general told the operator that he would not and that he would call back in fifteen minutes. Settling himself comfortably with his ham sandwich and his coffee, he took off his Russian wristwatch and placed it in plain view on the low table. After fifteen minutes, still chewing (the general liked to eat slowly), he called back to the hotel with the same negative results.

After fifteen minutes had elapsed (which interval he used to have a grey-faced little rabbit of a man with bushy eyebrows bring him a bottle of vodka and some good, plain bread), Dvat downed his first shot of the stuff, chewed on the bread, and called the hotel again. This time he got through, informing Shawn that he would like to come to see him immediately. When asked to identify himself he said: "You will remember the insurance money? I should like to come over and discuss this with you." Shawn told him that it would be all right.

Next, General Nicolai Dvat pressed himself into one of three ill-fitting plain suits of dark blue, in which he looked like a retired sea captain, once again told himself in the mirror that he was doing this for Russia, and ordered a stretched limousine which arrived presently. The suitcases were placed in the trunk and front cabin and the general asked to be driven to the train station, where he got out, paid handsomely, had two porters carry the suitcases to a platform for boarding the train to Nyon, some 16 miles east of Geneva. Once in Nyon, he checked the suitcases at the baggage room, and wandered a labyrinthine pattern about the near-deserted streets surrounding the station. This diversionary tactic would, the general assumed, throw off any possibility of his being followed. When a sufficient time had passed, he approached a young lad near the station, and paid for his assistance in retrieving the suitcases. With the help of the boy and a driver, they loaded the luggage into still another taxi - which delivered the general and his precious cargo back to Geneva. He arrived at the Royal Palace Hotel within two hours after he had made the last telephone call to Shawn. And he was admitted without fuss - despite his three bellboys and his suitcases - by the guard at the door to Shawn's suite.

An extraordinary thing now occurred. As soon as the two men saw each other, the one a battle-scarred veteran of front-line combat and now one of the most powerful military men in the world, the other a young prince from no one knew where, they loved each other. This was not a common love, either, but the manly love of two who instantly recognized each other's strength and beauty, though in the case of General Dvat the beauty was that of craggy rock and required great vision to be recognized in its entirety.

They tried unsuccessfully to usher each other into armchairs, to make each other comfortable, to assure each other that they should feel at home, because the general had long developed disdain for material objects. Furniture meant nothing to him. He had pissed on Hitler's couch, darkened the great floral pattern once thought inviolable in the Reich's Chancellery. Wherever the general found himself, in hut, palace or bungalow, he felt that nothing there mattered and that everything placed there was placed at his whim, so that in every sense of the word he, General Nicolai Dvat, was at home there. He had earned this right by killing nine men, eight of these in honourable combat and one in the context of an execution.

Not having succeeded in making each other conventionally comfortable, the general simply laid all eight suitcases on their sides on the floor, opened them one by one and said: "My dear young man,

I brought you eighty million dollars in shiny new thousand dollar bills all the way from Moscow. This is Russia's gift to you for your excellence and your contributions to the field of parapsychology and related psychic phenomena in which, as you may know, I happen to be more than commonly interested."

Shawn knelt to look at the bounty.

"The suitcases themselves," said the general, "are a personal gift from me to you. They are made of camel leather. I trust you will have use for them."

Shawn showed no great surprise, but he did remark on the fact of eighty million instead of the fifty he had demanded. The general shrugged, at last, allowing himself to be accommodated by the furniture. He said, "I do not believe that our American friends will dispense even with thirty million of their dollars. They do not like what they think of as blackmail, do you understand? They are a little sensitive in that area, and I have seen them get very angry at the slightest whiff of what they call extortion. Then, what constitutes blackmail and extortion can be widely disputed between them and us, even by a humble general in the Soviet Armed Services such as I am. Personally, I like to think of this money as payment for a valuable lesson you have taught us. I've had plenty of time to think about what this lesson has actually been, and I think you have shown us the meaning of modesty. After all, you could have asked for *all* our money!"

Shawn looked at the visitor and the general looked squarely back. Then the Durstli Man began to smile. It was his customary, celestial smile but with a difference, having been touched, it seemed, at the edges with the recognition of a terrestrial quality relatively new to him - the quality known as irony.

"Now," said the general, "I should very much like to open a bottle of vodka with you, Kaluga will do, and find out if we can come to some agreement for the future. I have something you want, I believe."

Still smiling with the pleasant shock of meeting this simple, straightforward human, Shawn ordered the vodka. By the time it arrived and the general tossed down the first glass, Shawn found himself engrossed, though he drank sparingly, while the suitcases, closed once again, stood neatly in a corner awaiting their new master's disposal.

"The Central Committee and myself recognise your importance," said the general. "Naturally we cannot know who you are or where you come from or what havoc precisely you could wreak should you choose to do so. Still, we are not entirely behind the times in Moscow. I think in this instance we even have the jump on our American friends. As soon as I had assured myself that Slavo Stentorian, the man you sent back so efficiently, was not a raving maniac and that what he claimed had happened indeed, I realised that unusual measures were warranted. Fortunately I am respected in the Soviet Union. It was not easy, but I finally did persuade my comrades that we would have to move fast in order to make a friend of you. Contrary to the bourgeois and the counter-revolutionary idea that one cannot buy love, I feel that a great deal of money can buy not only love but loyalty if it is based on intelligent strength, which you possess I'm sure. *N'sta-rovya!*"

He raised his glass in a brief arc and tossed off another vodka. Shawn sipped from his. Dvat shook himself, grimacing. "No," he went on, "our American friends won't give you fifty million. They'll probably send somebody with five million, or they'll just put it in your account, if I know them right, and hope for the best. I like them. They have learned that if a man stridently asks for fifty he'll gladly take five. This is naturally the rule in the world. We know this, too. But there is something beyond that, the exception. You are an exceptional man, if a man you are. More than that, you are unique. Even among the unique you're unique. When you asked for fifty million, I knew that we should give you eighty. I knew this with great certainty. But what is money? It is not nothing, as some say, nor everything as others want us to believe. Money is itself, it has its own precise value. I brought these eighty million not merely to demonstrate goodwill, not merely to outbid the Americans, not merely to surprise you and to show you that I respect you, nor to buy friendship. I brought them primarily so you would listen to me, which is what you're doing. *Skol!*"

He drank again but did not grimace this time. "Everybody says don't trust the Russians. Everybody thinks we are stupid," he said. "That's true. We *are* stupid. Russia is stupid. I am a stupid man. Look at me! I am short. I have a thick neck, a flat face. My legs are bent. My left leg is shorter than my right. I have many scars. I could have killed a thousand Germans. I killed only nine. I was stupid then too. This money... that is stupid. What can be more stupid than eighty American dollars? Did I say eighty? Well, if eighty American dollars are stupid, can you imagine the stupidity of eighty million?"

He sat back, roaring and shaking with laughter, slapping his thighs. Shawn's smile deepened. He said: "What is your name, old man?"

"Forgive me," said the general, "I must truly be getting senile. I thought I had introduced myself."

He rose and bowed, still laughing.

"Nicolai Constantin Dvat," he announced. "And now you must tell me what your name is."

"I cannot," said Shawn.

The general sat down again and drank some more. "Good," he said. "This Kaluga is not bad! No, the money is just a good tidy sum. But what I came to tell you is this: this is money! Do you understand? Time equals money, which means that money equals time, also. An American saying. I got here before they did with more money than they will bring to tell you that time is money, and that if, as you've said, you want money and time, you've got both. Eighty million is plenty of time. Drink up, my boy!"

Shawn did as he was told, smiling at the general. The general too, drank.

"The Americans are not true capitalists," said General Nicolai Constantin Dvat. "In this instance, they are losing simply because they are going to the limit of the time limit you gave them. If they give you money, they will give it to you at the very last minute. But the very last minute can be too late! Ah," called the general with a happy voice that frayed into a croak, "this calls for a celebration, for music, my son."

He whipped a small harmonica from one pocket and held it up.

"This harmonica saved my life near a town called Gusev, in East Prussia," he said.

It could have been true, because the harmonica was twisted out of shape, bent and torn apart in the middle.

"That bullet still cost me two ribs," said the general, "but two ribs is better than one life!"

He blew into the harmonica, holding it high between thumb and middle finger of his right hand. He began to play what could have been a tune composed of three notes, each one of them tortured to the limit. As he played on he lifted the bottle of vodka with his free hand and began to filter small amounts into his mouth. After having set the bottle down, he played on for a while, one-two-three notes, one-one-two, two-two-one, three-two-three notes, one-one-two, two-two-one, three-two-three and one-two-three again. When he was through he stated: "To drink and play at the same time I could have had a molar removed, as the man did who taught me this trick. But I was a purist, I learned to do it without the gap. Do you like the tune? It's called Dvat-Dvat-Dvat, and could you have guessed? Three notes - that's all a man can get out of this piece, but to me those three notes are the voices of the angels who saved my life that night."

Shawn was smiling infinitely at his visitor, "Old man, Mr. General," he said, "you've brought me a lot of money. You've brought me a lot of time. I have one further wish, I want a name."

The general brought his great fist down and smashed the harmonica on the table. He brought his flushed, flat face forward like the face of some great red-arsed baboon! "Do you want a name?" he croaked. "Take mine! I give it to you. Dvat! Not a great name, but a good one. Eighty-million-dollar name, my boy, eh, what do you say?"

Shawn had begun to laugh. It was clearly terrestrial laughter, fuelled by vodka. He laughed so hard he lost his balance and fell to the floor. He began to roll around on the floor, pounding the carpet, rolling toward the suitcases, kicking them.

The general had raised the bottle high, took a long, long draft, set it down, wiped his lips, stared with bulging, insane eyes. "Ahhhhhhhh," he roared, "money, yaaaaahhhhhhh!"

Shawn was still rolling around on the floor, moaning with laughter. He formed words, a sentence, something that could not be easily understood. It sounded like: "Go... show him, Pat... show him!"

Patrick Young stretched out his hands. They looked more or less like two normal hands on a single man but one was not entirely complete. The fingertips were missing. In their stead there was a wavering, shimmering mass of light, like five ethereal misty thimbles.

"Show him," Shawn said more intelligently, "tell him, Patrick!"

"I'm Patrick Young," said Pat. "I lost my hand when I was killed, blown to bits. This one!"

He held up the hand that had been lost.

"A new one is growing, as you can see, sir, and when it's done I shall be allowed to live again, as before."

"Yes," Shawn confirmed. "It wasn't easy, General Dvat."

The general nodded benignly.

"I see that our money has not been misapplied," he murmured, "not misapplied at all."

"Good-bye Patrick," said Shawn, and Patrick Young disappeared.

"We are stupid," mumbled the general, "but the Americans are also stupid. Where are they now? Young man, how would you like the name Father Russia? I give you Russia. You take her. You take her and make something of her, I command you! Call yourself saviour or tsar as you like. Call yourself Mr. Future, who cares? Take over the world, why don't you? Show these rotten dogs what can be done. Ohhhh, my good boy, my son, you would have to be very intelligent indeed to imagine how stupid Nicolai Dvat is. Very, very intelligent."

Dvat sank back into the upholstery. There were tears in his eyes. His cheeks were wet, tears no doubt mingling with vodka. The harmonica lay forlorn on the table, twisted, bent, torn like the heart of this humble warrior. But when he spoke now his voice was deep and steady.

"My son," he said, "now that you have money and time in one, I will tell you how to get a name. In order to get a name you must destroy. The more you destroy, the bigger will be your name. Look at me, I have destroyed only a handful, a large handful of men, but Russia trusts and reveres me. So it is not necessarily a matter of numbers. It may be a matter of quality. Destroy the greatest living man and you will have a name. Destroy the ten greatest living men and you will have a name. Destruction is the answer. You can build, too, but what is built, no matter how large, can be in turn destroyed. Destroy the pyramids! Destroy the Great Wall of China. Yes do that, that especially, my boy! Haaaahhhh, what an idea! What a stupid, stupid idea!"

The general collapsed, sobbing and laughing in one, tears of real grief streaming down his great, grinning ape face.

25

TRY

Shawn looked down on the Soviet general who was twitching and shaking in a comatose fit, waving his hands as if to ward off evil spirits. He looked down on the general with a look that was not human. There was neither pity nor hate in it, nor even indifference. He looked at the general in a way that was also utterly non-religious. He looked at him as if a man were looking at a puddle of rain water.

After a while the general began to calm down. His legs stopped trembling and kicking, the hands came to rest and at last he lay quiet, though his breathing was still rough and noisy. A grin had frozen on his face. His eyes were not quite closed but obviously he saw nothing. He was unconscious of the world.

Shawn's mind, too, had become unhinged. When Dvat first appeared, he had thought it might be Oba in the body of Dvat for a confrontation. He looked forward to it. He enjoyed jousting with Oba, who was a very powerful Councillor, but also one bound to the status quo, sworn to maintain the order that had been established. Shawn could defeat Oba at anything, hands down, simply because Oba could not live in alternate worlds, he would have been destroyed on the crystal planet. But now Shawn saw that this was not Oba. This was indeed General Nicolai Constantin Dvat, and he was slowly coming around, opening his eyes, staring, coughing, sitting up unsteadily and immediately reaching for the bottle. But, of course, sitting on the floor as he was, he completely misjudged the distance, his hand grasped air and he toppled over again, howling with laughter.

"One little bottle of vodka can do this to an old man," he screamed. "What tragedy for Russia!"

Again he managed to right himself. This time he sat steadily, grinning up at Shawn. Shawn smiled back down.

"General," he said. "why do you come here with all that money?"

"To give it to you, as you demanded."

"General, why do you want me to believe that?"

"It is the truth. I *have* given you the money, it is yours now."

"Yes, but for how long?"

"Ahhhh, ahhhhh ...." groaning, the general got up on all fours. Like a dog he pawed in the direction of Shawn.

"For how long, General?"

"You ask too many questions," rasped the general. "Don't you know the trouble with money? You have to let it go, otherwise it's no good to you. You must spend it. So, this money here for example, it must be spent."

"Yes, General. It will be spent."

"Well, in that case," Dvat said, suddenly appearing much more sober, "I have some good suggestions how you can spend it." Now at last the general regained his feet and wobbled over to an armchair where he sat down.

"My situation at this moment is a dangerous one," he said. "I've persuaded my government to lend me this money for this performance. I insisted that it be real money. Not many people know this, but I am an admirer of great movies. I love them. There was a director in Hollywood, I believe the Austrian, what's his name, the one who loved to wear German officer's uniforms, I'll think of his name. The director once filmed a scene of an orgy and this orgy involved officers of an army and, of course, many beautiful women. Ah, yes, von Stroheim, Erich von Stroheim, I knew I would remember. Now in this orgy scene he wanted absolute authenticity, this von Stroheim. And so he insisted that even the officer's underwear be tailor-made. The officers wore cotton shorts, with their individual initials stitched into them. What a notion! Yet I can understand him well. I, too like everything to be realistic. This is why this is real money. I could have tried to fool you, but it would have diminished the performance. And now, my good young man lost on our cruel planet, let us see if you can dodge a fast bullet as well as smothering an exploding grenade."

From his bulky coat Dvat pulled out his shiny revolver and pointed it at Shawn. Shawn laughed and lifted his right hand, extending the index finger, pointing back at Dvat. "Bang, bang, bang," Shawn went, kinking his middle finger as if pulling the trigger. "That's the solution here on Earth, isn't it? If it bothers you, shoot it, eliminate it. What a waste of time."

"What do *you* know about time?" Dvat said hoarsely.

"I've learned a great deal since I came here," Shawn replied. "When you kill a man you increase time."

"What?"

"When you kill a man you increase time."

"I don't understand."

"Every man, woman or child who is killed, murdered, blown up, increases the volume of time, can you understand that?"

"No, but it doesn't matter."

"Yes, it does. Don't be foolish, General Dvat. I like you. You are like a child, a son. I could be your father. Don't be fooled by time, by the difference of your skin. Before you try to kill me, listen. How many people died in World Wars I and II?"

"Ah, how many - a good question. Sixty four million, perhaps more. Many people died in those wars."

"Yes, good. In every war the burden of time is vastly increased. For time is the burden of Earth while the killing goes on."

"I dislike killing a poet," Dvat said with equanimity, now apparently quite sober, "but better a poet kick the pumpkin than I do. I've personally vouched for bringing back this money. I can't go home without it."

"That is all unimportant, general. Listen, when you kill a person, that person becomes your dependent in another world. How many dependents do you have?"

In reply the general aimed carefully at Shawn and fired.

As he did so he was looking squarely at Shawn. He had aimed not at the head but at the heart, and he was ready to fire again if he missed, though there was little likelihood of that at this distance. But as he watched, the picture before him changed. In a curious way he had the impression that the target at which he was firing was receding at phenomenal speed, much faster than the bullet, so that, in a few instants, the bullet had spent itself and fell, its destination hopelessly out of reach. And yet the same man was still sitting there meters away, looking back at him. The general fired again. And again the bullet entered that impossible race with the receding body of Shawn. And again it lost.

"You see," said Shawn, "you fired in space and time, but space and time is *your* burden, your responsibility, not mine. You should have fired at my toe, because I have a toehold in space and time, no more. You might have hit my toe, General Dvat, my Achilles' toe."

The general groaned. He lowered his revolver. Then he raised it again and placed the muzzle in his mouth, biting down on it.

"General Dvat," said Shawn, "before you go, wait!"

The general did not instantly squeeze the trigger, but kept the tip of the barrel resting on his lower lip which gave him the appearance of a large, ugly, pouting child. He stared at Shawn out of wide-open, wild, eyes.

"If you wish to travel swiftly without physical impediment of your body, General Dvat," said Shawn, "why not let me help you? Where would you like to go?"

Further startled by the question, General Dvat slowly pulled the revolver out of his mouth and lowered it.

"The Crimea," he said.

"The Crimea," Shawn smiled, "a pleasant region on this planet, I'm sure."

"Yes," nodded the general, "sunshine, vineyards, champagne, violins, and beautiful dark-eyed girls with skin as white as alabaster and fire in their hearts."

"The Crimea it is, then!"

"You are going to send me to the Crimea?"

"Yes."

"That will be a waste of time. I'll only have to go on to Moscow immediately."

"Don't worry about that, General. It would not be good if you continued your present life-style at this time. First of all, I don't want you to take this money back with you. And further, you deserve a vacation. When would you say the Crimea is most beautiful?"

"In June," said General Dvat.

"Is there no pollution in the Crimea?"

"Well, perhaps. Of course there is pollution everywhere now, and we..."

"But not a hundred years ago, General Dvat. It must have been magnificent in the Crimea a hundred years ago."

"Yes, I'm sure, but..."

"Champagne, dark-eyed girls with alabaster skin and fire in their hearts - and no pollution. General Paradise. I am sending you back to Paradise."

Even as he gestured and General Nicolai Constantin Dvat

faded into that other, more perfect Crimea of a hundred years ago, Shawn felt a pang of human regret and a surge of memory of the crystal planet and the messenger of the female principle with whom he had been granted merger. He had a vivid impression of a lion sinking his fangs into the unblemished throat of a lamb.

26

LOVE

"One day," said Slavo Stentorian to Vera, "I will have to *kill* the pig." Slavo said this while encircling Vera's waist with his arms. He said it drowsily, uncertainly.

They had woken almost simultaneously, Slavo first, then Vera. By his watch it was five minutes past three in the morning. They had woken at an ungodly hour - he had told her it was about three-thirty and had added that, come to think of it, all hours were ungodly in Russia. She had chuckled under a pillow in order not to wake the neighbours through the paper-thin walls.

"You could have killed him," Slavo whispered after a while.

"Yes," said Vera, "I could have, I think I took the starch out of him."

"Yes, you did," said Slavo, and they traded chuckling whispers again. "Let's get married now."

"In one room?" she teased him.

"It's not just a room," Slavo told her, "it's a room with bed and music."

He got up, tiptoed to the record player, and put on a record. They were beyond considering the neighbours. He turned the volume very low and hopped back into bed. It was Duke Ellington - "Caravan." They lay listening to the entire number. When it was over, Vera whispered to Slavo that she thought "Caravan" had been inspired by *Ravel's Bolero,* and he agreed that it was possible. "Caravan" was followed by "Black and Tan Fantasy," and Slavo had to jump up again to turn the volume down even further. They talked very little until the whole side had run off, then Slavo said, "I know it, Vera, this Shawn killed Dvat. I'm sure of it!"

"You still trust Nihilev," she told him, pulling herself closer. They lay face to face, belly to belly. She told him she thought General

Dvat had been framed by Nihilev and higher-ups in the Party Council. She told him he was sent to Geneva to be killed and Shawn would sooner or later be charged with the murder. "But," she said, "the corpse has not been found, and that doesn't fit. If they killed Dvat, they would have prearranged to have Shawn trapped with the body. That part I don't understand."

Slavo got up and turned the record over. "Oh," whispered Vera, " you shouldn't have got up, we were perfect." He told her that they could be perfect again and slid back into the same position with her. "Perfect?" he whispered, smiling in the dark. "Perfect!" she replied.

"What good would it do them to have Dvat killed?" Slavo asked himself as much as his fiancée. "I know that Dvat took money to Geneva. I don't know how much, but probably a lot, though if you want to kill a man, you don't give him millions of dollars for the road, unless you want to give him a real sense of security. But that wasn't necessary, either. It fitted. All they had to do was give Dvat a million and tell him to look up Shawn. The rest would have been easy. I admit that it sounds right, but it's much too obvious, much too smooth. I mean it isn't clumsy enough. Certainly it doesn't sound like Nihilev's idea. I think Shawn killed Dvat and made his body disappear."

"But what would be his motive, Slavo?"

Even lying on his left shoulder, Slavo shrugged, shrugging himself closer to Vera, who kissed him lightly on the shoulder. They were both wide awake now.

"He doesn't need a motive," he said. "He's young, impetuous. He's crazy. He can do anything he wants. A whim, an impulse. Nothing he does has to fit. I saw our planet from an orbital point of view, Vera! That boy orbited a conference room in his hotel and nobody noticed! Then he teleported me from Geneva to Moscow! I have to keep repeating these things, because I must continue to account to myself, tell myself that they actually happened as they did, as I know they did. Motive! Does lightning need a motive?"

"Yes, master," Vera breathed on his shoulder. "Lightning needs a motive, and so does rain, don't you think?"

"So that is what they taught you at the university? To counter poetry with science? Well, my sweetest, poetry is winning the contest! Science is dead. Shawn doesn't need a motive. And General Nicolai Dvat is no more among the living, though at the boy's whim he, too, may be resurrected, reconstituted, rematerialised - whatever we call it - like that Englishman, Young. Yes, like Patrick Young!"

The last strains of "Mood Indigo" vibrated through the room, then the turntable switched off.

"Do you love me?" Vera wanted to know.

"I love you," Slavo told her.

"Would you defect without me?" she asked.

"I would defect without you," he whispered, "but I would make certain you had defected first."

She kissed him again, keeping her lips on his skin after the kiss. "Where would we go?" she asked. He told her that they would have to go to the land of Woody Herman, Benny Goodman, Lionel Hampton and Duke Ellington, if they possibly could and she agreed. "I could work in the household of a wealthy family. I could operate their dish-washing machines, their laundry machines," she said. "I could cook and take care of their children and teach them Russian lullabies. We could live in Georgia," she said.

Slavo wanted to know why Georgia. "Because that is where the great Joseph Stalin was born," she joked, purring against his chest. "We could start out in Georgia and then work our way to California on a train. I know they need waitresses and maids on their trains. Americans need good servants, I know that, and I know I could be a good servant. I don't want to work in an office in America. I don't want to type."

"We might have to tell them everything we know and take a different name," Slavo said to Vera. "I don't mind changing my name. I like my name but I wouldn't mind changing it. If it were necessary I would certainly change my name, cut my hair, and dye my eyebrows. We would have to live incognito in America, start a new life, become Americans, become like Americans."

"Your name could be Paul," said Vera, "your name could be Paul or John and a truly American family name. How would you like Paul Newman?" she giggled, pronouncing Newman like Nyoomunn. "We would have to learn to sing the American National Anthem," she told her lover. "We would place our right hand on our heart, like this ...."

She pushed her hand up between their bodies and placed it on Slavo's heart, and Slavo did likewise, placing his right on her heart. "That is how the Americans do it. Did you know that my mother has a good friend who knew Marina Oswald well?"

"I think you told me," Slavo said.

"Yes," Vera went on, "Marina Oswald became a good American. She changed her hairdo. She looked very pretty. She began to spend a lot of time at her hairdresser's until her husband was arrested."

Vera's breast felt so plump and so beautiful to Slavo's touch that he began softly to knead it. "Would you kill Nihilev if he touched you like this?" he whispered.

"He would be dead long before he could touch me like that," Vera Verovna replied.

"Why is it that a thing that can be the joy of one man's life," Slavo murmured, "will be the death of another? Or let me put it differently: is there a man whom you would not kill for touching you like this?"

"Paul Newman," Vera giggled. Slavo shifted his weight slightly and his hand found new caresses.

"Would you kill him for touching you like... like *this?*" he asked.

"You," sighed Vera after a moment had passed, "you are the only man on earth who may touch me like *that* and not be killed for it."

"Shawn," Slavo said, "is much prettier than I am, if he did *this* to you, *this,* as I'm doing now, tell me, would you kill *him?*"

"Oh, Slavo, oh," Vera sighed, "I could... oh, I could try." She turned and opened her legs, pulling Slavo on top of her. She helped him in with both hands. Slavo began to move around inside her, his face earnest in the dark like a man who has come home after a long day in the woods and must get used to the dimensions even of this familiar room in which he spends so much time. Vera began to moan. She began to move up against him and he down into her on a straight line. They were on a seesaw line with each other now and there was no stopping as they settled into their own special rhythm. He had told her once that the way they made love should be studied to replace nuclear energy, if it could be harnessed. It did not last very long. It lasted two, three minutes, this ride of fission. Toward the end their voices began to merge in the chant that has shaken the world since time immemorial. Then they subsided, staying for a long time, resting inside each other. Just then there was a deep, muffled crash in the adjoining apartment, also a one-roomer. A crash and a long oath, not in the least muffled. Then there was silence. It was four thirty-five, Slavo noticed.

"When you were in Geneva," Vera whispered, "I had dreams about you, but I can't tell you what kind of dreams."

"Tell me," he mumbled, allowing himself to sink more softly and more deeply into the bed. He was lying on his back. They were holding hands.

"I can't," she said.

"I had dreams about *you*," he told her drowsily, "dreamed we were making love the way we just did. Then we made love again the way we just did, and we kept on making love for a long time. When it was over you asked me if I wanted to make love again the way we just did..."

Slavo Stentorian was falling asleep very gently. Vera still lay awake, thinking about Shawn and about General Dvat's disappearance. She had closed her eyes and watched the slow, undulating dark waves she still saw inside her lids. She thought she had been asleep for a short time only when she suddenly sat bolt upright. Her eyes flung open. Slavo's gentle snore turned into a snarled grunt. In a very loud and clear voice she heard herself call out: "The lamb is the lion!" The sound that came across from the adjoining room was unmistakable and it was accompanied by a thunderous trembling of the wall at the head of their bed. A fist had been smashed into the wall from the other side.

27

BLOOD

Dimitri Nihilev was a vain man. It bothered him that the hair grew slowly over the area on his head that had had to be shaved when the wound Vera had caused was stitched. The stitches had been taken out, the crust of dry blood had fallen off, but a spot some three inches long and two wide was still bald. He was standing in the bathroom, examining the area with the help of a hand mirror and his bathroom mirror when the doorbell rang. It was Vera.

Nihilev quickly recovered from his surprise and handed her the hand mirror, saying: "This is a good time for you to inspect the damage you did, Vera Verovna. You look pale. Sit down. Would you like some champagne?"

Vera, the mirror still in her hand, sat down. Nihilev returned to the bathroom, combed hair over the bald spot, brushed some dandruff off his shoulders, though it might not have shown on the white shirt he was wearing. He strolled back smiling and polite into the living room, traversed it conscious of Vera's glance, and went into the kitchen, from which he returned before a minute was up with a bottle of champagne and two glasses. He sensed why Vera had come and it gave him an ugly self-confidence.

He began opening the bottle, saying: "My dear Vera, you have come to apologise, haven't you?" Vera said nothing. "There is no need for it," said Nihilev. "I insulted you, I was beginning to get drunk, you overwhelmed me. In return for that you smashed me. I deserved it. That makes us even, doesn't it? And so," he added, loosening the cork on the bottle, "I shall propose a toast to the old cossack saying that only a fatal wound can never be forgotten!"

He held the bottle at a steep angle, gave the cork a final nudge, and a merry shot reverberated in the room. Champagne gushed, adroitly caught by Nihilev in a glass which he handed Vera, who took it and drank immediately, without waiting for the toast to be proposed. Nihilev made a ceremony of it nevertheless, raising his glass to her, saying: "Only a fatal wound can never be forgotten. A fatal wound and bad champagne!" Then he drank.

Vera's face was still pale as she set down her glass. She began to tell him why she had come. It was not to apologise. It was to tell him that, if he wanted to, he could have her. In return for this, she wished to go to Geneva with him.

"Do you know," Nihilev said, "that I could arrest you right now? And Slavo Slavovich, too? Only he could have told you that I'm going to Geneva. But I shall overlook this little slip, my delicious and saintly martyr. I shall overlook the insult of your offer. I will not even ask you why all of a sudden you're so anxious to go to Switzerland. Instead I will tell you that I strike no such bargains. I make no deals of this kind. At least, my good Vera, not when I'm sober. And there isn't a champagne in the world that can make me drunk. So, of course I still want you. I may have phrased it badly just before you hit me, but the desire was genuine. How my palms have itched to cup your sweet breasts! How I have seen all your perspectives in many dreams. Bloodflecked dreams, I may tell you. You shocked me, my little one. You shocked me badly. Are you certain you wish to stand against my fury?"

In reply to his speech Vera began to undress. He filled up her glass again. She was dressed exactly in the same way she had been when they met in the café. There must have been blood on her sweater, he could not help thinking. She has had it cleaned! And that shiny gold-buckled belt! She was unbuckling it. She pulled the yellow sweater over her head, revealing a sweetly pink brassiere held together at the centre by a bouquet of shiny blue silk forget-me-nots. Touching, how touching, thought Dimitri Nihilev.

She unhooked the brassiere and presented her breasts. They were everything he had seen in his convulsive dreams except that they were not bloodflecked. And that, he decided, could be changed. He got up and walked into the bathroom and nicked his thumb with a razor and came out, holding his right thumb to his mouth, sucking on it. Vera Verovna stood in the doorway to his bedroom, totally unveiled in her full, pale innocence. Nihilev took in the picture in one thick gulp. He swallowed. He walked up to her and let the blood from his thumb drip slowly first on her left breast, then on her right.

"There," he said, "my dreams are coming true!"

Vera embraced him. He was thick and pudgy, but muscular underneath the layer of fat. For a moment she thought he would kill her. She felt faint. He picked her up effortlessly and carried her to the bed. He laid her down. He took a pillow and pushed it under the small of her back so that her body convexed. He dripped more blood, this time on her belly. Then he put the thumb to her mouth, telling her to taste it.

"It's good, revolutionary blood," he grinned. "Isn't it sweet?"

She had closed her eyes and was sucking his thumb. He pulled it away from her. He was erect and ready to enter. She reached for his testicles and began to caress them with both hands. She spread her legs wide and tried to pull him in. "No, no," Nihilev said," no, not that! Take it! Yes, like that! Take it in your mouth!"

She obeyed. He knelt with spread legs over her and she used her tongue to caress his penis. Nihilev's palms were pressed against the wall for support, his eyes closed. "When it comes," he said loudly, "I want you to swallow it. I don't like women who are afraid of semen! Are you?"

She shook her head without interrupting her work. "If you do it good," he said, "I might just take you to Geneva. I don't need a secretary, strictly speaking, but I'm entitled to one. Funny how things turn in a circle, isn't it? What made you want to go, anyway? Has that psychic done this to you? Has he made you crazy, too? Are you like those women that committed suicide, are you one of them? I should think you're thinking of him right now, aren't you, tell me, are you?"

Vera shook her head again, without stopping. Once he had given her the idea of making love to Shawn, she could banish it only by thinking of Slavo.

Nihilev made sudden, vicious thrusts with his pelvis. She tried to ride them out by yielding, drawing her head back deep into the pillow. Nihilev cupped his hands over her head and held it, thrusting deep. She gagged. He let go of her head. She continued with her work. Then Nihilev inundated her. Vera swallowed, swallowed, swallowed - thick hot stuff. She must not gag, she must not cough! She must not spoil his pleasure! Slowly, slowly his stream subsided in small spurts. She felt his thighs tremble. He sank down on her and she managed to make him slide off sideways.

Dimitri Nihilev lay like a baby, on his side. Though the bleeding of his thumb had probably stopped, he was still sucking it. He did not pull away from her.

When she dared open her eyes, she saw only his great quivering belly. She closed her eyes again. Her right hand slipped casually off the bed and found her leather bag. She unzipped it slowly and brought out a knife. For a moment she hesitated, wondering why everything had gone wrong. But then new certainty rushed through her. She swung the knife up and into his belly, pushing hard. She let herself slip off the bed, onto her knees. Nihilev's hairy arms clasped spasmodically, hugging nothing to his chest. Again she plunged the knife deeply, from the end of her outstretched arm. She pulled it out and began to stab him in earnest, no longer caring about his arms and hands. Stabbing him, in the heart, in the chest, again in the belly, she came closer, like a lover. Nihilev was dying fast. They were both covered with his blood. His blood smelled clean - intoxicatingly clean. Her stabbing arm was growing weary. Her face, in the effort, lay almost upon his and she felt his last breaths cool her bloody lips.

She did not know how long she lay in a stupor of exhaustion. Her eyes wide open but unfocussed. When the bedside telephone rang, she reached for it with precise robot movements.

"Comrade Nihilev?"

The voice came through slick, obsequious. Vera said nothing.

"Comrade Nihilev, are you there?"

"Nihilev is here," she heard herself whisper.

"What?"

"He is here."

"Who are you? Let me talk to him!"

"He can't talk," she said. "His mouth is full of blood."

"Blood?"

The receiver slipped from her hand and bumped the carpeted floor. She sat up. She was covered with Nihilev's blood. She tried to get up, but her legs trembled violently and she collapsed on the bed. Her senses were gradually coming back. She was on a bed, next to a corpse, the corpse was Nihilev, she had killed him. She would get up, no, sit up, call Slavo. She sat up, bent down to pick up the receiver. Her head seemed to be carried off on a black wave in a black sea. Cautiously she righted herself and sat staring, trying to think. Time passed when it should not pass. It was too late to call Slavo. She had to .... had to .... Again she tried to get up. This time she made it, and stumbled to the bathroom. No time to shower. Wash hands, face, dry them.

Back into the bedroom, found her brassiere on a threshold. She pulled the yellow sweater over her head, the skirt, the belt, buckle it, now, stockings, stuff them into .... where, where is the handbag? By the bedside. And the knife, where, still where? No, not, it couldn't .... in Nihilev. She had left it in him, still in him. She had to pull the corpse, shift its weight to get the knife out. Hands bloody again. Time, time!

Now she was dressed, no, hands bloody, wash, bathroom again, water, towel. She flew through bedroom, living room, out the door, down the stairs. One landing, two, first floor, landing, ground floor, through the inner door into the vestibule, then .... then shadows rushing up to the thickly glassed double door to the street. She should turn, but did not. She composed her face, walked forward, indifferent looking, bland, knew nothing, had seen no corpse, no blood. They rushed past her, she caught the heavy door, was outside. One foot forward, step down, the other, again, dream-walking down the stairs, halfway down now ....

"Stoi!"

KGB! Instantaneously, the thought flashed through Vera's mind.

She did not stop but kept walking. One of them was on her from behind and pushed her down the last two steps. She lost her balance, stumbled forward and felt searing pain in her breasts from the impact against a parked car. Rough hands spun her round and her coat was torn open.

"Ah, you ....!" the same, servile voice.

She kept her face down, tried to close her eyes but saw Nihilev's blood. It had dried but not fast enough. It made an abstract pattern in the yellow fabric of her sweater, something like a large butterfly with broken wings.

The car door swung open, there on the brown ragged back seat was a haggard, handcuffed Slavo.

"It's execution or Siberia for you both," uttered one of the agents as he slammed the door shut behind her. "Which do you prefer?"

28

MIRACLES

In the twelfth day of his marathon levitation, Carl Dobzhov, though he was breaking all previous records, had become something of a nuisance. His diatribe against the state before General Dvat had been only a prelude. He had continued to spew forth insults, threats, obscenities and once he had actually vomited, no doubt as a result of his refusal to accept any kind of food except beer.

It was not easy to deal with him. To arrest him and put him on trial for treasonous sentiment and behaviour would not have been wise. For one thing, there was the problem of how to get him down. While the Advanced Studies Ministry had at first been inclined to trumpet Dobzhov's fantastic achievement to the world, invite the international press in for direct observation and make political hay while the sun shone, it became quickly apparent that there was more of the freakish than the scientific in Dobzhov's condition, especially in his perpetually drunken states. Nor would it have been good to deny him beer. All the consultant doctors agreed that in the absence of ordinary food, beer was a passable substitute. The last thing the Advanced Studies Ministry wished to do was to create an emaciated martyr, a starving saint. There was beginning to develop too much of a religious undercurrent as it was.

The peasants in the area, still relatively backward and superstitious, had long tended toward adoration. Their temperament lent itself to the anticipation of the arrival of saints and saviours, and in that department there had been a long drought in Russia. As Carl Dobzhov became internationally known, it had been difficult for them to hold back. There had been unpleasant incidents, heralded by a basket containing potatoes, bread and salt, the traditional offering of hospitality and friendship. This basket had been left on Dobzhov's doorstep three years ago. Since then there had been other, less harmless offerings: a whole sheep, ritually sliced at the throat with the heart exposed; a dead rooster sacrificially presented with its head between its legs; and finally, a basket of fruit arranged to highlight a dove, bloodflecked, innocent, motionless. Now that Dobzhov was rumoured to have been in the "exalted state" for over a week, the peasants sent a delegation of twelve who camped outside in the bitter cold that still gripped the land. At night they made fires and passed the time chanting and drinking. During the day they stood wrapped in blankets, motionless, with the faces of believers enchanted by a miracle. They, too, did not fit into the plans of the Advanced Studies Ministry in general, and its Psychkultura Section in particular.

On the fourth day of this vigil, the peasants were approached by the local party boss, accompanied by a political educator and two men who did not identify themselves in any fashion. The peasants were told that there was nothing for them to see here, to disperse and go home. But they were adamant, insisting that they be allowed to enter and witness the great miracle of exaltation of Carl Dobzhov, and that they be allowed to pray in his presence and with his blessing. They were told that Dobzhov was not a religious man but a good comrade and socialist worker, whose life was dedicated to the state and to the people, and that a visit such as they imagined would not be merely an embarrassment to him but an insult. Did they wish to insult Comrade Dobzhov?

The spokesman for the peasants, a large man still further enlarged by a heavy overcoat, fur cap and bulky boots, apologised for giving the impression that they wished to disturb Dobzhov. He said: "We know that our brother Carl Dobzhov has been blessed with states of exaltation in which his physical weight is rendered meaningless and he floats above the earth like a cloud. We know that the Almighty God of All the Heavens has bestowed this grace upon our brother so that our eyes may behold it, may feast on it, and that in our hearts that faith may be strengthened. Let us see the miracle! Then we shall return to our homes and fields and continue to work for the common good of our great Socialist nation!"

The educator, himself of relatively diminutive proportions, certainly when compared with the spokesman's bulk, looked up into the peasant's face, smiling indulgently. "Ah, comrade," he said, "I see that your dedication to the great ideals of our nation is true and tested and I, too, wish to apologize to you. I see now that you would never find it in you to disturb Comrade Dobzhov in his most important, scientific work, his experiments in levitation which are studied by scientists the world over and which carry the glory of our people to the far corners of the earth. Still, let me remind you that what you call the 'Almighty God of All the Heavens' has long been understood by our great scientists as the inexorable forces of nature which move all and permit all to rest. There is nothing mysterious about it. Carl Dobzhov will help us learn more about disturbances in the magnetic field of the earth, which temporarily offset the pull of gravity in certain susceptible individuals and make levitation possible. All you good men and comrades, go home now and leave us to pursue this important work in peace!"

"I shall not," said the spokesman, assuming for the first time an individual stance, perhaps because he realized that to refuse to obey such a direct order was an act of individual obstinacy or fortitude not necessarily approved of by those men whom he represented. But behind him eleven voices echoed: "We shall not go home!"

The educator shrugged his round shoulders, turned abruptly and walked back to his automobile. The others followed in his wake, except for the local party boss, who stepped up very close to the large spokesman and said: "You are a stupid man, Ivan Ivanovich! What you are doing is a crime against the state, hooliganism. For this you will freeze your fingers and toes at strict discipline. I do not care. I care only how stupid you and your friends will look before the world, interrupting an important scientific experiment stupidly as you are doing! But I will tell you this - if you go home now, I will see that nothing comes of it, that you will not be punished. Don't make it difficult for yourselves. Go home! Go home, all of you!"

But neither the big man nor any of the others said anything. They stared over, through, the man as if trying to pierce the walls behind which they knew the blessed Dobzhov hovered in his exalted state, which (and this they could not know) was rapidly deteriorating.

A few days earlier, efforts had been made to bring Dobzhov down but these had not been successful. First a few men had stood on chairs and tried gently to steer him back down to a sofa, but Carl had not budged. Then, when they had applied more force, he had cursed at them and told them that they were hurting him. So they had brought ladders and ropes and tied the ropes around him after throwing blankets over him to distribute the pressure evenly. Then they had tried to pull him down, while he cursed and spat on them. Still he had not moved. It had become obvious that conventional methods would not work. Many alternatives had been discussed. Perhaps, it had been assumed, the magnetic disturbances were less powerful at night and so, that very night, again they had tried to pull him down, and again they failed. The following day a pale-faced, bearded observer from the Advanced Studies Ministry had suggested a solution that struck everyone as brilliant in the extreme. "If the mountain will not come to us," he had told them, "then we must go to the mountain. Why not *elevate the house?*"

And so they had arranged the sofa in such a way that when the house was elevated, Carl Dobzhov would come to rest on it directly. They had brought in powerful cranes, lifts and earth-moving machinery and worked throughout the night. In the morning the new supports stood ready and the house was lifted to the height calculated to bring Dobzhov down to the sofa and a more conventional position. At last their efforts had been crowned with success. At the last crank and heave, Dobzhov was properly in place on the sofa. He was immediately secured there and blankets were placed over him to hide the ropes that held him down. Then a bulletin was issued stating that the internationally famous psychic, Carl Dobzhov, was recovering from a state of prolonged levitation during which important scientific data had been gathered on this exceptional condition and that these data were in the process of being evaluated by Soviet scientists.

"I'm still levitating," Dobzhov had told them, "and you know it! You won't be able to fool the world with this ridiculous manoeuvre. It's just another example of childish minds at work. More beer!"

By now he was being treated more or less like a patient in a mental hospital, in return for which he cursed and swore and would restrain himself only when Nina Dumbatse came to see him, which was frequently. She had become his mother confessor. In long conversations he would pour out his heart to her. Once, he said: "Nina Ninanova, weep for me. Behold this wreck of a man before you and weep. I'm in a state of dissolution, as is the world, I know, but I'm afraid my own decay is proceeding more rapidly. I won't live out the month!"

"Nonsense," Nina would tell him.

"What do you think," he continued, "I can't eat and even the beer doesn't help much any more. Listen to what I am saying, do I sound like a hopeless drunk? No, not at all. I've guzzled down three barrels of beer and come out reasoning with you. Do you know, you do know don't you, that I'm still levitating? You know that, don't you? I can feel it. I may seem to be in an unenviable position, but I've been thinking, Nina. I am beginning to see things very clearly, I am! I used to think that levitation was fun. I considered myself fortunate. But now I know that it's more than that. Believe it or don't Nina - and you know me and know what a cynic I have been - but I feel the pull, I feel the tug of the divine. Yes, Nina Ninanova, my lovely Nina, I shall ascend, I feel it!"

True to his word, the ropes did not hold him down, and once again Carl Dobzhov levitated higher to within reach of the ceiling of the elevated house, the bonds on the sofa still intact, unbroken. From a scientific point of view, when this new feat was discovered in the first light of the morning, it should have made everybody happy, since it proved that a material object, in this case Carl Dobzhov, could pass through other solid objects, like ropes and leather thongs.

But all that had happened, in fact, was that Carl Dobzhov was turning into a bona-fide saint, attracting bigger crowds from the surrounding villages, which finally had to be dispersed by police and militia, a step that was taken very reluctantly by the authorities. Both of the big Ivan's legs were broken accidentally when he stepped into the path of an armoured vehicle during the turbulence following the arrival of police and troops. And Dobzhov stopped cursing, which at last might permit the introduction of a few, selected journalists. Nor was there any question now of elevating the house once more. Anyone could see that this might become an interminable process, with Dobzhov finally perhaps still levitating in a house atop some modern Tower of Babel. But there were voices now which, instead, cautiously suggested removing the ceiling and a portion of the roof so that, if this should come to pass, he might rise as high as he liked or could. The impression that Carl Dobzhov could do as he liked would now have to be avoided at all cost. Nor could this performance become a circus act. Already there had been too much publicity. Fate herself, as so often in such cases, dissolved the problem. On the fifteenth day of levitation, during the night, Carl Dobzhov was shot through the head and died, still in a state of levitation. Nobody had heard the shot.

Nor had the guards allowed anyone to enter. They had been on duty, their account of the phases of that night checked. They had been chosen for loyalty, dedication, experience, but they were now in deep trouble. It was reasoned that they had either been negligent in the performance of their sworn duties, or else, worse, one of them had killed the unfortunate Carl. In either case they were guilty of a crime, though there was another alternative - that Dobzhov had been murdered by a ghost. It was decided officially not to acknowledge this possibility, in order to avoid adding to the fearful legend that was quickly growing around the levitating saint. The guards were taken away to be tried and sentenced.

If it might have been hoped that Dobzhov's death would finally bring him down to earth, such hopes were disappointed. Even in the lifeless state, Carl Dobzhov continued levitating. After a day of heated conferences in Moscow, a construction and engineering unit of the army drew up before his house and began filling it with cement, all the way to the top, entombing the floating man. When the work was finished, Dobzhov's home was declared a National Monument and transported to Moscow to become a permanent display at the great People's Hall of Scientific Achievement. No one could say how, but it was then that a rumour began to spread that Carl Dobzhov had been executed by General Dvat. Or, worse, that - though the general's body had not been found - Dobzhov had been shot by Dvat's ghost.

29

MESSAGE

There was, of course, good reason why the general's body was missing. It - he - was in the Crimea of the 19th century. There was no pollution, the young women's alabaster skin was of exceptional and stunning clarity, and the champagne was excellent. But there were other problems.

General Dvat found that the small amount of cash he carried on him was worthless, and that he was being stared at for his dark-blue serge suit, which, for all its ill-cut bulkiness, must appear foreign-looking and futuristic even to the peasants who, to Dvat's eye, seemed colourful and picturesque.

It was a sobering fact to find himself transported backward in time and Dvat was instantly involved in the daily struggle for survival. He had no roots here and he needed time to think of a way to utilize his knowledge of the future. Fortunately, the small Black Sea resort town of Yaku, where he had spent a few vacations in recent years, was only a few miles from where Shawn's whim had deposited him, in the heart of the wine country, and he persuaded a vintner to take him there by horse and cart. Since he could not pay the man, he had to make up a story which had to do with a special mission, a government mission. Even though this convinced the vintner, Dvat noticed that it did not elicit friendly spontaneity, but something more like cowed obedience. It was brought home to him forcefully by the man's behaviour that the revolution had not yet occurred and that a tsar ruled in Moscow. Who this particular tsar was, for the moment Dvat found himself unable to recall - an embarrassing circumstance.

Yaku was there, but the hotel which had accommodated him so recently, and which he had always assumed to be over a hundred years old, had not yet been built, though, he found out, plans were already drawn up for the magnificent edifice, the future pride of the

Crimea.

Bluffing his way in, with a mixture of craggy charm and bullish persistence, Dvat obtained accommodation in a much smaller inn, ordered dinner served in his room, and allowed the innkeeper to select a regular red wine of the region, rather than champagne in order not to appear extravagant. The notion that somehow he was an emissary from Moscow spread quickly and it brought more sullen cooperation. It was clear that the Tsar was not popular in Yaku.

Having dined, and finding the wine stimulating, General Dvat now sat by the window and looked out over the vast, dark waters of the great inland sea. The inn was built into the hillside and the town itself, really still no more than a growing village, arched away along the beaches of a shallow bay. There were palms, hibiscus, rhododendron, and the familiar variety of succulents and evergreens, even some ornamental cacti. It looked familiar enough. From where he sat he could even see the spot where he liked to walk early in the morning for a refreshing swim. Dvat snorted and shook his massive head. He was trapped, no question!

To begin with, he would have to obtain clothing suitable to the period. It would not do for him to walk around in this suit of his. Then he needed money. In fact, he needed the money first. Then he could order clothes. On the other hand, with a bit of bravura, he might succeed in clothing himself and getting billed for it. Why not? After all, if the Tsar employed him it stood to reason that the Moscow coffers would pay for everything and an accounting would have to be made which necessitated strict billing, even before payment - certainly, that was the way to proceed.

But Dvat stopped himself short. This was defeatist thinking. What was he doing trying to make himself comfortable in this inapplicable period of history, while some insane renegade from outer space prepared to rule the world from a hotel in Geneva a hundred years into the future!

Dvat realized that all this knowledge of future history was suddenly reduced to the fantasy of a deranged ex-soldier. It had got woolly enough in Geneva, at that. Was there not something, though, which he knew of that could be applied to this backward locality at this time - something that would establish him and allow him to create a base from which to return to his own time?

The general was not a man technically inclined. His main assets were courage, a cunning intelligence, persistence and experience with human nature, acquired through long tough years of living, struggling, and dodging bullets and shells of large calibre. He would have been hard put to name the major components of the internal combustion engine. Assuming that the year was 1880 or 1890 (he had not dared inquire which), the internal combustion engine had in any case already been invented. People were experimenting with the possibility of flight, were they not? It would not be much of a prophecy for him to predict airplanes. What about the submarine, then? No, the submarine, too, had passed through an embryonic stage. Some German duke had sponsored its development in the 1870's if he remembered correctly. There was penicillin, of course, or Vitamin C. He had discovered very quickly that the reason for the beautiful girls' sombre faces and absence of smiles was the generally bad condition of their teeth. Vitamin C would be a very great boon in this community this year, but how could he get his hands on some? It had not yet been extracted, the procedure wasn't known and even if he had brought some along with him, it would be an experiment that took time, without immediate benefit. Nor could the villagers be expected to trust him, since he had made the mistake of aligning himself with the Tsar.

A few hours went by as Dvat twisted this way and that in his mind, letting go of first one desperate plan and then another, slowly boxing himself into a corner. He was two years past sixty. This was at once what had allowed him to impress the innkeeper and at the same time was a great impediment. How could a quickly-ageing man like himself be expected to begin a new career in this out-of-the-way village? He would have to go to Moscow, would he not? And there he might, with the appropriate reading in the public libraries, establish a reputation as a political prognosticator or something in that direction. Then it suddenly hit him, with terrible impact - the Romanovs were in power in the 1880's were they not? The Tsar's name was Alexander, wasn't it? These were the very people whom the revolution would smash. Damn that crazy man in Geneva. If only he had sent him back *two* hundred years - his chances would have been far better at the time of the French Revolution, when Russia was swept with a wave of popular liberalism.

On the other hand, Dvat reasoned with himself, I might be able to look up the young Lenin and spread out before him his destiny, apprise him of his fate. A bleak prospect that, too! And there is no money in it! Damn again, I know too much and much too little!

While he sat, drinking, thinking, he had been doodling absently with a standard, government-issue ballpoint pen, a thing which, like many others before it, had begun to leak. Not that Dvat cared. The stains would not show on his dark, heavy suit, but the smudges gave him an idea. Somehow he had to get a message through to someone. Crazy as it seemed, he had to write a note for help. Make it succinct and convincing. If there was a hole in time, a tunnel through which he had passed to get here, that aperture might dilate again. If it did and if he saw it, if he could not squeeze in himself, at least he might have a letter sucked through to the other side. If people in the future knew about this predicament, they might bring pressure to bear on Shawn to bring him back.

This, if anything, was an idea even less realistic than the others he had rejected. The plain fact of the matter was that General Dvat was exhausted and the wine was going to his head. Still, he walked out to the top of the stairs and, in his best authoritative manner, demanded to be brought paper and sealing wax. The sealing wax was something that occurred to him might be appropriate at this time in history for an emissary of the Tsar adrift in the provinces.

When paper and wax were brought, Dvat, with a look at the almost empty wine bottle, ordered another one. Then he settled down to write. He began as follows:

Help, I am adrift in time, out of time and lost.

You who read this must help me ....

He had been writing very slowly. When the bottle came, he did not pour into a glass but drank directly. He sat, staring, then grinned at what he had written.

Why were there candles here? Had not electricity already been invented - the telegraph, the telephone? There were no signs of them here. There was a mail service, was there not? Who had invented the mails? A French king, *n'est-ce pas*? Dvat's survival instincts were beginning to assert themselves. For the first time since coming here, he managed a more detached assessment of his situation. The fact was he had eaten well, was drinking good wine. It was true, he was lost in time, but this development could also be thought of as a vacation. A hundred years ago, after all, could not be so different from a hundred years hence. The credit principle seemed to be already at work, he had not yet needed cash. In that sense it was already modern, wasn't it? Damn!

He shook the ballpoint pen. They probably had ink and quill in this place! He crossed out the message and began again, directly under it, on the heavy paper:

I, General Nicolai Constantin Dvat, am stuck in Yaku, in the year ....

He did not know what year it was. In the morning there might be a newspaper, though he doubted it. He could, without arousing suspicion, ask a boy. But, then, he could not be sure of the answer, either. And for a courier of the Tsar not to know the year was unthinkable. Tomorrow, early in the morning, he would go to ....where? ....ah, to church, yes. He would know the day, the month and the year of our Lord. It was, damn the prospect, religion that would allow him to orient himself. Grinning now, his mood rapidly improving, the general wrote.

.... here among the palms and evergreens, spring arrived hundreds of years ago and never left. Yaku, the Pearl of the Black Sea.

He crumpled up the paper and stuffed it in his pocket, having suddenly developed an urge to go down to the beach to his quiet little spot of a hundred years from now.

General Dvat was feeling no pain. He stuffed the bottle behind the broad waistband of his trousers, buttoned his coat, and made his way down the stairs, striding through the large downstairs guest room without looking at anybody, eyes slightly downcast as if deep in though. It befitted a man in the Tsar's service to be deep in thought, did it not? Still, he noticed that there were a number of men at a table in a darker corner who wore clothes which, by some stretch of imagination, could have been thought of as resembling his own in style. From the way the table was placed and from their demeanour, Dvat judged them to be either indigents or working men of a very low order.

He easily found his way down to the beach, simply allowing gravity to guide him down the hillside. On the beach he continued walking close by the water, to the right. The last huts of the village receded and he was alone. The beach looked different from the one he had been on only three years ago. Different but similar. When he got to the spot where he thought he had gone for his morning swims, he sat down in the sand, pulled out the bottle, uncorked it and drank. A fine, bluish opalescence hung like a mist over the dark sea. What was this, where was he, and why was he here?

Dvat felt his eyes fill with tears. Thirstily he drank more. A deep, black, star-studded sky vaulted above him. Dvat fell back and looked up. There, up there, somewhere was the world from which the crazy conjuror had come! Which one was it? Why was it? Dvat wept and wept like a child.

When the bottle was empty the general sat up. He lifted it up to the skies and "wrung" it by its neck, as he had learned to do during the drinking bouts of his youth. He was happy now, happier than he had ever been. He stood up, swaying slightly, about to heave the bottle into the water. Then he had an idea. He pulled out the crumpled paper, smoothed it, folded it, rolled it and pushed it down into the bottle. He put the cork in and pressed it down firmly, made sure it fitted fully. Then, pretending he was tossing a grenade, he drew back his arm and threw the bottle. His shoulder followed through in the throw. His great, ugly face pale in the starlight, smiling happily, saw the bottle outlined against infinity, even saw it flash, saw fire, and explosion, heard the sound still.

The bottle hit the water as the general, face down, hit the sand. Damn! This is war! I've been shot, he thought. His very thought became a musical incantation - war, bottle, message, space, time, shot, dying.

He could not see very well, could not feel very well that he was turned over. His eyes were breaking, giving way. His smile was breaking. The bottle with its smoothed-out crumpled message was in a current to the stars, as was Dvat. But he forced himself to linger, tearing open his lids by willpower alone, allowing his smile, forcing it to stay, for now, long enough to speak to the assassin, or the two assassins, or three or many. There was a crowd around him, staring, he could not be sure. There were beautiful young men, with alabaster skin, and the fire in their hearts shone also in their eyes, but they did not smile. Their teeth were rotten. "The Tsar will hear of this," said General Dvat.

30

MURDER

Soon after the disappearance of General Dvat, Shawn's standing with the Swiss authorities took a distinct downturn. The ancient Pampini displayed at Durstlimas, and the entire new village of Morgendurst which had become something of a target for pilgrims - a sort of space-age Lourdes - these were the tangible signs on which Shawn's reputation was based. But now a noticeable change had occurred. The Soviet Embassy had cautiously approached the Swiss Government, voicing the suspicion that Shawn was responsible for Dvat's disappearance, and the Swiss had seized the opportunity to develop a tangible case for the deportation of the survivor of the Durstli crash.

The Government of the Confederatio Helvetica prided itself not only on its neutrality, but also and especially on its internal security. Though it was a haven for foreign agents, outcasts, misfits, and revolutionaries, for plotters and schemers and soldiers of fortune of every ilk and stripe, the disappearance of a great visiting Soviet general and dignitary was an embarrassment of no negligible proportions. What made it worse was that not everyone took the Dvat affair seriously. It became a feast for cartoonists. In one particularly biting cartoon, the artist showed the territory of Switzerland as a swamp of quicksand. The cartoon was done in three sections. In the first, a Russian bear with Dvat's features was stepping into the swamp. In the second, he had been sucked in up to his chin. And in the final section a realistic map of Switzerland showed a great, frayed hole where Geneva had been. The caption read: *Bears Beware!* There was absolutely nothing funny about it.

Shawn was brought to the Palais de Justice inconspicuously in an unmarked car. For the occasion he had chosen to wear a dark blue *après-ski* outfit somewhat less flamboyant than the silvery garments he usually sported. He looked healthy and relaxed and his customary smile had not deserted him. The men who confronted him were top-level agents of the Swiss Government.

"Now sir," he was asked, "we would appreciate it if you told us all you know about General Constantin Dvat, especially when you last saw him and what the occasion of your meeting was."

Shawn nodded casually, having flung himself into a comfortable armchair in the heavily over-furnished room.

"Gentlemen," he began, "before I go into the details of General Dvat's visit, I have to tell you some things that are necessary to your understanding - that is, if you are interested in understanding what is happening."

There was a brief discussion in subdued tones among the interrogators, then he was told to go ahead and speak.

"You have already noticed," he stated, "that I am no ordinary man. I can do things no one else on this planet can do, things that are considered miraculous. The people of Switzerland have shown great appreciation of my talents. I am very popular here, and everywhere in Europe. I expect that I could live in other countries, too, if I so chose. But, curiously, the Swiss Government has shown no overwhelming interest in me. This has surprised me, though by now I've become used to it. And, while I'm at it, I should also say that, while other governments have shown much more interest, my feeling is that they mean to exploit me for purposes of international power play. Nowhere has there been any attempt to find out why I am here, where I come from, what my mission is. The people of Earth, as represented by their governments, have been apathetic. They have shown no curiosity to plumb the knowledge I have. They have not wished to hear about the cosmos and its denizens.

"Now, to me this is very curious. Imagine if you lived on an island in a very simple civilisation that knew only canoes and fishing. And one day a helicopter arrives and sets down. People get out. They bring all kinds of gadgets and electronic gear with which they can reproduce faces, voices, make magic. The smart islander is the one who is curious to find out where these people come from, who they are, and how they can create such magic, especially how they have learned to fly. The smart islander realises that from that moment on all his future is going to be linked with theirs and that the time for adapting to their life-style is here.

"In the same way, among the billions of people on Earth, many should realise that Earth is an island and that I have arrived from another island or from another continent in space. From the moment of my arrival, the process of adaptation should have started. Whether or not people realise this consciously, that is what is actually happening, but there should have been more who would be consciously curious. Not so.

"Since being sent here I have learned a bit about human vanity. I had hoped that it would be understood that vanity is not my motivation during this sojourn. In fact, it has been necessary for me to exercise restraint to avoid catastrophes of a certain kind as a result of employing powers which, in other contexts, I may routinely use. You have heard me speak of the symbols of the Lion and the Lamb. The lion symbolises destructive power toward the lamb. If a lion lies peacefully with a lamb, the lion must exercise restraint. In your history there arose a figure, Jesus of Nazareth, whose divine innocence had been likened to that of the lamb, who has in fact been called The Lamb of God. Jesus came to this world, to this particular world to make peace, to pacify it. The peace he made has universal application. But the creatures of my world, creatures of God like yourselves, are more appropriately represented by the symbol of the lion, even though there are no lions where I come from. So, my lesson to you has been that power must be harnessed.

"It is understandable that the people rely on their governments to lead them and expect certain information and knowledge which requires a great, concerted, organised effort to be engendered by the government. When the government is apathetic in this regard, it shirks its natural responsibility. This is not a matter of money or bribes. When I came here I knew nothing about money. Now I have more than most. It makes no difference whatever. It will be left behind.

"It has been said that I am a dangerous person who could wreak destruction. That is true. In theory, it is in fact possible that I can destroy Earth. Make no mistake, this is no idle boast. I can do it!

"I am here to introduce a new reality. Until I arrived, science had monopolised thinking, creative thought. Academic procedure even now dominates and harnesses the natural creative processes, inhibiting and often destroying them. That an exploding hand grenade should kill a man or at least tear apart the hands of him who holds it, is self-evident. That is, it was self-evident until I demonstrated that there can be a different reality in which this is not inevitable. People have asked me: Well, so what, so you did that, what does it prove? It really proves nothing. It is a transcendent demonstration and only the beginning of a process in the mind which will lead to the acceptance of a new reality.

"That I come from another world, a world not even in this, your galaxy perhaps, that I live here like a human body, that destroys the illusion that people of Earth are alone in the universe. But, especially in the modern age, all knowledge has been founded on the assumption that humans are singular, unique, and essentially unrepeated expressions of divine creation. It was an illusion which, along with a technological emancipation, was becoming dangerous to humans. A suicidal delusion! Now that I am here, some of the pressure of such fantastic assumptions has been relieved. I suppose that has been part of my mission. The reason I say that I suppose this to have been part of my mission is that I had only an idea, before I came here, that there was such a planet as Earth. I was sent here by what you could call a court, as part of a sentence for what you would call rebellious behaviour. But these terms only remotely touch the meaning of such a sentence. Where I come from, no-one is ever sentenced without concern for the community as a whole - even communities as remote from our world as yours. That means there is no such thing as a punitive sentence. That may appear to you to be a simple statement and perhaps a simple fact; but if you think about it you will see how difficult if would be for you here on earth to pronounce a non-punitive sentence upon an offender, and especially a sentence that would not affect other distant worlds. Earth simply has not as yet become effective in its own galaxy, let alone in ours.

"Even concerning God there is still division on this planet. That is, there is division not only between those who believe God exists and those who do not, but among those who believe in God there is a division concerning the divine nature. Such a mental condition is extremely and dangerously fantastic. It is that which is called insanity on Earth. By the standards of the enlightened creatures of the cosmos, the people on Earth are essentially insane. Now begins a period where some of this insanity can be healed, and in time all of it will, of course, be healed. It is a period of integration of a crazed asylum of lunatic savages into the peaceful and harmonious community of this and other galaxies.

"What has not been understood on this planet is that what you call 'time' is a condition very much like a sentence. It is in iteself non-punitive and it is coming to an end. I am the harbinger of the end of this sentence of time under which Earth has laboured for good reason. It will be lifted, but before it is lifted it will become optional for some humans instead of mandatory, as it has been for all. That is the beginning of the end of time on your planet. I ...."

Shawn was interrupted by one of his interrogators. It was pointed out to him that he had not been called here to lecture, but to answer certain questions. Among these questions, he was informed, was one that had to do with a message that was found in a bottle on the shores of the Black Sea near the resort of Yaku. The Soviet Government had been kind enough to place it at their disposal for this occasion. Would he care to examine it and comment?

A wine bottle without cork was handed to Shawn, along with a cracked and yellowed paper with fading script. He weighed the bottle in his hand, read the message and smiled.

"Here is General Dvat's name," he said. "Did he write it?"

"It has been determined by Soviet experts that this message was written by General Nicolai Constantin Dvat approximately one hundred years ago."

Shawn, still smiling, shook his head. "Yes, that makes sense," he said, "when one considers the mandatory and incircumventable condition of time on Earth."

"What do you know about this, Mr. Shawn?"

"Well," said Shawn, "if this message was written by General Dvat, it shows that he must have been somewhere on the shores of the Black Sea about a hundred years ago. I have already told you that I sent him there. So this message found in a bottle supports my claim. What we should ask, though, is: Will this satisfy the scientists?"

Since he had smiled in his usual fashion as he said this, he was reminded that the purpose for this discussion was very serious indeed; namely, to determine if there was cause to indict him for murder and/or deportation.

Shawn said: "If General Dvat wrote this, he must have thought he needed help. In fact, there is a passage crossed out, but the word 'help' is still legible. Then he writes that he is stuck in Yaku. Now, that doesn't make sense if it was written this week, because a high-ranking officer of the Soviet Armed Forces would not be stuck in Yaku on the Black Sea unless he had been put in prison, and in that case he could hardly have got out a message in a bottle. Also the passage: '*.... here among the palms and evergreens, spring arrived hundreds of years ago and never left ....*' shows a certain preoccupation with time. It seems to me that ...."

His interrogator interrupted him now: "We have been informed by the Soviet Government that research indicates that in the year 1890 in Yaku, a murder was committed. A stranger who allegedly travelled under orders of the Tsar was killed on the beach by anti-Tsarist revolutionaries. The overall description of the man fits General Dvat."

"That must be so," Shawn smiled, "especially if the Soviet Government has unearthed these circumstances."

"The point is," Shawn was told, "that if this man who was killed was indeed General Nicolai Constantin Dvat, then you are responsible for his murder and must stand trial."

Shawn could not help himself. An irresistible wave swept over him, shaking him with laughter from toe to head. It took some time for him to recover. At last, when he did, even the slightest trace of a smile had left his normally friendly face. He looked cold and enormously stern as he said:

"You are joking! Do you wish to become objects of derision in this world? Will you accuse a man who is by all normal and acceptable standards no more than twenty five years of age of a murder committed a hundred years ago? No, gentlemen , there is entirely too much sanity in such an accusation for the present state of this world. I sent the general to Yaku, yes. I sent him back in time. But what happened to him there is his business. It was foolish of him to pass himself off as a government official. It was unnecessary. I sent him there to have a good time. Well, perhaps he did have a good time. And isn't it also possible that he emptied this bottle before he entrusted the message to it? He may have died a happy man. And that, you will admit, was not likely to have happened as the world is now constituted. If I sent him there, I did him a favour. His time may have been up, in any case. Perhaps he attacked me. Perhaps he was sent by the Soviet Government to kill me. Would you presume to tell me what actually happened when we met."

The interrogation went on a bit longer. The Swiss officials

earnestly tried to pin down their elusive visitor. They were becoming increasingly frustrated. When they thought they had him against the wall, he slipped away with an infuriating smile.

"You must understand this," he told them finally. "The history of your world is studded with martyrs. Some of them knew they were martyrs, others didn't. But the true martyrs of the world are the innocent children who die at the hands of adults. I am neither a child nor a martyr. There is no possibility of my suffering on this planet simply because I have survived and learned to love planets whose very atmosphere would dissolve your bodies. I have walked in storms that carried tons of fragmented crystal in each cubic metre. The 'I' of which I speak is immortal. But nor will I permit you to destroy this body which was fashioned for me by application of divine law. You are insane children. I shall leave you to your doomed games. Goodbye! May time be merciful with you!"

With these words he rose and walked out of the room, out of the Palais de Justice. Outside he broke into a jogging trot and did not stop until he had arrived at the Royal Palace Hotel where a crowd had formed around a large vehicle, brightly painted, bearing on each side the legend:

JACK BALDWIN'S CRUSADE FOR TRUTH

Jack Baldwin, microphone in hand, was standing by this vehicle, haranguing the crowd.

31

SALVATION

Since that night in Paris when he had met that strange apparition which had identified itself as Oba, Jack Baldwin had not felt like himself. But, he had to admit, it was a positive change. He felt not merely more energetic than he could remember ever having felt - even as a young man - but was actually brimming with vigour. His need for sleep had decreased so drastically that it had taken him time to get used to it. He slept no more than an hour now, two or three at the most. And - something seemed to have happened in his mind. It felt as if it had been hitched to some great source of knowledge and energy. It was, in fact, as if he, Jack Baldwin, as he had known himself to this time of his life, had become an appendage of sorts to something else. That something was incomprehensible to him.

Though he knew that he was being used in some fashion by this Oba, whatever or whoever he was, Baldwin did not mind. Not that it would have helped him to object or struggle - there had never been a question of that. Impulses arose with such force that he found himself doing things that did not make sense to the old Jack Baldwin. For example, outfitting the "Crusade for Truth". When the idea had occurred to him, it had come more as action than as thought. He had walked into the nearest automobile showroom in Paris and bought an all-purpose van. He had paid extra for immediate delivery and driven it straight to a garage for a paint job: JACK BALDWIN'S CRUSADE FOR TRUTH.

The slogan was corny, to say the least. Still, he liked it, but had no idea what it meant or to what it would apply until he was on the road to Geneva, on the freeway, when mind-pictures went tumbling through his brain, in which he saw himself already in Geneva- driving up to Shawn's hotel, parking, and using the public address system he had installed to address the crowd. It should have been a disturbing idea, knowing the Swiss and their love of peace and quiet. Even if he did such an outrageous thing, he wouldn't last five minutes. The police would stop him instantly. Nevertheless, the thought had raised pleasant anticipation in him.

Nor was his thinking fuzzy in all of this. Baldwin realised that indeed this Oba had gained a powerful hold on him and was making him act in this fashion. Even though through his years of interest in occult phenomena, he was familiar with demonic possession, he found himself unable to diagnose his own case this way. Why should the devil have taken the form of some extra-terrestrial intelligence that wanted to challenge Shawn? Made no sense at all! The devil, to the best of Jack Baldwin's knowledge, didn't work that way. It was too complicated and irrelevant an approach. Nor, if the reports of demonic possession he had read implied anything, would the devil become involved in discrediting an extra-terrestrial like .... Mr. Jack Baldwin broke off this thought and was instantly and painfully aware that he had thus admitted to himself that Shawn was not from this planet. And that assumption, through all these turbulent weeks since the Durstli crash, had been the rock and foundation of his position. Well, he shook his head as the van rolled along - now on the road that would lead into the Jura Mountains via the mustard town of Dijon - it didn't matter! What mattered was to confront Shawn. And that, too, could be left to his new personality, his new power.

Baldwin had noticed, for example, in dealing with the usually rude, stubborn French, that his own French had become amazingly fluent and that he seemed to exert upon the people an almost hypnotic effect. This was something he knew to have been absolutely missing in his life until his meeting with this Oba. He had always had to strive for attention and to make certain that people knew he was around. He had not minded, but he never kidded himself about that, either. Now, by contrast, the shop assistants in Paris, so frequently ranging from surly via sullen to churlish, watched him with hawk-like attentiveness and hurried to interpret his every gesture like well-trained domestics. And in other contacts, too, he noticed that something awesome was developing. It seemed that whenever he looked at an individual, instantly between them was established a bond of highly charged energy of which he, Baldwin, was aware even on a physical level as an electric, prickly sensation. It went so far indeed that the other person or persons became or seemed to become like shadows of himself or filings to his magnet, turning when he turned and following him compulsively until he discouraged them or, even, instructed them to obey his commands, which they would instantly do.

There was also another and vastly intriguing dimension which Mr. Baldwin's normally ordinary mind seemed to have acquired: a growing awareness that he had become involved, as an important player at centre-stage, in a play whose scenario did not originate on Earth. This was frightening. He felt as if a six-volt battery (Baldwin) had been hooked to a multi-million-volt power plant (Oba). He could blow out any minute.

Other analogies that occurred to him in picture form - and it should be noted that the regular Jack Baldwin was in no way prone to pictorial metaphor - was a glass fist (Baldwin) at the end of a steel arm on a steel body (Oba). Or: a hammer fashioned of ice in the hand of a great, muscular carpenter about to bring it down on a real nail. It was quite clear what would happen. The glass fist would shatter, the hammer would break. And, in the case of the hammer, not only would it break but then it would melt as well and become non-existent. Whatever lay ahead for him in Geneva, Baldwin began to think that he would need a great deal of luck indeed to survive.

Of course, there was still that other part of himself, that familiar part of himself, which kept chanting its familiar refrain of magic and stage trickery and hypnotic influence and nonsense and tomfoolery cunningly applied to fool the people and to discredit reputable investigators like himself. That old part of himself kept relegating all this to the fantasy-and-science fiction department. And that part, too, could never have done anything as outrageously direct as parking the van across from the Royal Palace Hotel and whipping out the brand-new microphone, and telling the people (who slowly, in Swiss fashion, gathered to listen) in excellent French, that Shawn, the Durstli crash survivor, the man from another world, was an out-and-out fraud and not worth a second thought, if it weren't for the fact that a lot of young people thought he was real and important.

Baldwin didn't understand why he was saying all of this when he himself had actually just begun to realise that Shawn might very well be what he claimed to be. But he was in no position to resist these impulses. He continued lecturing the crowd.

It surprised him, too, that the policemen who strolled by made no effort to stop him. Had he thought about it, it might have occurred to him that Shawn, prior to being officially expelled from Switzerland, had become a person in limbo who enjoyed for the moment a certain fool's freedom. In the same fashion that a condemned man is granted a request for his favourite meal, so he, Shawn, and by extension perhaps all those involved with him, had the freedom to lead one another one last merry dance. Then they would all be banished from the Western version of Paradise forever.

But Baldwin did not think that way. Mildly surprised though he was, he spent no time on analysing the situation. Instead he continued to tell the good people of Geneva of the trickery of the man they called Shawn. He heard himself say things that he recognized as very clever, much more clever than anything he had ever said. And, after a while, he began to listen to himself as he spoke:

"This man, friends ...." (speaking in French he actually said, "*Cet homme, mes amis*") " this man is an example of great cunning. He has introduced a sort of mystical imagery into his fraud, that of the lion and the lamb. And there is a certain relevance and validity to this symbolism. He is an animal of sorts. We have met such as him before in history, a corrupter of youth, a wolf - namely, a wolf in sheepskin. Even a lion, if you will. He is a wolf and a lion of corruption. He is misleading the young by substantiating their wildest fantasies of outer space. He is pandering to those parts of their minds which put stock in comic-book fables. You know yourself what they may lead to. Your children, your sons and daughters will begin to - have in fact already begun to - ignore the long-established truths of science in favour of wild fantasies of other civilizations in other parts of the cosmos which, can you believe it, pick out tiny planets like Earth to send a messenger to?"

Baldwin's voice at this point became dripping with irony. But, in fact, the people gathering around his van were intrigued not by what he said, of which they could make little sense, but by the spectacle itself, so rare on Swiss streets, of a person freely expressing his opinion, and loudly at that. Of course, they recognized, this was a crazy American, they were already familiar with his face from television and the newspapers. To the Genevans he looked like a mad preacher of the type which abounded in America, and they were amused by his performance, even though some appeared to be taking it in with more earnest attention.

Shawn himself, who had jogged into the lobby and quickly

strode to the elevator, was now watching Baldwin and his van from the window of his suite. He saw also the arrival of television crews and was able, in a short while, even to hear Baldwin on direct transmission. He had instantly recognized Oba in Baldwin and had seen that this was the beginning of the last round of this game that had been played out on the territory of Earth, in the far-flung corner of the universe. Now Oba would make a final push!

Shawn did not know what to expect. The council's decision to send him to Earth, following his exile on the Crystal Planet, had always seemed to him nebulous. That was the way they sometimes proceeded. It was the way he, as Nonomine, and others like him before, wanted to change. He had to grant them and himself that he had no image for a different, clearer reality. He had been acting by compulsion and it had earned him exile, and now Earth, and beyond here he knew not what destination.

Even as he listened to Baldwin/Oba spin his net below by the lake shore, he fell into a trance of recollection. His merger with the messenger of the female principle recurred; the reality of the Crystal Planet which so far and so majestically transcended this individualized reality of suffering and stupidity on this beautiful planet they called Earth! It was so much easier to live here, and so much less possible! Yet, here, now, some important decisions were being made. Oba down there, in his usual, methodical fashion, was laying, within the limitations dictated to him by the human minds and bodies through which he was obliged to work, the foundation for a foothold with which, once and for all, he would subdue the rebellious Nonomine. This was the demonstration which perhaps had been placed so far away from home because of its nature. Was it too embarrassing, too primitive? Did it reach too far back to the beginnings, to dimensions in which there had been no councils, no elders, no messengers, no mergers, no exiles? And hence dimensions in which there had been no rebellion, no extreme behaviour? Yes, especially the latter! In the beginning there had been no extremes because all was extreme. When the masses cooled, when energies subsided, then the peaks and valleys could appear, then there could be high and low, hot and cold, storm and calm!

Here, too, in this remote part of the universe, intelligence was locked in writhing combat with itself, mind had sunk its fangs into mind, the lion of mind and the throat of the lamb of mind! Mind blood was flowing here on earth, plenty of it! The children of Earth could not see that they were wading ankle deep in it. Soon it would be up to their knees! One day they would see it. Then their wails and lamentations would transform their planet! They would see what they were doing to one another, what they had done to themselves, how they hacked each other to pieces even into the luminous selves of their immortal bodies. Hunger, wars, pollution and suffering was the lot of Planet Earth. He, Nonomine as Shawn, had been placed here and allowed to play. Ah, yes, perhaps they had sent him here to recuperate from the Crystal Planet. What irony to exchange magnificent solitude for solitary magnificence! And yet the human Jesus had accomplished salvation from the dungeon of savage human ignorance, as had he, Nonomine, been saved by the Son of God in a different garb - in the form he had been instructed to describe as a lion to the people of Earth.

He saw Baldwin gesture down there, fixing the growing crowd with wide-open eyes. He heard him saying, in his room, on television:

".... cannot be ignored. Shall superstition again be rampant as in the dark ages? Will witches and warlocks disguised as emissaries from outer space again hold sway over the credulous and gullible? I am not speaking to you emptily. I know what I'm saying. I can repeat every trick, perform every clever thought through a quote, unquote 'miraculous feat.' I will, in a moment, give you a demonstration of how one contains a hand grenade with both hands, how one stops a bullet fired from an ordinary handgun, how one melts glass. I will go further than that. I will show you exactly how I perform these tricks. Then you can judge for yourself if he has done the same thing, or if he has been able to do this as if it had really been done the way it appears to be done."

The crowd, at last moved to a smattering of applause by the prospect of a magic stage show, seemed to draw a little closer to the podium near the door of his van where Jack Baldwin stood. In this movement, Shawn suddenly saw a wispy breath of a wave, something luminous, an airily printed dress draping itself around the waist of a young woman at the edge of the crowd. It was a movement not of this world!

32

BLISS

Having recognised the messenger of the female principle in the crowd below, Shawn sprang from his room and impatiently stamped the carpet by the elevator doors. When the elevator arrived, he lunged through the still-opening doors and glared at the operator who hastily closed the doors again.

She was waiting for him in the lobby. She had a human body, perfectly fashioned for her, but he barely saw that form. What he heard was the familiar warbling whistle of home, so delicate and high-pitched that on Earth it was inaudible to Terrans. He advanced toward her and together they walked to a V-shaped constellation of couches and armchairs and sat down.

She reached out and their hands met as they immersed themselves in trilled and whistled giggles.

So they sat, wavering shapes of light beyond their Earth bodies, whispering, jabbering, gossiping, tumbling in and out of each other.

She told him of the Council's decision to allow him to return home, ending his mission on Earth. It was up to him now, he could do as he pleased, for while he was free to return, he was also free to stay, or go anywhere he pleased, naturally.

Only in the surge of sweet energy from home did Shawn as Nonomine feel the withered and parched core of himself, the terrible dehydration of Earth. Boldly, he demanded merger and she immediately granted his request. Those who saw them sitting in the lobby of the hotel noticed nothing unusual except perhaps that the famous young man sat rather rigidly upright, as did the beautiful young woman who sat there with him. In truth, the aliens had entered union and out of their union spun the threads of cosmic harmony in all directions at once to the farthest reaches of the universe, making them spiders of love safe in their own web.

In their embrace, a long heartbeat of eternity passed. It was something which they had not calculated in the rush of coming together. That heartbeat occupied three Earth days and these were days during which they had become desensitised and impervious to distraction. At first, of course, no particular notice was taken of them. Then after an hour and twenty minutes, the rigidity of their state was commented upon by the assistant manager and valiantly acknowledged by the manager himself.

Immediately, measures were taken to remind the two, discreetly of course, of their whereabouts. But when spoken to, they did not reply. Gently tapped on the shoulder, they did not stir. It was also noticed that their eyes were glazed and seemed unfocussed. Her left hand rested in his right and his left hand in her right. Their torsos were turned at a ninety-degree angle, so that, while their lower halves sat conventionally, knees pointing into the lobby, they were actually facing each other on top in what appeared to be a simple yogic position.

Still, it was apparent even to the laymen who managed the hotel that some sort of professional assistance was needed and very quickly two doctors were mobilised to examine the two petrified bodies. While the doctors felt their pulses and found only a slightly delayed rate of heartbeat with, however, an arythmic and rather severe flutter or fibrillation at certain unpredictable intervals, for the moment they could not think of a way to dislodge them from their trance state.

The two doctors were joined shortly by an Indian mystic who happened to be staying at the hotel while lecturing in Geneva, Sri Bhagavan Ji. Mr. Ji hastily called a conference in the heavily furnished business offices of the hotel and informed those assembled that the two young people on the couch in the lobby had entered what appeared to be the state of Samadhi, a state of pure bliss which was not at all easy to attain, particularly not in union, and especially not in union of male and female.

"I don't wish," said Mr. Ji, "to go into the detail of the disciplines essential to the accomplishment of such a feat, but they are considerable. From a physiological point of view, in my experience, there is nothing to fear here. The natural course of this state is that it will end and the two lovers will 'return to earth', so to speak. But naturally, if you like, I shall continue to be watchful of their condition."

The Royal Palace management breathed an audible sigh of relief. Sri Bhagavan Ji was thanked profusely. Only the two physicians, having been brought up staunchly in the no-nonsense tradition of Western physical sciences, muttered disagreeably, but finally could not bring themselves to object to Mr. Ji's diagnosis. It would not, in any case, have been a discussion among peers: Sri Bhagavan Ji was wearing a loosely fitting robe of bright orange red, and the white and yellow smudge on his forehead that vaguely looked like a whirlpool galaxy created the impression that in his arsenal of knowledge he commanded weapons which the two good doctors would not be able to match. So they reluctantly concurred and left.

A number of finely hand-painted Japanese silk screens were now placed around the picturesque couple on the sofa, and the entire area closely roped off so that any casual passer-by would assume simply that repairs or alterations of some sort were in progress and pay no further attention to the scene.

But, naturally, word of this event got out and the news media, already in agitation because of Jack Baldwin's Crusade for Truth, now began to concentrate in earnest on the hotel. It was generally felt by those in the know, many foreign newsmen among them, that things were brewing in the matter of the man who had survived the Durstli crash. The disappearance of General Dvat, the coming out into the open of a professional challenger in the form of the reputable Mr. Baldwin, and now the most recent extraordinary occurrence in the hotel lobby, all of this combined to keep Shawn in the news. Also, it was surmised, things could not go on like this for much longer.

Switzerland, of course, had a great deal of experience in how to deal with undesirable outsiders. In most cases this never came to public attention; it was done as a discreet routine. Italian labourers without work permits were quietly handed tickets home and shunted back across the border. Money launderers were approached inconspicuously while purchasing their obligatory Swiss Rolex watches and informed, ever so politely, that their time in Switzerland had run out. American CIA men, Israeli Mossad Agents and PLO Activists were handed a parting gift of expensive polarised sunglasses and instructed to pack their bags. Fallen dictators sought by the Secret Service of their own country were sent on route to a more hospitable and less particular France, unfortunately only a stone's throw away from downtown Geneva. But every once in a while publicity could not be avoided as, for example, in the case of General Dvat, who had not been expelled from Switzerland but had done something infinitely more damaging to the Swiss image.

When all these factors and the history of the Swiss behaviour toward undesirables were added up and considered, it seemed only a matter of time until the expulsion notice would be served on Shawn. The question that now had arisen was: How could such papers be served? When the undesirable seemed in some equally undesirable state of rigidity, staring into space, holding on to a beautiful young woman whose role in all of this was also still undetermined? When the whole world was watching to see how the cagey Swiss would extricate themselves from this dilemma? When, to make it all even more difficult, there was no precedent at all for such a situation?

On the second day of the inexplicable state of the two on the sofa in the lobby of the Royal Palace Hotel, Sri Bhagavan Ji declared himself ready for an experimental mission. He would, so he said, himself enter a state of divine bliss, Samadhi, and in loving union persuade the two young people to allow their distant spirits to return into their bodies so that these might be activated for more mundane, workaday reality. This invitation, since it involved neither expense nor risk for the hotel, was gladly accepted, though it was realized by the government agents who were on surveillance duty in the lobby that Mr. Ji's generous offer tended somewhat to contribute to a circus-like atmosphere that developed, especially with Jack Baldwin's Crusade for Truth showing no signs of abating on the other side of the lakeshore drive. Still, the Indian holy man arranged himself on an upholstered footstool near the petrified duo, placed his hands on theirs, rolled his eyes heavenward in the direction of the spiral mark on his forehead, and, so it appeared, was instantly gone from ordinary consciousness.

The two doctors, who sensed interesting medical developments, were present to supervise the Indian mystic's excursion into the unknown and, if necessary, to render the simple medical assistance Western physicians were known to be capable of rendering on occasion. They had equipped themselves with a bagful of drugs, emphasis on stimulants, and stood ready to revive the mystic should he show no signs of flagging. Quite to the contrary, within a space of minutes, perhaps a quarter of an hour, Sri Bhagavan Ji began to tremble violently. His face turned first red, then darker shades of purple, tending finally toward a very unhealthy-looking violet streaked with lines of deathly pallor around the nose and the corners of his mouth, which was now firmly even grimly set in his face, jaw muscles rippling recklessly. Then Mr. Ji's purplish lips parted and a thin flow of saliva, bubbly in places, began to dribble down his chin. Now, again, his jaws abruptly clamped shut and finally his breathing became laboured and noisy and he seemed in danger of suffocating.

The two doctors, syringes at the ready, were about to intervene, when Mr. Ji's eyelids fluttered like the wings of a disoriented hummingbird, his head jerked from side to side, he let go of the hands he was holding onto and fell backwards, regaining consciousness as he fell, managing by only a magnificent reflexive twist of his shoulders to avoid banging his head on the carpeted floor. There he lay for a moment, eyes still restlessly roaming in his head, recuperating from what had obviously been an unpleasant experience of some kind.

He managed, assisted by the doctors, to get up and was escorted to the business offices, where he feebly asked for a glass of water. Having refreshed himself, he cast a long significant glance around the room and said: "I escaped death by a very narrow margin."

He drank again and inquired if the press had been kept out. Assured that it had, he continued: "It has been assumed that the state of Samadhi connects an individual with the godhead itself in loving vibration. The individual achieves, if I may be forgiven an analogy, contact with the hem of the divine garment at the very least, and this is in itself enough for him or her to wish never to break that contact. A great deal of discipline and experience are necessary to make certain of return within a reasonable period of time. That is, at all times the human practitioner of this advanced form of yoga must remain aware of his physical body and its placement in time. Time, in fact becomes an essential and essentially limiting condition of the state of Samadhi. As soon as I entered the state, I could see that the two beings who are linked in it out there in the lobby are of a very highly advanced spiritual order. So highly advanced, in fact, that I could not classify them other than in the angelic realm. You can, therefore, imagine my shock at seeing two angels in a state of unutterably intimate union. Even though I began almost immediately to develop a concept that their condition was beyond my interference with it, I tried. Clinging firmly to the safe staff of my own personal, divinely inspired mantra, I tried to dislodge them. Instantly I was swept up along a curved beam oscillating at a phenomenally high frequency, a beam one might imagine as the arch of a very steeply constructed bridge, a bridge such as one might see in a Japanese ornamental garden. I was on the outside of this bridge, being drawn into dimensions I had never entered, and then shot back into my body, and drawn out again. Being bounced about like that in the spiritual realm is a terrifying experience. I'm still shaky from it. And at no time did I participate in the intimacy of their Samadhi, as I had intended. This, I would venture to say, is impossible for any human. The two beings you see out there are of an angelic order, having chosen for reasons of their own the guise of human bodies. My advise is to leave them alone. They themselves will decide what to do next, and when to do it." About halfway through the mystic's narrative, a steep frown had appeared on the forehead of one of the doctors. Now he could hold himself back no longer.

"That is despicable nonsense, sir," he roared, "and you are an idiot and a fraud. Do you sincerely want to make us believe that two perfectly human youngsters on a couch are angels, even if one of them claims to come from outer space?" He found immediate support from his colleague, who had also been boiling.

"Enough is enough," said the latter. "I've gone along with this charade because I believe in fair play. You've had your chance. But now we will have no more of this voodoo and witch-doctoring. It is my professional opinion that the two people out there are in the grips of a muscular seizure and I recommend a mild dose of a relaxant to be administered by intramuscular injection."

"No, no, please," protested Mr. Ji. "You gentlemen don't know what you are doing. Any form of physical shock might sever the thin connection between their spiritual selves and their physical bodies. An injection might well create such a shock. You would be murdering two angelic beings."

"Balderdash!" said the first of the doctors, a Swiss citizen who had studied at Oxford.

"This is a medical emergency," snorted the other doctor, "and I won't stand here while two human beings are in *rigour extremis.* Enough is enough!"

"Gentlemen," cried the mystic, "let's compromise. Give them twenty-four hours. It is likely that they will return to their ordinary state by then. Waiting twenty-four hours will not endanger them physically, and there'll be no risk of shock." Their vanity mollified, the two doctors, after a brief whispered consultation, agreed that a twenty-four-hour wait was a reasonable compromise. The reporters were told that the condition of Shawn and his mysterious companion was such that it required a careful analysis by medical experts to arrive at a diagnosis. Doctors were being consulted and would convene as soon as possible. By tomorrow a course of action would be decided upon.

As night fell, the vast lobby lay deserted, the customary evening traffic having been diverted through a side vestibule. Only Sri Bhagavan Ji sat just outside the roped-off area, his legs folded easily in a comfortable semi-lotus posture. It was the stance of a man who had just realized that even sainthood can be relative.

And outside, the media encampment grew as more newsmen arrived. Their hunting instinct told them that a dangerous beast was at bay in the hotel. They had come to watch it make its move.

33

THEFT

Dr. Barry Conrad, Cg., in a sense was an unfortunate man, having been blessed with an intelligence as profound as it was slick and as slick as it was profound. No one could ever have taken exception to his ideals, but he had a way of transforming them into everyday reality that often, to put it mildly, expanded the frontiers of what was conventionally acceptable in the medical profession. As a result, he had made a name for himself and a pile of money to boot.

The "Cg." behind his name stood for cryogenetics, a term he himself had created and reinforced with a $250,000 donation to the Free University of Milwaukee, Wisconsin, in return for the establishment of a Chair in cryogenetics. The budding branch of science so named rested, for an initial while almost exclusively, on Dr. Conrad's premise that too little was known about the coding process of human genes and that, therefore, these had to be preserved via cryogenic suspension until such a time as science began to master the process of coding and could then begin to apply such knowledge in practical terms - i.e., true genetic steering with a view toward upgrading the entire human race without embarrassing any of its many racial components.

This was the full profundity of Dr. Conrad's work in the world, and it had withstood the immediate onslaught of the most erudite, earnest and eloquent of academic critics from the ultra-liberal camp. But, if Dr. Conrad had been able to confess to the truth in the most secret sanctum of his heart, he would have had to say that cryogenetics, for all its complexity, was only a red herring constructed to draw attention away from a dangerous hobby which had begun to possess him. It had happened gradually, but in accelerative fashion, and it had come out of the consideration that the purest way of preserving human genes was by preserving human semen. Ergo, the good doctor had established the Cryogenetic Seminar Corporation, with its pun fully intended and much appreciated by Dr. Conrad himself.

C/S Corporation, at the time, had been in operation for almost two decades and had done, under the direction of Dr. Conrad, a great deal of pioneering work in the field. Its primary purpose was to permit mechanical fertilisation of females whose husbands or mates for one reason or another could not accomplish insemination, usually because of infertility. Literally thousands of letters of grateful acknowledgement from happy mothers testified to Dr. Conrad's efficiency.

From the very beginning of his work, he had kept meticulous records. Some of the children so conceived via the Cryogenetic Seminar Corporation were now in their late teens and many, if not most of them, showed keen intelligence, good physical health and above-average looks. All of this was due to Dr. Conrad's screening process for semen donors, which was rigorous in the extreme. And it had been this phase of his work which had started Dr. Conrad thinking seriously about the future of the human race. While, he realized, direct manipulation of the genetic coding was premature at this time, a process of indirect weeding out could begin almost instantly; indeed, he had been involved in it without quite being aware of it by selecting only the healthiest, keenest applicants for semen donors and thereby encouraging a development of positive genetic traits in the recipient females, though, of course, all this was done discreetly and anonymously so that the females never knew who the male donors were. But Dr. Barry Conrad, Cg, knew.

For over a decade now, Dr. Conrad had been working on a grand plan to chart the course of humanity, and in this work he had come across many intriguing and sometimes frightening possibilities. Being a conscientious man he had discarded most of these, but the idea that, somehow, a superior race could be evolved more quickly than by the laborious method he now employed, i.e., upgrading of the relative handful of sons and daughters born to women whose mates could not impregnate them, had taken a firm hold in him. It was clear to him that this would have to happen through male continuity. With this in mind he had already succeeded (though he kept these statistics strictly to himself) in producing three males out of four births from donor insemination. These would, cumulatively, continue the strong strains he introduced in the great human stream of genes. But, of course, it was only a drop in the ocean.

Fate, however, now smiled on Dr. Conrad. Even when Shawn first came upon the scene following the Durstli crash, Dr. Conrad's imagination had been stimulated. What, he had asked himself, if this man is really from another planet, some great distant civilization? Patiently and with keen interest he had followed Shawn's career, short as it was. He had taken note of the phenomenal occurrences attributed to the Durstli Man, and from week to week the conviction had grown in Dr. Conrad that here was not merely superb genetic material, but, if his hunch was right, material that could accomplish a mutational leap for humanity. If the foundling could be induced to donate semen to the Cryogenetic Seminar Corporation, even at a rate of compensation higher than that paid to ordinary donors, well, the potential was incalculable.

Immediately Dr. Conrad realised that this was not merely a tricky and delicate matter, but that the slightest error would ruin everything. Because of this consideration he forced himself to be patient, when his natural inclination was to rush in and talk Shawn into donating semen. But finally it had seemed that the Durstli foundling was getting involved in dangerous situations and it had not been beyond the good doctor to imagine that his precious potential donor might be kidnapped and/or assassinated and a great opportunity for mankind thus be gone forever. He had, therefore, prepared to jet to Geneva and make a try for it, just when the news came of Shawn's curious trance in the lobby of the Royal Palace Hotel. With the natural certainty of an intuitive genius, Dr. Conrad had recognised that this was opportunity knocking at the door, and he wasted no time.

When he stepped into the lobby of the hotel in the early afternoon of the third day of the couple's trance state, Dr. Conrad was fully equipped to accomplish his great mission and to do so in utter secrecy. Once again circumstances were in his favour - as they usually are when a man is moving in the magnetic field of his own self-realized fate. A small group of doctors, both medical and psychiatric, had examined the two entranced aliens and, having found them in good physical condition, had just left. Dr. Conrad now recalled seeing them outside the hotel, hailing taxis for a late lunch. He walked to the manager's desk and with a tone of quiet but steely authority in this voice said:

"I am Dr. Barry Conrad from Milwaukee, Wisconsin. I was

delayed en route here. I wonder if I might be given a moment with the subjects of this trance. I have encountered a number of similar cases before and might conceivably be of help."

The manager, at heart an eminently simple man of Gallic extraction, shrugged good-humouredly. He, too, was late for lunch and could see no harm in another, obviously respectable, doctor from the United States adding his opinion to that of the other eminent scientific experts who had just left.

"Our pleasure, sir. The couple are in the enclosure over there, behind the Japanese screens. Would you like someone to assist you?"

"Oh, no," smiled Dr. Conrad suavely, "that won't be necessary, thank you."

He turned and walked briskly toward the screens. So briskly did he walk, in fact, that he did not notice the security agents nor the squatting figure of Sri Bhagavan Ji who sat, now in the full lotus position, eyes closed, humming mantric incantations. Some of his youthful disciples had taken up positions at a respectful distance, smiling knowingly and adoringly at their master. Dr. Conrad almost stumbled over the seated mystic but veered at the last fraction of an instant, nearly whacking Sri Ji a good shot with his shoulder bag, which contained a single, battery-powered instrument of his invention and manufacture - a Seminal Extractor that worked on the principle of high vibration.

Once inside the enclosure, Dr. Conrad swiftly set down his bag and zipped it open. Then, remembering his precarious position, he quickly peeked out in all directions through the slits in the four screens, but the lobby appeared empty and safe. No one was approaching. With his heart beating high in his throat - for even this enterprising scientist had never done anything as adventurous as this - he quickly and, for someone accustomed only to unzipping his own trousers, very deftly unzipped Shawn's. Fortunately for Dr. Conrad, Shawn wore no shorts. The doctor gently but with great determination bared Shawn's member, picked up the portable Seminal Extractor and placed the exposed penis on a concave, elongated rubber portion of the instrument called "the trough."

The Seminal Extractor looked externally like a compact hand-held vacuum cleaner. The opening, roughly the diameter of an average penis in erection, was where the suction hole would be on the vacuum cleaner and once Dr. Conrad had switched the machine on and Shawn's penis began quickly to be engorged with blood, the doctor gently pushed the now-erect member into the hole and advanced the switch to "Full Power." In an instant Shawn's body shuddered and it was over.

Dr. Conrad quickly withdrew his gadget, placed it in his bag, zipped the bag and then, even more hastily, stuffed Shawn's penis back inside the *après-ski* outfit and zipped it up. Paying no further attention to the involuntary donor, the doctor had just turned to leave when Shawn, and almost simultaneously the young woman with whom he sat, opened their eyes.

"Ah, hello," smiled Dr. Conrad. "How interesting."

"Hello," said Shawn, letting go of her hands and luxuriously stretching his magnificent frame.

"I'm Dr.Conrad," said the doctor quickly, "I was just about to examine you. You have been in a trance state for a number of days, you know, and you had all of us worried."

"Ah, well," said Shawn, looking dreamily at the current embodiment of the messenger of the female principle whose gaze likewise had not departed from his. "I am back and I feel wonderful. How many days do you say have passed?"

"Almost three days, I believe."

"Yes," said Shawn, smiling a smile ravenously generous, "that explains how hungry I am. You will join us for lunch, Dr. Conrad, won't you?"

"That," beamed Dr. Barry Conrad, Cg, "will be my profoundest pleasure."

34

CHALLENGE

Even though it was becoming increasingly more likely that Shawn would be expelled from Switzerland - and his three-day trance in the Royal Palace Hotel had certainly not diminished this probability - the Durstli survivor was in great spirits during a long afternoon lunch.

Dr.Conrad, who had safely stored Shawn's involuntary seminal donation in a portable hydrogen/nitrogen freeze tank for transportation to the U.S., proved a charmingly eloquent guest. And the female form of the messenger so suffused the hotel's dining room with her luminous presence that, even though the sophisticated world travellers at the other tables tried their best not to show their burning curiosity, she was the centre of the vortex of everyone's attention. She was more than a star or superstar. She was *from* a star.

"So, Dr. Conrad," Shawn was saying, "if I understand you correctly, you believe you could, under certain conditions, mutate a core of humanity in a few generations to a level inconceivably higher than the present one."

"Yes," nodded Dr. Conrad eagerly.

"But you have failed to tell us what these conditions would have to be," smiled Shawn.

Dr. Conrad was in the enviable position of a poker player who has been winning all night and participates in the final game only to show that he is a good sport. Still, he approached the matter from the point of view of securing a further professional advantage. To him, even though this might be the last round of the day, why not try to win it?

"I've figured out that a single ejaculation, properly used, can create one hundred million humans in three generations, roughly in sixty years. This is based on the assumption that one potent ejaculation yields enough gametes for about two hundred inseminations. Considering factors of mortality and the roughly fifty-fifty ratio of male to female births, and other variables, out of the theoretically possible two hundred million certainly one hundred million potent males should result within, at most, seventy-five years. That is, if the programme is conducted on a scientific basis, of course."

"Yes, yes," smiled Shawn, "but *whose* ejaculation?"

"Yours, sir," Dr. Conrad said boldly and solemnly. The young man did not show surprise. He took the messenger's hand and gazed into her eyes. Having been granted union with her a few hours earlier, he felt only the bond of celestial kinship. And his terrestrial body, secretly relieved of its procreative essence by the cunning doctor, was also at rest, free from lust. She smiled at him. Then she said: "What an amusing idea!" Dr. Conrad could have jumped for joy at her words. But he held himself back. It was just possible now that the alien could be persuaded to donate additional semen.

Shawn, as Nonomine, was considering all of this very carefully. It was all too open and too easy. He did not, of course, distrust the messenger. She had come to take him home. But to leave behind him an ingredient that would, in one third the space of his exile on the Crystal Planet, change the core of Terra, did this not border on a new provocation to the Council?

Nor were there any guidelines to follow here for, after all, there was no precedent for this situation. He would have to follow his instincts. And since he did not feel like ejaculating, he would not ejaculate.

"I think not," he said. "The people of Earth must work with their own genetic material and bring up out of their own essence the very best for the continuation of the planetary race. But you, Dr. Conrad, are engaged in most important work. How are you doing financially?"

"Can't complain," grinned the doctor. "But, of course, I'm really no more than a small businessman."

He sighed dramatically, showing his palms in a gesture of mock despair. "To do everything I want to do I'd need one hundred million dollars!"

"Well, I can't give you one hundred million, but I can give you fifty million!"

"Fifty .... million?" The doctor gulped incredulously.

"Yes, why not? If you have no plans, meet us here in the

morning. I will make the necessary arrangements with my bank."

"But .... fifty million! You don't even know me!"

Shawn looked thoughtfully at Dr. Conrad. He nodded agreement. "I like what you have told me about your work."

Dr. Conrad still could not believe that Shawn was serious. His hands fluttered, gesturing a bit nervously. "I must tell you that there is some disagreement in the scientific community concerning the validity of my principles of experimentation. I've been severely criticized for my racial theories. You may know that only a few decades ago tens of millions of people died because of a man named Adolf Hitler. I have been likened to him."

"How can that be?"

"Well, the idea is that I, by advocating advancement of healthy human stock in a disciplined and organized genetic continuum, discriminate against the genetically less advantaged. In that fashion, according to my critics, I am actually advocating the extermination of millions of humans whom I consider of 'inferior' quality."

"But you have no intention of destroying life, have you?"

"None."

"Rather, you wish to create a new, healthier core race, am I right?"

"Absolutely."

"And you want to accomplish this systematically through as many generations as are necessary, that is, by the method of birth, not of death?"

"That's exactly it," said Dr. Conrad. "Now, if I could do this with *your* sperm, there could be no question of the superiority of genes, and the mutational potential would not merely be heightened, it would be assured."

"Well," smiled Shawn, "fifty million dollars will accomplish two things. It will console you for the loss of my semen, and it will put you in a position - if I have understood how money works in this world - to silence your most insistent critics."

Dr. Conrad had to admit that this was true, and he said so. Even as he spoke, thanking Shawn profusely, he realized that he had won again - in fact, that he had broken the bank. He would go home from Geneva with fifty million *and* the Durstli man's semen. It was a little more than he could bear. He felt a shadow snake its way up his spine and spread like an umbrella over his brain. He raised one hand to shield his face. His head slumped. Then the attack passed. This was as close as he had ever come to losing consciousness at a luncheon table.

"It would be amusing," said the beautiful young woman, "to return here a hundred years from now and find your children, Nonomine!" She had said this in their native warble, too finely pitched vibrationally to be detected by human hearing.

"Yes," said Nonomine, "but the last time I amused myself I was exiled for it. Perhaps I should allow this opportunity to pass."

"Perhaps my hero," she twittered almost painfully at him, "is ready to become a Council member himself. Oba might retire and create a vacancy."

Nonomine, as Shawn, again held one of her hands. "Oba is out there speaking through a man named Baldwin," he said. "He has been told that the experiment is over."

"I'm sure he has."

"Have *you* told him?"

"No."

"Do we have freedom to move as we wish?"

"Yes."

"Would you stay with me on Terra?"

"Yes."

"And you will go home with me?"

"Yes."

"Can the male principle fully inflame you?"

"Yes."

Nonomine, as Shawn, sat back, letting go of her hand. "This is a tough planet," he said.

"I know."

"Women are jealous creatures, second only to men in their jealousy. Fear reigns supreme. Their minds are cowardly. But consider the beauty of their bodies."

He sighed deeply, his gaze enveloping her. She raised her hands. With the heel of her palms, inhaling deeply, she traced the outline of her magnificent torso as if this body had always been hers. Dr. Conrad, who had watched this pantomime with half-open mouth, saw the beginnings of a savagely divine mating dance as Shawn's shoulders rose and angled forward. It was wild and perhaps just a bit embarrassing in its wildness.

"What a wonderful afternoon," he said. "I ...."

A woman had entered the dining room. Though she was small of stature, her entrance immediately commanded attention. She wore traditional Japanese attire, her hair arranged in a towering complicated cascade. Her pale, lustrous skin supported the dark and dangerous fire in her eyes. She walked directly to Shawn's table and curtsied.

"I am Nanita," she said to Shawn. "I have killed three men to free myself for you. Who or where or when is unimportant. I am your future on Earth!"

Shawn nonchalantly indicated a space at the table, inviting her to join them.

"I will not sit," she said.

"If you are my future on Earth," he smiled, "then my future is confrontation with obstinacy. How can confrontation with obstinacy be my future on Earth?"

"I am not lying," said Nanita. "You will be the father of my children."

Dr. Conrad fidgeted on his chair. There was a great deal of explosive potential in this situation. The Japanese woman looked fierce, reminding him of a samurai warrior.

"Madam," he said politely, "won't you join us? We have ...."

"Shut up!" she told him.

Shawn's free hand rose slowly. The gesture was compelling, seeming to calm even Nanita momentarily.

"I respect your vision," he said to her. "Only a powerful vision could have brought you here at this time. Re-examine it. Find in it the kernel of reality. Speak to me again when you have found it."

Nanita stood slowly veiling the fire in her eyes. Her left hand moved. From the folds of her robe she drew a delicately painted fan. Inclining her head sideways and changing the angle of her slim hips, she began to fan her face in studied fashion, pivoting slightly.

"Master Shawn," she cooed coquettishly, bowing, "my Lord of Infinity!"

"Rest now from your exertions," Shawn smiled, "I shall see you tomorrow."

"My Lord," she bowed, taking little backward steps. Still fanning, she turned, walked through the dining room and out. Dr. Conrad heaved a great breath of relief, winking involuntarily in nervous reflex. He had a feeling that an extremely dangerous confrontation had just taken place - a battle, in fact, which had ended in the defeat of the Japanese woman. Hastily he raised his glass.

"Allow me to propose a toast," he said. "I drink to the beauty and the passion of women!"

35

GATHERING

Those who knew Switzerland had often remarked on the stand-offishness of Swiss natives. While the Swiss had become used to accommodating foreigners of every hue and cry and persuasion of thought, they dealt with them distantly and politely, no more. Occasionally the facade might crack and there would be an outburst, but in general this somewhat hypocritical system worked very well. Since the Swiss had not distinguished themselves as thinkers or poets in the history of the world, it had been difficult to accept their condescending manner. Even the innocent arrival from the skies above the Durstli Massif, Shawn, had noticed it. But Pat Young had settled the matter by explaining that to the Swiss, Switzerland was Paradise and was it not natural that Adam and Eve should resent sharing the Garden of Eden with intruders?

Shawn had not understood much of this terminology, and Pat had told him that, as soon as he mastered English, or at least as soon as he could read, he should read the Bible. As the cogs in the machinery that took care of the expulsion of undesirable foreigners from the paradise of Switzerland began slowly to grind, Shawn was now indeed immersed in the study of the world's most popular book.

The life of Jesus of Nazareth, an authentic terrestrial hero, especially fascinated him. And whenever there was something he did not quite understand he would summon Pat, whose new hand was almost completed, to ask questions. Outside the hotel, however, the world was not so peaceful.

As could have been expected, Shawn's statement to the Swiss government agents that he could destroy the Earth had been leaked to the press. In the one night it took to be printed and distributed, it became the top news story in the world, overshadowing even the Middle East turbulences and the bloody massacres in China. There it was on every sensational front-page of Europe and America, in bold type: I CAN DESTROY THE WORLD!

The more serious, more objective, more analytical newspapers and journals set about investigating the phenomenon of this man to whom and to which they had not paid much attention recently, because there existed still a very large stratum of the scientific and intellectual world which pooh-poohed the Durstli man as a bold hoaxer, a clever young man intent only on publicity, money, women - probably precisely in that order. In the professional forums of the world, Shawn had not been taken seriously.

Now that he had become the centre of political controversy, the great publications of the West saw an opportunity to bring in his name and photograph. That their circulation figures stood to profit from this sensible move was so self-evident that it needed no mention.

In front of the Royal Palace Hotel now occurred an incident which further polarized public opinion and which was thrown into the balance against Shawn. A girl was killed. It happened in this way: The local chapter of the Durstli Man Fan Clubs United had begun to demonstrate in support of their hero. About three hundred women ranging in age from pre-teens to one seventy-two year old had been parading up and down in front of the hotel with posters and placards clearly stating their support. SHAWN, WE LOVE YOU! they read. And: MORE POWER TO THE DURSTLI MAN. And even the most militant: GO AHEAD, DO IT! This latter presumably in reference to the destruction of the world.

About two o'clock in the afternoon, a shot rang out and one of the demonstrators fell dead. It was determined that the shot had come from the lake shore and that immediately after it was fired a motorboat had been seen, speeding off. This was more fuel on the fires of the newspapers, especially those of the *Nouvelle Genève*, a morning sheet that now published an extra edition denouncing the Durstli man. With gallic gusto, the girl was sanctified, martyred, enshrined and the *Nouvelle Genève* was the first paper directly and openly to demand the expulsion of the flamboyant amnesiac who claimed to have descended from space to destroy the world, as it now turned out.

If the collective consciousness of Switzerland could have had a voice, it would now have heaved an audible sigh of relief. Expulsion was the favourite method of the Swiss Government to deal with undesirables. No-one was allowed to soil Paradise, and in the case of the Durstli Man this was clearly the best way of dealing with the situation. But the President of the Durstli Man Fan Clubs United, Geneva Chapter, went on television that very night to declare her suspicion that the girl had been killed by hired assassins, agents either of a foreign power or, worse, killers directly or indirectly linked with the Swiss Government itself. This statement struck like a bomb. Never had the Swiss Government been accused of using political assassination as means to an end. It was so outrageous a suspicion that it needed strictly speaking not be dignified with a disclaimer, but to everyone's surprise it was, though the denial was only semi-official. It came from the Stadtpräsident of Geneva who let it be known, in a lapse of temper during casual conversation with newsmen, that Switzerland didn't need to kill innocent girls to throw out undesirables.

The rumour was a stubborn one. Too much had been written about the behind-the-scenes bickering for Shawn's services to dismiss the notion that a foreign power wished to discredit him further. Some of the more intelligent publishers and editors reasoned that it would be in the interest, certainly, of the great powers Russia and America if the Durstli man were deported. If money had not persuaded him to go to Moscow or Washington, then expulsion from Switzerland might.

Within hours after the new killing, the streets around Shawn's hotel were cordoned off and barricaded by police. The expulsion order was expected any moment, and it was considered only a question of how long the government would accord him to leave Switzerland. Beyond the roadblocks, the crowds started gathering. On the surface and in the immediate perspective, it seemed merely a matter of watching the forcible removal of a wealthy and celebrated young man from his luxurious lair. It was a rare occasion in the sense that most expulsions from Switzerland occurred indirectly: residence permits expired, people on the run chose quietly to yield to pressure. Once in a while, a moustachioed nonentity from South America was accused of plotting the overthrow of the legally constituted government which had sent him into exile. Such a picture would flash across the evening news, the morning papers and would be gone. The Durstli Man in his colourful *après-ski* outfits, with his golden hair, bright blue eyes, his regal stride and the great, galactic smile he bestowed on everyone had become a flamboyant sight in Geneva. Even so, all of this considered would not have brought the Genevans out in droves. They had learned a long time ago that money rules the world, too, and so not even Shawn's rumoured millions impressed them. In Geneva, every little clerk had money. No, there was something else: the feel and texture of a historic event, an imminent event of global significance. For the first time in years the populace was truly excited.

It had all happened so fast, had seemed at first only the customary series of pictures in the kaleidoscope of world events. The Durstli Man had provided entertainment more colourful than the grisly cross-section of common brutality that made up everyday fare. Still, these had only been pictures. Now the pictures had become three dimensional. The Durstli Man would walk out of his hotel and be taken to the airport, as was customary in such cases. There were few now in Geneva who would have missed seeing him go.

36

TEARS

Speechless, Patrick Young stared up at the familiar facade of the *Inter-Europe News* building at 15, Rue des Brumes in Paris. He grunted. He didn't have the foggiest idea why he was here or how he had got there, but managed quickly to gain a certain inner equilibrium. In a gesture of habit he brought up his left hand with firm fingertips, no misty oscillations. He had a new hand, a hand that fitted perfectly, although, when he placed his hands next to one another, the new one looked younger, smoother. That made sense to him. Assuming that there had to be a reason for his presence, he walked in and up the well-worn stairs directly past the receptionist into the office of Mr. Kirkley Evans who was hunched over some illegible piece of copy and not in a particularly charitable mood.

When Evans saw Young his mouth fell open and even the shadows in the concavities of his pockmarked skin turned pale. "Pat..." he squeezed out. "No, you are not, you can't be!"

Patrick Young sat down and smiled pleasantly at his former editor, saying: "Take it easy, old man!"

"But," bubbled Evans, "you were blown to bits, they found your hand. I saw it myself, your ring and everything! It was a positive identification!"

Young held out his left hand, saying: "Shake, Kirkley, feel for yourself!"

But the editor retreated in his chair, pushed himself away from the desk, swivelling to avoid Young. "Now look here," he said, "what kind of woeful prank is this, who are you and what do you want?"

"Don't be a sissy," Young told him. "I have a story for you that will set you back on your ears, and I will give it to you exclusively but it has to be printed word for word as I give it to you. Call Larry!"

"Mr. Coalwaller is attending a luncheon in honour..." Evans

tried, but Young cut him off, saying: "Call him now, tell him to come here, I don't have time to fool around. Meanwhile I'm going to give one of these typewriters the pleasure of my touch, if you don't mind."

Still pale, Kirkley Evans dialled for the restaurant, got through, asked for Mr. Coalwaller, waited and then started talking. What was said at the other end could not be heard but it could not have been pleasant judging by Evans' response. "No, sir, no, certainly not. No, of course I cannot vouch for this man's... no, sir. But he looks every inch Young. Yes. Yes, sir, he has two hands. He showed them to me. He is alive. Fresh as a daisy, sir. Yes, sir, I'll ask him."

Turning to Young, muffling the receiver, he said: "You are not an impostor, are you?" Patrick shook his head. "No, sir," Evans spoke into the phone, "he is not. He has assured me not only by his presence but by shaking his head that he is not an impostor. Yes, sir, I'll tell him that. Thank you, Mr. Coalwaller."

He hung up and said to Young: "He's coming over straightaway, but you'd better be Patrick Young. You'd better!"

Patrick Young, paying no attention to the staring staff, walked to a free desk with a typewriter, sat down, put in paper from a ream and started typing blithely. THE TRUTH ABOUT THE DURSTLI MAN by Patrick Young (Special Exclusive).

"I have known the so-called Durstli Man ever since he was found in the eternal snows of the Durstli Massif after the mysterious crash of an antiquated 1938 Pampini aeroplane back in March of this year. I was there when he thawed out, though he should have been dead. I was there when he spoke his first words, made the first sounds of a budding consciousness. I became his friend and adviser. I know whereof I speak!

The man whom I call Shawn is now embroiled by controversy and in imminent danger of expulsion from Switzerland with no place to go in the world, due to vicious slander, character assassination and adverse publicity disseminated by the media. I myself am guilty of having contributed to this atmosphere in a series of articles I wrote in March for this publication. I want to set the record straight. It is time that the world found out the truth about the mysterious foundling who has caused so much speculation and rumour. That is why I'm writing this article.

This man, Shawn, is in truth an emissary from a planetary civilisation in our galaxy. To call the society or family which sent him to us advanced by our standards would be a severe under-estimation of the situation as it exists. Those who have sent him here are not simply and merely 'advanced', because the term advanced, implies that we, too, can eventually gain the level of existence which is theirs. Nothing could be further from the truth. Shawn's presence on earth is, by my best judgement, a playful fluke, a galactic whim, something that could not have been anticipated in any fashion by the inhabitants of this planet. It is an outside event, a gloriously fortunate circumstance from which humans may benefit if they recognise it and seize the opportunity. To call the Durstli Man powerful, again, would be erroneous and dangerous. He alone, as a single individual, has the power to destroy this planet in the ultimate, physical sense. In other words: he can blow the globe to smithereens! And this brings me to his much publicised statement: I can destroy the world!

How can such a statement be taken seriously? To take it seriously is to assume that a single individual is capable of destroying the world, but to assume such a thing is to give the greatest, the ultimate importance to the Durstli Man. In that case, should not the representatives of all the governments convene immediately, perhaps under the auspices of the United Nations, and invite this man to address them to learn what can be learned? That is what I am proposing. Rather than deporting him, let him address the U.N. Allow him to speak. Give him the freedom to explain himself and the world. We could all profit from it! If we do not act wisely now, perhaps the Durstli Man will carry out his threat. Perhaps the world will be destroyed!"

Patrick Young leaned back in his chair and looked at what he had written. Then he pulled out the paper, tore it to pieces, wadded it up and threw it deftly into a wastepaper basket. He got up just as Lawrence Coalwaller came in and stood aghast when he saw Patrick Young. "This is impossible, Pat," he said, "is it really you?" To affirm the fact, Young put out his left hand and they shook hands, warmly. Coalwaller, who had had advance warning, was not as shocked as Evans had been but still his eyes were not entirely steady as he inspected his former employee closely. "I suppose it must be you," he said finally, "and damn to that, Young! This puts me in a fine mess. Now I've got to bring in the occult, the otherworldly, spiritism, dig up the old tracts, and all because you couldn't stay in pieces! Ah, but I have a good idea what happened. It's a hoax, am I right? It was convenient for you to disappear for a while and so you arranged for your blow-up, am I correct? But the hand, the hand doesn't fit, so tell me, how did you do it?"

"What does it matter?" Patrick said lightly. "I was going to write a piece for you to print, but it was not good. I'll tell you what I think is going to happen. I think Shawn is going to blow us all to kingdom come, you and you and all of us included. I think we don't have much time left, either. I've had a little time to think about it while I was typing, and I think he's going to do exactly as he threatens. Why not, why shouldn't he? He'd be doing the galaxy a service, don't you think?"

"Doing the .... galaxy a service?" ooohed Coalwaller. "What in heaven's name do you mean?"

"Oh, Mr. Coalwaller, I'll explain," Patrick said perched on the side of a desk, long legs blocking a well travelled passage, "this is France in Europe on Earth in the solar system at the rim of a galaxy!"

"Come on, Pat, I know you've been through a lot," Coalwaller said, "but you don't seriously go in for all that psychic stuff now do you? It's all bogus, isn't it? A fad, a fashion. People love to think that there's life in 'Outer Space'. Escapism, that is what it is, nothing else! Now this Shawn, you know I've never told you what I think about him, but I'll tell you now. I admire the youngster. He has what it takes, he's got chutzpa! He's going for the Big Lie and he's sticking with it. What else can he do, still, it's a temptation. He could cop out, couldn't he? No, not really he couldn't. He's said he's from up there and so if he admits now that he isn't, that he's just like you and me, then he's through, isn't he? Good! Now they're throwing him out of Switzerland. It's happened before to others you know. The way I understand it, he's loaded like a freight train. He'll have no problem. He can go almost anywhere with his money, but I wouldn't bet a dime on his future. I think that he's through. It'll be an expensive funeral but I'm afraid, my boy, that no-one will weep. And, talking about doing a piece for us, you'd be the ideal person for an obituary!"

Patrick Young looked quietly at his former boss. Then a smile spread over his face. "That's right, Coalwaller," he said, pushing himself away from the desk, "an obituary! I've read the piece of trash you printed when I died! You didn't even get my birthdate right. In fact, Coalwaller, you're all wrong on everything and you always will be! Goodbye!"

He stalked out of the room and building and took a taxi to the airport where he noticed that he had no money on him. The cab driver began a long oath with occasional pauses of muttering. He called a policeman, to whom Patrick tried to explain the situation in basic French, saying: "Vous voyez, Monsieur, je regrette énormément, but j'ai oublier mon argent. Actually, and you may have a certain amount of difficulty to understand this, Monsieur, but ...." He broke off, realising that the truth would not only get him nowhere, but complicate matters considerably. He searched his pockets. No credit cards, no identification either. Nothing. "I'm Patrick Young," he said. "I'm a friend of the Durstli Man, you know, in Geneva, the man who came from space and ...."

"In that case," he was told, "it might be a good idea for you to come along and make a deposition to the effect that you are penniless and owe this man fifty-two francs fare from - where did you fetch this gentleman?"

"Numero quinze, Rue des Brumes," said the cabbie.

"Numero quinze, Rue des Brumes," repeated the policeman, "to Orly Airport. Fifty-two francs."

Patrick decided to gamble. He addressed the policeman, saying: "Monsieur, no doubt you have followed the important news concerning my friend, the Durstli Man. No doubt you have heard the rumours of considerable amounts of money having passed hands on his behalf. I assure you that all of it is true, he is wealthy, and the sum of fifty-two Francs can easily be paid by me, but I must go to Geneva immediately. You must trust me, both of you! My friend needs me, believe me!"

"So," said the policeman, "and how is it then that this man can make people fly in a moment over long distances, that is what I've heard, and cannot transport a friend from Paris to Geneva?"

"He can, he can," Patrick assured his questioner, "but he has his own mind, his own reasoning. He may be doing this in order to find out where *you* stand in this matter."

"So," said the policeman, "and he is going to destroy the world, eh? My family, myself, this uniform, this airport, this honest, hard-working taxi driver, his automobile, everything, eh, your friend, he has said that, that is what I've heard!"

"A figure of speech, believe me," Patrick said, a little desperately now because he could see the battle going against him. "Believe me, he didn't mean it. How could he have meant it, Monsieur, ask yourself. How can a single individual destroy the whole world, please, that is not possible is it? He is a young man. Remember your own youth, would you! He exaggerated a little, no more, believe me. It was boastful of him to say that, a boast."

"So then," said the policeman, "is he going to apologise for making us afraid. Is he going to take it back?"

"I," said Patrick, "I myself will apologise for him, right here, right now. I take it back for him. I'm sure he would want me to do that. Let me give you my signature, a piece of paper, my assurance that I shall not pay fifty-two francs, Messieurs, but one hundred, yes, one hundred francs within three days. That is a bargain, is it not?"

"True," said the policeman, "that would be a bargain."

Turning to the cab driver he asked: "What do you say to that?" The cabbie nodded, reluctantly. A piece of paper was found and Patrick wrote in terrible French that he owed one hundred francs within three days. Dated. Signed. About to turn and be off when the policeman stopped him.

"You are going to Geneva now, Monsieur Young?"

"Yes," Patrick said.

"So you will need money to pay for the flight, will you not?"

"Oui, Monsieur," said Patrick Young.

"So," said the policeman, "will you accept my help in this matter?"

Patrick looked at the man, thunderstruck.

"Yes," the policeman went on, "you impress me as a trustworthy man. And I confess that I like the way you stick up for a friend. I placed myself in the position of being your friend and I found that perhaps sometime soon I should like to sit down with you and drink a bottle of wine, if you like. My wife especially has been interested in the entire Durstli affair. We've had many lively conversations and arguments about it. I'm sure she would like to meet you to hear some firsthand news. If you will do me the honour to accept the plane fare and whatever is left over of the, let me see..."

He took out his wallet and started counting off the bills, saying finally: "Yes, seven hundred francs, that should see you through. My name is Duluoz. This is my telephone number. Please call me when you have news."

He handed Patrick the money, saluted and walked away.

"Monsieur," Young said to the cab driver, "here is your hundred francs. Tear up the note I gave you and convey my sincere gratitude to .... no, wait, I'll do so myself."

He ran after the policeman, caught up with him. "Monsieur," he said, touching him on the shoulder. Slowly, almost heavily, the policeman turned. His face was red, puffed up and glistening with tears.

37

CALL

Shawn was in bed, leafing through the morning papers. "Here, look," he said, "they have finally come up with it. I'm the Lion. Look at this one: *Is the Lion Getting Ready to Leap? And on Whom?* Ingenious!"

She stood naked before the full-length mirror, admiring herself, studying the body that is customary on Earth, one such as she had been given for the first time.

He sighed. "All that would keep me on this planet is your body."

She thrust out one hip, slanting the muscular ridges so that shadow filled the shallow concavities, accentuating the hillscape of her flesh.

"If I'm the Lion, then you must be the Lamb. And did we not lie peaceful together through the night?"

They warbled, giggling at each other. She had raised her arms and her hands clutched above her head, turning, turning in slow rotation.

"They call flesh gravity here," he trilled at her.

"Gravity?"

"Yes, that is what they call flesh!"

It was immensely amusing to be filled with love in the face of such terrestrial eccentricity. It was very clever of them to equate flesh with gravity, she thought.

"Look out the window, is Oba still preaching?" She walked majestically to the window on the tips of her toes, all ridges still tensed. She bent forward lightly at the waist to see. She trilled at him yes, Oba was still preaching, or preaching again. A great crowd was there.

"Stay like that, in that pose. Don't move. I must absorb this."

"Then I shall lose this body again. You wish to take only its essential imprint," she giggled.

"I don't know now."

She stood for a long time, enjoying the confines of her flesh. She had no desire to leave this vessel. Inside it was warm, firm. Energy bubbled everywhere. A fine, tickling sensation filled the dome, the head. No wonder there were so many humans. They had all come here like this, from other places, and got to like their bodies like this.

"It is not fine enough to become used to," she said. He read at random from a paper:

".... and the government is expected to act at any moment. In the wake of the disappearance of General Nicolai Constantin Dvat and the most recent occurrences in the Royal Palace Hotel, public voices are clamouring for expulsion of the charismatic figure known as Shawn. No one knows when ...."

"Precisely," said Shawn, "no one knows when!"

"Time would become important to me, too," she smiled. "Time is flesh and flesh is gravity. Gravity is time and time is velocity."

"Perhaps the two of us could become ordinary," he whispered. She still maintained the stance into which he had thrown her. She had made it one movement of a long dance. She could keep it not only for a long time, but if she chose could take it out of time.

Nonomine, as Shawn, pulled off the sheets and got up. He walked to her, naked as she, and stood very close, assuming a pose complementary to hers. Then he could again have asked to be granted a merger, but that would have been dangerous. He would have to decide soon.

"Come," he said, "let's do some shopping."

"Shopping?"

"Yes, buy things."

"Things?"

"To amuse ourselves!"

"With money?"

"Yes, I want to buy crystal," he said.

"Where?"

"In a crystal shop!" he trilled, and she filled the room with a warbling giggle that brought them dangerously close to union again.

Now at last, she moved. They began to dress. She put on the same gossamer silk dress of muted blues and greens. She pulled it on over her body. She sandalled her feet, combed her hair. Shawn dressed in silver.

Guards outside his suite had kept reporters away from their floor, but in the lobby they were set upon by a sweaty mob of newsmen and bold celebrity addicts. Shawn's mild glance cut a swathe through them, parting the crowd as if it were water.

The Japanese woman was waiting for him at the entrance. She said nothing, nor looked at him. As they went out into the street, she followed them. And Dr. Barry Conrad was almost cut off by the crowd that closed in behind the trio. But at the very last moment he slipped from the revolving door into the open area around the Durstli Man.

"Good morning," he said. "Have you seen the papers? They have a new name for you - 'The Lion.' Kind of catchy, don't you think?"

Shawn smiled a generous smile. "Let's go to the bank first," he said.

A loud call came from Jack Baldwin's travelling Crusade for Truth van across the street. It was aimed at Shawn. It had a quality recognizable only to Nonomine and the messenger. It was Oba calling through Baldwin, but it was not a call of challenger. It was a call of friendship and .... a call for help.

Shawn walked across the street as the crowd opened before him. He stood looking up at the body of Jack Baldwin.

"Good morning, Mr. Baldwin," he said, "so nice to see you. Have you been entertaining the people with magic?"

Baldwin sadly shrugged, shaking his head. "They are here waiting for you," he said.

"But all my tricks, all the things that we can do, you and I, do you mean to say that you no longer do them?"

Jack Baldwin stood gazing down thoughtfully at Shawn. He felt neither anger nor hate. He had a good notion of himself standing on a small platform like a barker for a travelling sideshow. How had he got here, why was he here? What had he been trying to prove?

"A very fine morning, sir," he said. "A fine day for all of us!"

"Yes, Mr. Baldwin," smiled Shawn. "That being true, let us enjoy it while we can!"

He turned and, surrounded by his retinue, began to walk away.

"Sir!" Baldwin called after him. Shawn stopped and turned. "You win, sir!"

Shawn said nothing, but turned and continued walking.

They walked along the edge of the lake to the Rousseau Bridge and turned to cross it. At the middle of the bridge they stopped to watch the swans and to listen to the rushing waters that fell into the deeper and narrower bed of the emerging Rhone.

All day long into this afternoon the swans had been arriving from distant parts of the lake. Across the shoreline boulevard before the Royal Palace Hotel they gathered on the water, what seemed like hundreds of them. People boating on the lake reported that they came from as far away as Nyon, Lausanne and St. Gingolph and were still coming. They, the swans, and the Durstli Man were the exclusive topic of conversation in the crowds held back on either side of the hotel by police.

People, pretending to be promenading, were following them at a respectable distance. Shawn was holding the messenger's hand, gazing into the turbulent waters. Nanita had placed Dr. Conrad between herself and Shawn as if he were a shield. Dr. Conrad had just entered that paradisiacal state of bliss that comes upon man when he knows that he has finally met and fused with his destiny.

They walked on slowly, the messenger's dress being pressed against her by a mild breeze from the lake. Swans followed them with proudly held necks. They left the bridge, strolled across a square, and into the Banque Centrale du Lac. This time no glass melted, no shoe got stuck.

Shawn and his party were ushered into the executive offices, where he signed a transfer paper for fifty million dollars. The whole procedure took less than fifteen minutes, and they were given a guide to take them to the nearest establishment where crystal was sold. This turned out to be a small shop of octagonal shape, cleverly lighted to bring out the beauty of the crystal on display.

"Now I know," Shawn smiled, "now I see!"

What he saw was a sampling of the treasures of Earth and proof of the evanescent, transient nature of man. When all earth had worn off, when the sea had washed away the last grain of sand and soil, when the fiery core of Earth had melted and swept away the cities and the artifice of man, then this would be a new home for crystal, a nascent crystal planet in its own right! Here was the proof, here were past and future in one!

He stood for a long time, gazing, holding the messenger's hand.

Dr. Conrad broke the silence.

"See anything you like?"

"Yes. That!"

Shawn pointed to a long piece of crystal - milky colour, five-edged, terraced, the diameter of a wrist.

"That," he repeated. "What is it?"

"Monsieur," said the shop owner, "that is a piece of quartz crystal. An exceptionally fine piece, a sample from Minas Gerais province in Brazil, it is the female type because of its opaqueness."

"Please show it to me."

The man slid back the glass door and carefully removed the piece. It was of approximately the length of an arm from elbow to fingertip, but a slender arm. He handed it to Shawn, who took it and held it up against the natural light from the window.

"Please," said the owner, "examine it outside, if you wish." Shawn went out and looked at the crystal. In the daylight it turned even paler, its quality now more profound in the subtlety gained from natural light. Shawn walked back into the shop.

"This will do," he said.

The owner could not refrain from raising his brows, but he quickly regained his composure. His feelings about the Durstli survivor were ambivalent, but he suspected that the young man was wealthy. Therefore, when he told Shawn the price, his voice was even and appeared disinterested.

"This is a fine, rare piece," he said. "I have cautiously priced it at eight and one half thousand francs."

Shawn turned smiling to Dr. Conrad.

"Please buy this for me, Dr. Conrad," he said.

Dr. Barry Conrad had not found much occasion in his recent years to blush. In a way, he had become a man incapable of surprise. But now he blushed fully to the tips of his ears. And, indeed, tears began to form in his eyes - tears perhaps no less precious, in view of their rarity, than the most beautiful pieces of crystal in this boutique.

He hastily whipped out a plastic wallet and said: "Will you accept U.S. travellers' cheques?"

"Certainly, sir, with pleasure."

While Dr. Conrad signed the travellers' cheques, Shawn and the messenger of the female principle, followed by Nanita, walked across the street and sat down at a table under a red and white striped umbrella. Shawn ordered lemonade. He handed the crystal to Nanita.

"Since I am to be the father of your children," he smiled, "this is my gift to them."

She held the crystal, her eyes averted. He took it from her. He handed it to the messenger who took it lightly, balancing it precisely on the ridge of her right index finger.

"It is of Earth," she said.

He took it from her and weighed it in his hand. The lemonade arrived and they all sipped through straws. Dr. Conrad came charging out of the shop, rushing across the street to join them. He fell into a chair, laughing.

"This is a great day," he called out happily, "the finest day of my life. The lion of your generosity has awakened the lion of my gratitude, sir. Command me, please, I beg of you."

"Well," said Shawn with sudden seriousness, "we have all escaped a harsh verdict."

He looked at his celestial bride.

He trilled at her: "The Council cannot itself form judgements. No council anywhere can. It is empowered merely to pass on that which it receives. When it is judged, it judges. When the judgement on it is mild, it judges mildly. When it is judged harshly, it judges harshly. To be a Councillor is to be an administrator of judgements which one does not form oneself. To be a rebel is to form one's own judgments."

"Which do you prefer?" she warbled back at him.

"The rebel and the Councillor are one," he smiled. He held up the crystal. He lowered it but kept it above the table. He began to shape it with his hands. It became like putty in his hands, a smooth, rounded pipe. His hands kept shaping it. He held it into the light, pleased. It was now a pipe, pointed at one end. He put the pointed end to his lips and seemed to blow. Then he laid it down on the table, it could be seen that his breath had tunneled through the crystal, shaped a narrow circular passage. Shawn nodded at Nanita."

"Take it," he said. "Play!"

The Whore of Japan picked up the crystal flute and blew into it. No sound emerged.

Shawn leaned forward and touched the flute. He gently pointed it toward the lake, in an easterly direction.

"Now blow!"

"Keep blowing!"

Nanita blew the crystal flute. She blew it for a long time,

pausing for breath now and then. At last she stopped. She sat back, pale, looking exhausted. Dr. Conrad, too, looked bloodless. His cheeks seemed sunken. His eyes were dull. If she had continued playing this instrument any longer, he would have tried to stop her. Shawn trilled at the messenger, who warbled back. They giggled together, though none of this was audible.

"Do you see," Nonomine giggled, "do you see what music from their *own* crystal does to them?"

In her own terrestrial body she was luminously radiant. Women and men alike stared adoringly across tables. Some had raised their hands as if to touch her.

"It is changing," she trilled at him. "It is changing. It is coming."

"Yes," said Nonomine, as Shawn, audibly, "it will come!"

38

METAMORPHOSIS

That the town of Durstlimas in the Canton of Valais in Switzerland had been put on the map, so to speak, by the Durstli crash, was at best considered a mixed blessing by Antoine Delacroix, its postmaster. With the tourists had come a great increase in the volume of mail.

Before the crash he and his wife had had no difficulty handling the postal business of the remote Alpine spot, but now they found themselves hard pressed. It was not only the sorting of mail and its delivery and the great number of outgoing letters and postcards and parcels (some of the latter no doubt containing mementoes and souvenirs illegally obtained from the phantom village site of Morgendurst and/or even from the Pampini out on the square), but there was also a greatly increased volume of incoming money orders. Many of the tourists, particularly the newsmen, had become quasi-permanent residents. Monsieur Delacroix did not like the idea of handling considerable sums of money every week.

All around, business had tremendously increased in Durstlimas, and while the merchants considered this a fortunate development, Antoine Delacroix's normally jovial demeanour had suffered deterioration. He had requested funds for hiring at least one part-time helper. This request had been denied. Consequently, a frown had settled on his brow. He no longer had time to chat or exchange pleasantries. He was turning into a harried, hurried, citified official and he didn't like it. He had been obliged to shorten his lunchtime from two hours to one, and of this one hour he needed every minute to relax a little, smoke a pipe of tobacco, and let his mind drift away from the business at hand.

Early this Monday afternoon he had wandered out into the square to see how the two guards by the airplane were doing. Tickets for inspection of the machine were sold at the tobacconist's, and some of the proceeds from this brisk business were used to pay the guards. The rest went to the Canton Council. So far as the citizens of Durstlimas were concerned, this was a far from satisfactory arrangement. They felt that these funds should be used for improvements in their town. They were also making representations to be allowed to use the funds to finance the seat-lift to the Morgendurst site, contending that substantial profits could be realized.

The guards were young men, unarmed, glad of the opportunity at once to earn a leisurely living and be part of a situation that attracted more and more international attention. While at first they had not been uniformed, their appearance was by now streamlined. They wore light-blue windbreakers of nylon, and matching trousers. To give themselves an air of authority, they had sewn broad rectangular strips of yellow cloth to their jackets, serving as shoulder pieces. And they had agreed not to smile in the photos for which they posed in front of the Pampini. Their job was to prevent the theft of souvenirs and to supervise the often considerable crowds that lined up, having paid twenty-five francs each to enter the airplane and sit at the controls that had so mysteriously functioned - or malfunctioned, who knew?

Normally the post office closed between 12.30 and 2.30 p.m., but now it closed only for one hour between 12.30 and 1.30 p.m. to handle the extra work. Delacroix had locked it at 12.32. He had then walked directly into the kitchen of his adjoining apartment and sat down to a brief lunch. Before going out into the square he had checked the clock. It had been precisely seven minutes after the hour of 1.00 p.m. No more than a few words of greeting had been exchanged between himself and the guards when the Pampini, as Delacroix later put it, "shuddered." It must then have been either 1.09, or 1.10, or at the latest 1.11.

According to Delacroix, ".... it changed colour a bit. It became darker, more substantial. It happened very quickly, and I didn't have to tell the guards - they had noticed it, too. I used to climb around in these mountains, you know, and so I thought that the shadow of a cloud had fallen over the Pampini and looked up. But no, no cloud. There were no clouds."

When Monsieur Delacroix looked back down, the initial "shudder" had turned into a steady trembling. Though there was no sound whatever from the engines, the trembling became rapidly stronger.

The three men rushed through the gate of the fence around the site and Delacroix, who got there first, put his palms on the hull. There was a strong vibration. In a matter of moments - Delacroix estimated ten, maybe twenty seconds - the entire plane was shaking so violently that they were forced to step back.

Though still no engine could be heard, there was now a loud tearing, scraping sound caused by the hull against the support struts. Delacroix sneezed vigorously a couple of times because of the dust that was stirred up. The plane by now was bucking violently and one of the guards tried to board it but could not get a firm hold. Tourists began to pour into the square from the hotel and restaurant, where they had been waiting out the lunch break, and the guards had to take up positions to stop them from getting to the plane.

Along with the intense trembling and bucking, the silver hues of the old Pampini underwent further transformation. The metal pulsated, turning lighter and lighter until the entire plane had a silverish lucidity as it became more and more transparent. In the crash the Pampini had broken into many pieces and it had been repaired just sufficiently to permit safe inspection; but now, according to Delacroix: ".... the thing was repairing itself!" Dents and cracks disappeared, one part appearing to melt and flow into the other, until the Pampini was whole again - a sleek, gleaming airplane.

At this moment the telephone rang in the post office. Monsieur Delacroix's wife, Cecile, answered to learn that up in the phantom town of Morgendurst startling things were happening. No one had been hurt, but the buildings were turning into what looked like snow and ice to blend into the glacial landscape. Some of the tourists up there were in a state of panic and help was needed!

Cecile Delacroix rushed out to call her husband. She got there just in time to see the Pampini rise. The aeroplane rose, even though its propellers were not turning. In fact, the airscrews had disappeared altogether. In their place were streamlined, bulbous outgrowths of what looked like opalescent, jade-like material, all of it blending into the fuselage. The entire thing rose slowly to a height of perhaps 50 or 60 feet above the gaping-mouthed and wide-eyed mob. There it stood absolutely still in the air, hovering silent and motionless.

Those who witnessed the event disagreed on the length of time the Pampini, or rather that which the Pampini had become, hovered there. It might have been anywhere from thirty seconds to five minutes. Some said it was even longer than that, but all agreed that it seemed like an eternity.

Then, at a leisurely pace, according to Delacroix: ".... much more slowly than the slowest helicopter I ever saw ...." the pale, now almost translucent machine began to gain height, at the same time banking in a great curve. Delacroix: ".... it had a majestic sweep, like an ocean liner at sea. It seemed incredibly large and powerful now, even though I do not believe that it had changed size."

It moved lightly and soundlessly, yet with the irresistible force of a great mass and weight. It seemed not to be concerned with gravity.

As the rejuvenated, transformed Pampini drifted off balloon-like in a westerly direction, everyone ran to the north side of Durstlimas, the side that overlooks the Rhone Valley. They clicked their cameras and watched it for a long time in the clear air as it gradually appeared to pick up speed, shrinking to the size of a dove in the distance. Finally it was no more than a wavering spot, and then it was gone from sight around a far bend of the river valley. Thousands along the way saw the strange, palely luminous craft without propellers and with what now appeared to be no more than vestigial wings. They watched it on its silent, steady drift from Durstlimas down the Rhone Valley, following the river almost directly west, unmistakably in the direction of the great Lac Léman, which is also known as Lake Geneva.

39

THREE

It had taken someone largely unhuman like Shawn - in fact, it had taken *Shawn* (whom the newspapers called The Lion) - to make the Swiss Government over-react. What had been going on was simply too dangerously confusing, and the military mind, which on many occasions in the long and glorious history of the oldest democratic confederacy in the modern world had saved the day, meant now to save the day again. Albeit, it chose the wrong moment, the wrong approach, the wrong subject.

Rather than routinely delivering a twenty-four-hour expulsion notice, as was customary, a detachment of some thirty crack regular troops, supported by a platoon of armed militia, pulled up in troop carriers before the Royal Palace Hotel in a misplaced show of strength. The reasoning behind this had been that the citizens of Geneva would be reassured that their government could not be intimidated, even when confronted with phenomena over which it had no control. The Durstli Man had become a legendary figure in a few short months and the Swiss were in no mood to fool around any longer. He had tried, strained, and finally broken what they considered their patient hospitality. Now they would not merely expel him, but bodily throw him out and humiliate him in the process.

The arrival of the troops was ill-timed, Shawn was out shopping. Even Jack Baldwin, who was hastily pulled in, could tell them only that he had seen him walk away in the direction of the Rousseau Bridge. And to complicate matters, another obstruction now arose in the form of Sri Bhagavan Ji and a group of his followers, about three hundred strong. The mystics had taken up positions squarely around the military convoy in such a fashion that if the soldiers wished to move, they would have to move through or over a double line of human bodies. Ji was ordered to get out of the way. But he refused.

The commander's first impulse was simply to break through the thin line, but he got hold of himself in time and approached Sri Ji, saying in English, "Please let us out, you are stopping us from doing our duty."

"Your duty is to refrain from the unwarranted exercise of power!" said Sri Bhagavan Ji.

"You are a guest of Switzerland," he was told. "You will respect Swiss law."

"I respect all law unless it interferes with the highest divine vibration, with the godhead itself," Sri Ji replied humbly.

The Swiss commander's modest command of English did not allow him to fully understand the meaning of what he had heard. To cover this up, he frowned.

"We will roll you down," he shouted and turned to climb into the command carrier. Sri Bhagavan Ji called after him:

"History will judge you, sir! You are about to commit a great foolishness! The man you are after is an angelic messenger, in harmony with the divine vibration. You cannot command him. On the contrary, you must consider yourself fortunate that he has not commanded you. Desist from your vainglorious course of action!"

In answer, the commander raised his hand, then brought it down. The command carrier began to move. Sri Ji moved also, with the speed of lightning, bodily flinging himself forward to break open the line of his followers. He tackled a heavy-chested woman in a long, not entirely clean robe which may once have been virginal white. He brought her down sideways. Not content with his manoeuvre, he rolled her against the sidewalk and up, out of danger. The men who had been next to her also jumped back, and one of them stumbled, going down awkwardly on top of the woman and the guru. A gap sufficiently large to let the troop carriers through was created, with Sri Ji shouting at the top of his voice, "Let them through, let them through!" The convoy rolled on in the direction of Rousseau Bridge and Sri Ji's own troops, quickly regrouped by the guru who seemed to be everywhere at once, followed in its wake, chanting the universal mantra: *Om*.

The great, dense crowd of Genevans which had gathered had been shaken out of their bourgeois lethargy by these events. Jack Baldwin, his arms flailing, his voice hoarse, screaming for everyone to go home, to disperse, to move along - in the fashion of a cop on the beat in his hometown Ossining - was helpless in the surge of agitated burghers who rushed in behind the guru's group. The result of all this was that a casual observer (if indeed casualness could be imagined at this time in this area) placed on the Rousseau Bridge, facing its northern ramp, would have seen an ominous phalanx of military vehicles, chockful of men in the white overalls of the foot soldier, leading a compressed but still colourful orange congregation of *Om*-chanting apprentice adepts, followed by a solid wave of Swiss citizens - all of this pouring around the corner onto the bridge and advancing in the fashion of a human millipede with a chain-rattling, armoured head of five troop carriers. Any observer, casual or otherwise, would instantly have known that here came trouble.

40

TWO

From the other southern side, a small band of people also walked toward the middle of the bridge, led by Shawn. It included a happy but slightly perplexed Patrick Young. Viewed from above, the classical scene had all the earmarks of a bloodbath in the making. No doubt the juggernaut of advancing machines and men from the north side of the narrowed lake would roll over and devour the frail unit of five advancing toward it.

And in the rapidly developing mix there was a third element: the transformed Pampini, gleaming pale like a large, floating tear-drop of jade, drifted in above from the east, escorted by a small armada of Swiss Air Force helicopters.

The troop commander signalled, the carrier convoy slowed. Slightly beyond the halfway mark of the bridge it came to a full stop. The soldiers dismounted and took up positions, forming a roadblock five-men deep across the entire width of the bridge. There they stood, a sparse forest that threw a thin lattice of shadows onto the asphalt, like medieval lances.

"Dr. Conrad," smiled the Durstli foundling, "is this a celebration of some kind?"

"If it's a celebration, it looks a little forced to me."

"Patrick, are you aware of a Swiss holiday today?"

"No, but .... I believe they mean *you*!"

Shawn walked on. Now they were no more than 160 feet from the convoy. Nanita carried the flute like a treasured possession, cradling it protectively in her arms.

A figure in an orange-coloured robe, Sri Bhagavan Ji, broke from the front line of soldiers who blocked the bridge. He called out as he ran, "Sir, watch out! Government troops, up to no good!"

Shawn had stopped and turned sideways, resting his elbows on the bridge parapet. He gazed up. The Pampini was now clearly in view, out over the lake. It was still approaching as three Swiss Mirage air force jets roared and passed above it. The helicopters maintained a respectful distance behind and on either side of it.

"Sri Ji," smiled Shawn without looking at the guru, "what are you doing here?"

"I came to warn you. I had a vision."

"You and your visions."

"A very serious warning, sir. Don't let them provoke you!"

"Sri Ji, tell me, how do you support yourself in the world?"

"Money comes my way, sir. I beg as well."

"And when you beg, what do you say?"

"I say, All Blessings Flow From the Godhead. Money Is Part of the Divine Vibration."

"But do you know how to handle money?"

"I don't know, sir. I have always been poor."

"Good!"

Shawn pulled out a cheque book and began to write. Dr. Conrad's curiosity prompted him to approach, walking slightly on tip-toes, but he could not quite bring himself to peek. Shawn handed the cheque to the guru. Sri Ji folded it without looking at it.

"Take care of this money!"

"I shall try, sir."

"And Patrick," Shawn smiled, "I owe you a new start. How much would you say your life is worth?"

"I really couldn't say, could I? I mean I couldn't put a monetary value on it, could I?"

"Do!"

"Ah .... one million, two, three? Certainly no more than five. Even by my own standards, five million would be tops."

Shawn wrote again. He handed another cheque to Patrick, who looked at it and grimaced, shaking his head. The cheque book and pen also were given to Patrick. Then the Durstli Man walked on toward the convoy and the other four followed.

When they had got within 30 feet, they stopped. As if to make certain they would not advance further, the commander took a few steps forward, slightly spread his feet and said loudly, "Are you the man called Shawn, the man from the crash near Durstlimas?"

Shawn laughed carelessly. The messenger, who stood next to

him, was amused. Neither of them replied.

"If you are," the officer went on, "I have orders to take you to Geneva Airport. An aeroplane is ready to fly you to any country you choose. I have a document from the Special Assembly here. If you resist, we will use force!"

"Nanita," said Shawn without turning his head, "play your flute for this man!"

The Whore of Japan put the flute to her lips and blew. A quavering, single note emerged. It steadied and became smooth. That instant, a shiver went through the still distant Pampini and it sank lower, now hovering only about one hundred feet above the lake's shining surface. Even through the noise of the chopping helicopter blades and the distant thunder of the circling jets high above, the gasp of astonishment from the crowd could be heard, for the old 1938, 12-seater aircraft now seemed to have turned into a near-translucent, membraneous piece of jade, a flying machine without propellors or windows.

41

ONE

What happened next was filmed by a TV cameraman who had been swept forward by the mob. The world would see this event later at regular speed, portions of it in slow motion, and one by one in stilled frames - excerpts from an incomprehensibly savage dance.

The celestial alien crouched. This first crouching motion was so swift that later, on the screen, it had a comical, jerky quality like footage from old films. Still crouching, he shot forward, a silvery streak in the sunlight, straight for the commander.

All of this happened so fast that there was no reflex from anyone except for the barest retraction of the commander's face as he tried to withdraw self-protectively. But Shawn came up short, inches before hitting the man. Leaning far back to his right he swung around, one arm outstretched, and flew towards his beautiful companion. Those who watched were petrified, entranced by the deadly grace of the moving figure.

Since the camera was focused on a portion of space rather than on Shawn, this part of the film looked like a staged sequence from some futuristic ballet. The woman, having anticipated his move, allowed herself to fall forward to meet him, her magnificent body gracefully curved at the waist. Shawn's arm caught her, encircled her. Only now were the keenest among the crack soldiers beginning to react. But there was no time to aim. In that same, unbroken sweep of muscular power, the female form of the messenger tucked in his arm, Lion Shawn pivoted into a ferocious leap - forward and downwards from the bridge towards the glass-calm waters of the lake.

42

ZERO

As Shawn made his lion leap from the bridge, the swans stopped preening themselves and shouted a wild, hoarse welcome. Patrol boats had kept heading off boat-loads of the curious who had thought they might get a closer view. At the periphery of the great armada of swans, confusion reigned as the birds were bumped and tried to avoid bows, oars and engines.

The sunshine falling directly on the Durstli survivor, created the illusion that there was no substance, only light, a great shiny apparition. The crowds had been caught by surprise. A deep, pained sigh rose from them, followed directly by a moaning sound. All of it happened so quickly that there was no time to speculate on what he would do next, but on one thing all agreed later that day: never had they seen a human being move with such force.

In these instants, too, the swans were turning to face out into the lake. As one they began to beat their wings, starting on the long run swans need to become airborne. In reflex before this unique spectacle, the people in the boats and even the water-police ducked and tucked their heads under their arms as the great birds whooshed past. And Shawn had reappeared, running among the swans, it seemed, running across the water now agitated by their wings and feet. The female messenger was still held tightly into the crook of his powerful arm. But by now she had become scarcely visible to the gaping multitudes. The earthly body that had been so admired had faded into a wispy, ethereal form that seemed almost to have merged into Shawn's own silvery, ghostly image.

That a man cannot run across water was so self-evident, so deeply ingrained in the human psyche and psychology that it constituted a fortress of immense proportions. As had happened so many times in the battles of remote and recent history, the fortress of this knowledge was nimbly sidestepped by the fact that a silvery man was indeed running full tilt in a great stormy cloud of swans in a southeasterly direction, past the famous fountain and pier, out into the smooth, sunny expanse of *Lac Léman.*

There was no way anyone on shore could properly estimate his pace. It seemed as if he ran at blinding, superhuman speed, but in fact some of the patrol boats whose crews had recovered from shock swung in after him and had no difficulty keeping up. They later testified that their speed had been perhaps twelve or thirteen miles per hour, so that the Durstli Man was running at the speed of a slow high-school sprinter. Most of the swans were airborne now. They had divided themselves precisely into two halves of a wedge formation at whose tip the Durstli Man ran. Certain experts claimed later that somehow the beating of the swan's wings had created a suction which permitted Shawn to appear to be running when in fact he was being drawn along in this vacuum, but this was flatly contradicted by the men in the speed boats who had a perfect view of the running man and swore that his feet actually touched and stirred the water's surface. According to them, unanimously, he seemed to be running through a long, shallow stretch of water, as if through a puddle.

Later, within three hours of the event, this entire portion of *Lac Leman* was combed with nets and sticks to see if perhaps a runway had somehow been rigged for the runner just below the surface, but nothing was found. It had been a desperate idea of the rational mind making a last stand against miraculous phenomenology. But, most incomprehensible of all, Shawn had not stood or walked majestically as Jesus had when he created the precedent. No, he had loped along in great, undignified, savage -yes, savage! - bounds. That is the image which remained fixed in the eyes and minds of all who saw it: a savage burst of speed, a savage run, a savage demonstration. That is what this had been, what it was, what it would remain - a view of how a savage defies the laws of gravity!

Meanwhile the young man was still running, had run over a mile, nearly two miles at this speed which, measured over this distance was turning into record pace, miracle or no miracle. Accompanied by his palace guard of swans that flew as one enormous winged body, he was still heading approximately toward the centre of the great lake, when at the other end, near St. Gingolph, the hovering Pampini began to move again. Thousands, by now alerted via radio and TV, were watching the spectacle. Now that the chips were down, the Swiss military commanders showed commendable intelligence. They had given orders not to shoot or interfere and to maintain a safe distance from the plane.

The Pampini flew - if flying describes what it was engaged in - at low altitude. Here, again, it was confirmed that there was no propeller action, in fact, no propellers, no windows. The thing seemed to have been cast from a single piece of pale, alabaster-like material which shone tantalizingly close to being translucent. With the Air Force helicopters at respectful distance in the formation of a flying shield, the former Pampini now gracefully slid even lower to a height of no more than thirty feet above the lake as it continued casually on its way west. It was apparent by now that the machine was headed for rendezvous with the Durstli Man.

Not much later Shawn, still running full speed, still escorted by the *Léman* swans, began gradually to change course, heading now due southeast toward the lakeside community of Evian-les-Bains on the French shore of the lake. The Pampini, too, slightly adjusted its drift in a shallow curve, slowed further so that the two, man and machine, moved at approximately the same speed. They were moving toward that predictable point of the lake where they would have to meet. The female messenger had now disappeared altogether, her ghost-like form having appeared to melt totally into Shawn's shiny body.

Helicopter pilots reported the incredible sight they beheld when they first saw the flying swans with Shawn's shimmering form like a silvery torch at the tip of their formation. But already he had slowed to a trot. The two halves of the swan wedge swung away in opposite directions flying a wide circle - one toward the southern shore, the other toward the northern - and returned, still in precise formation, to set down on the water in frothy flutter and turbulence.

Shawn walked the last hundred yards to where the Pampini hovered so close to the lake that it was hard to tell whether or not it actually touched water.

At this point the observers' accounts began to vary according to position and distance from the rendezvous spot. Some of them stated that a door had 'slid' open. Others maintained that Shawn had been 'sucked in' or 'absorbed into' the flying machine. But regardless of the method by which he entered the machine, the fact became incontestable that where one instant there had been the tall, shiny man miraculously standing on the surface of the lake by an eerie looking thing in the general shape of a twin-engine, twelve-seat 1938 Pampini, the next moment there was only the Pampini.

It remained still for what was clocked as precisely 42 seconds, then it began to rise. The increasing clamour of the helicopters contrasted with the awestruck silence of the watching crowd as the Pampini rose slowly at first, then gathered speed. Accelerating at an estimated angle of 30 degrees, it sped off towards the south-west, where the Mont-Blanc Massif was clearly visible. While the vast flock of swans, now bobbing at rest on the lake, all faced the departing machine, they made no move to follow.

The helicopters attempted to follow but the Pampini's speed was such that they were left hopelessly adrift. A wing of five jets, screaming in agonisingly steep ascent, also gave chase but fell away.

Seen from the bridge for brief moments, the Pampini was a priceless pearl falling upward into the azure ocean of sky above Geneva and the lake.

The soldiers' guns still pointed silently skyward. The commander still stood staring up, one hand clutching the envelope with the expulsion order. The alien's flute of quarry crystal was still close to Nanita's lips. Patrick Young still held the cheque book and the pen.

The world was caught and unprepared for this swift departure. Now, for what seemed an eternity, nothing could crank up the earthly machinery again. Seemingly no force in Heaven *or* on Earth could free these frozen figures watching in vain the darkening sky. Under the bridge, the waters of the Rhone had stopped rushing homeward from the lake. Nothing could make liquid again their dry lifeless froth.

No laugh, no touch, no tear could be. Nothing could happen now until the ancient sentence of time fell from suspension back into its coat of human flesh. It seemed that Creation itself had stopped... and so it had, like the sun over Jericho, until Pampini's mesmerising spell suddenly lifted - and the bridge-bound congregation broke into gasping sounds.

43

CLOUD

The pilots of the jet planes that had so fruitlessly attempted to pursue the Pampini later reported that at an altitude of around fifteen thousand feet above Mont-Blanc the craft had simply disappeared, vanished in what at first looked like a 'puff of smoke' but turned out on closer inspection to be an ordinary cumulus, unexceptional in size and composition.

This cloud was all the Durstli Man in his Pampini left behind. While it appeared normal in every respect, it did not move. Not at all. Not for an hour, not for a day. Not in fact for three days.

One could look at it, fly through it. Samples were taken again and again, but it would not dissolve. It would not even change shape. It hung there for perhaps no better purpose than to mark the spot where the Durstli foundling had disappeared.

The remainder of that memorable afternoon can be described simply as immersion in emotional and intellectual bedlam. To say that Geneva became the focus of global attention was not enough. In a matter of hours airlines reported capacity bookings from the great cosmopolitan centres of the world, carrying professionals and laymen alike, the greedy, the curious, the idle rich and all those who had somehow convinced themselves that going to the place where a godlike human had walked on water would cure whatever their affliction. The great battle for the minds of men had truly begun, and the lines were clearly and deeply etched: Sceptics and Cynics versus True Believers. There appeared to be no middle ground.

Reunited at the Royal Palace Hotel, Patrick, Nanita, Dr. Conrad and Sri Bhagavan Ji were joined by Jack Baldwin, who now displayed all the breathless fervour of a religious convert. Dr. Conrad had just announced his plans for an immediate return on Pan Am's flight number 119 to the United States, leaving that very same day. Sri Ji smiled wistfully.

"I, too, shall leave," he said. "I must go meditate on these events. I shall go to India, to my home without delay. I shall pass through the narrow portals of childhood memories into the broad and luminous pastures of unblemished perception."

"You do that," said Dr. Conrad, handing the mystic his calling card, "but don't forget to keep in touch."

Jack Baldwin gestured vigorously.

"Not me, not this boy," he gushed. "I'm not going home." Jack bubbled with the boundless energy of a newborn babe. Even his recent bizarre behaviour was already a fading memory. He did not care to dwell on it, especially with this group of people at the hotel. Something or somebody had got a hold of him, true. But he had been more fortunate than others who lose their mind: at least his particular something had had a name: Oba. Now Oba seemed to have departed, the devil had left. Good riddance! Jack Baldwin sincerely hoped that this Oba had gone back where he, she or it came from.

"No, no," he repeated loudly, "I'm not going home, I'm going back to Durstlimas. That's my base camp, that's where everything started."

Patrick Young nodded. Baldwin had a point. Deep in thought, he massaged his new hand with his old, a gesture already characteristic of him. Nanita, like a porcelain saint, sat cradling her flute. Patrick looked at her. Her pupils were so large that all of his image passed through without encountering the slightest resistance. He reached out and touched her shoulder.

"Go to Durstlimas with Baldwin," he said to Nanita, "I shall return to London. I have a book to write. It is crucial that I inform the world of Pampini and its miraculous departure."

A few hours later, the two were on their way in Jack Baldwin's van on which the legend 'Jack Baldwin's Crusade for Truth' still shone and sparkled in the spring sunshine. At the eastern end of the lake, where the broad glacial plain narrows and the deep slender gouge of the Rhone crooks into the Canton of Valais, Baldwin pulled the van over. He and Nanita got out to look back at the cloud. They shaded their eyes against the sun in an otherwise faultless sky. Jack Baldwin pointed to the cloud, saying, "With a little luck we'll be able to see it from Durstlimas, too." Lowering his hand he turned abruptly, his face strained. "No, no, Nanita. Our work is completed. Let's get out of this country."

Grasping the flute firmly, she inspected the surroundings. "Yes," she answered, "let's not go to Durstlimas. I have this strange feeling... there's something disturbing in the air."

They returned to the van, and rapidly accelerated downhill towards the French border.

44

TALK

Patrick Young was taken into protective custody at the hotel by government security men, some of whom he knew well from the early weeks after the Durstli Man's arrival. He was subjected to hours of harsh cross-examination in order to establish his identity, which was naturally questioned. His old hand was flown in from London on an Air Force jet and Patrick was confronted with it, admitting readily that this had been indeed his hand and stating that he, as could plainly be seen, had grown a new one. He told the whole story but he was at first not believed. Finally, it boiled down to the question of who or what was more credible: he or 'his' hand. This problem was eventually resolved in favour of the living man. To the miracle of Shawn's swift run on Lake *Léman* was added that of the resurrection of one Patrick Young, who was quickly whisked out of Geneva to avoid adding to the confusion. He turned up on a joint TV special of Eurovision, televised world wide via satellite looking smooth and confident, sporting a grin that may have been a poor imitation of the Durstli Man's victorious smile, but it was the best and the only thing the world had. Here, then, was Patrick Young, the man who had been closest to the miracle maker, flanked by a psychiatrist and a magician, both of whom had reached the pinnacle in their particular fields of expertise. These two men had been provided in order to permit the airing of an educated opposition to what to some appeared as a dangerous groundswell of a new, space-age fanaticism, a soupy wave of unreason and superstition that threatened to break on the already brittle shore of sanity and smash it to bits.

Patrick was introduced by the presenter modestly as 'the man who knew Him well'. There was no need to specify who had been meant by this 'him'. Since there was no written record of this broadcast it remained ambiguous whether or not the 'h' in him was meant to have been capital, but the feeling was that it was, indeed. Everything relating to the Durstli Man was capital news now, a scant twenty-four hours after his spectacular departure.

"No," said Patrick, "that I was blown to bits in London and returned from the dead is certainly no rumour, it is a fact, although strictly speaking I did not return from the dead. I was never dead. I was absent and during this absence I learned that all the so-called dead are merely absent, and that they are absent only from the point of view of those who consider themselves present here, on this earth. In fact everybody is always absent with most of himself. We're all toenails on our own bodies. What does the toenail know about the knee, and the knee about the chin, and the chin about the dreams of a man? Very little! I was more present when I was absent than when I had been present, you must follow me, do you?

"Well," said the psychiatrist, "everything you say is a not unusual expression of thought which is a product of the human mind and this mind, as we've seen countless times, is characteristically unreliable. In fact, for example, the schizophrenic condition is a condition of the mind, it does not-for example interfere with other emotional qualities such as love. A schizophrenic person may be in love, may love or be loved. So we see here the mind, specifically your mind, Mr. Young, expressing itself. There is nothing wrong with that that I can see!"

"Do I take it," asked the presenter, "that you deny the factual basis of Mr. Young's statement, I mean, are you contradicting the overwhelming eyewitness evidence of the great miraculous feats of Mr. Young's friend, the man who crashed at the Durstli, are you denying that?"

"Not at all," conceded the psychiatrist, "it would not be wise of me to dismiss the unanimous testimony of thousands of people, many of whom are professional men trained in recording their observations with all possible detachment and objectivity. No, they must have seen what they all say they saw. But we see often only the surface, in fact, we rarely see anything but the surface. I say that behind ...."

"Precisely," said the master magician, an elderly man with lively eyes and hands, impeccably attired, "in my country we have an old saying: The Hand Can Be Quicker Than The Eye. Well, I've taken the liberty to amend this. I say, the hand can be quicker than the eye, but no hand is swift enough for Speedy. Speedy is my nickname. I've caught literally dozens of fakers and impostors and if I'd been in Geneva yesterday it would not have surprised me if I had discovered the principle behind the trick that apparently allowed a fully grown man to run across or halfway across a lake. Unfortunately, I wasn't. My guess is that some sort of mass suggestion took place. There are many competent hypnotists in the world. I've taken the trouble to acquaint myself with what has been written about this so-called Durstli Man and it seems to me that the top men in my field could easily have duplicated most of his tricks, even though I confess that I'm at a loss in the resurrection department."

Patrick Young looked directly into the camera, saying: "It does not matter, Mr. Speedy, where you are at a loss. This is not your department, nor even mine. I'm not here to explain myself or my master to the world. I'm here to say what I feel like saying, which is, at this particular time, that both of you are full of - - - -"

The word he now used was 'shit' and though there was a ten-second lag in the transmission, it was decided that, in view of the importance of these events, it would be left in.

"Well," drawled the psychiatrist, seizing the opportunity, we mustn't lose our tempers, gentlemen."

"Quite," said the presenter.

"The world may be destroyed," Patrick said, "just as the Durstli Man said. Perhaps he will destroy it. Maybe he will keep his word. Now, in the primitive conceptions which are bandied about here and everywhere at this hour, in this crucial hour in human history, this to you can mean only that some unspeakable catastrophe will befall us. That there will be some kind of explosion, some kind of volcanic eruption, a tidal wave. No, it's much, much simpler than that, can't you see? What did he destroy, what did he really destroy? The religious myths? He destroyed hypocrisy, particularly religious hypocrisy. He destroyed the myth that a man has to be humble and good and long-suffering like Jesus of Nazareth to perform miracles. He destroyed the arrogance of man. He was flamboyant. He loved colourful clothes. He loved women and they loved him in a real physical sense, though he noticed soon that his passion was too powerful for these weak terrestrial creatures ...."

Nanita, who was watching this programme in a hotel room in Paris shook her head.

".... when he found out he stopped. He became celibate, not

because he enjoyed it, but because it was necessary. He was not modest, he did not speak in parables, he loved money and fame and if he had wanted to destroy this lousy planet, shit, he could have done so a long time ago!"

This second 'shit' was carefully edited out.

"Certainly," said the psychiatrist, who had begun to feel that things were going his way, "but let's not be hasty. There is still time. We may yet go up in flames!"

Patrick paid no attention to the irony, saying, "Yes, indeed, there is still time. But not much, not very much. You see, in my estimation, this is what has happened and this is what is going to happen. The basis of the Christian faith in the world has been destroyed. The mask of Christian hypocrisy has been torn away from the face and the face is that of a terrible, perhaps unbearable, an insufferable reality. So what are people going to do once they see this? I'll tell you what I think. I think they will panic. I think they will start the fire, the conflagration, and I think they will do it out of sheer desperation. Just think of what we've all missed if a creature such as this man can do what he did without guilt, without shame. He's taught us a lesson and the lesson is: you can be young, beautiful, rich, arrogant *and* perform miracles!"

"Well," said the psychiatrist, winking at the magician.

"Well nothing," said Patrick, "I've had enough of this. I'm getting out, and I advise all those who think as I do to do likewise."

"But," stammered the presenter, "out, Mr. Young, getting out to where? Where can we go, what shall we do?"

"That," Patrick grinned recklessly, "I cannot tell you. I can tell you this, however, and this is the best way I can sum it up for you and your viewers, for all of you out there. From this moment on, it's every man for himself!"

45

SNOW

The Durstli Man's departure had had the effect of adrenalin on the city of Geneva, which had awakened at long last from the drowsy state induced and maintained by its fortresses of finance, its charitable institutions and their calm daily routines. In one day it had become the centre of the world, bustling with hyper-activity. People were no longer asking themselves - they shouted religious slogans at each other. The newspapers, the radio, television tried to keep up with the quickening pace of ideas, but for once the man in the street was ahead of experts and analysts. Masses were celebrated in festive churches asking for guidance in this important matter. In villages like Durstlimas, where people were now forced to sleep in automobiles and tents and sleeping bags under the open sky, even the old folks, the peasants had been touched. They had brought out their Sunday finery and wore it as if it were All Saints' Day. And above Durstlimas, the ice-and-snow mirage of Morgendurst was sadly melting in the May sun.

About noon on Thursday, May 24th, almost three days to the hour of Shawn's disappearance, a new phenomenological development could be observed on *Lac Léman*. Swans were gathering, preening, testing their wings as if in anticipation of flight. This time film crews stood ready and the spectacle was captured for Switzerland and for the world. By 1.00 p.m. swans had stopped arriving from the distant parts of the lake and the great flock turned to face west. At 1.11 p.m. Thursday, they took off, flying in a circle as if to touch all points of the compass and then turning south-southwest in the direction of Annecy in France and its lake, where they were reported arriving at 4.04 p.m., just at the time when the first measurable changes were noted in the cloud that formed over the spot where the Durstli Man had disappeared.

Within an hour this cloud now shrank to half its former size while increasing five - six fold in density. Two air force helicopters that flew into it to take samples and report on these changes were lost without trace, forcing the Swiss Air Force to limit its activities to observation. Panic began creeping into minds of citizens in this small, neutral country.

At 7.32 p.m. on this fateful Thursday the cloud, or whatever it was, began to move. It moved at a leisurely twenty-five kilometres per hour ground-speed in a northeasterly direction, for all anyone could conjecture toward Zurich. As it moved it grew, until by the time it had reached a central position over the heartland of Switzerland it measured many miles in diameter and had expanded so rapidly that aircraft had to fly either very low or very high to avoid it, and some helicopters at the periphery never returned to base. By 11.00 p.m. that night it covered all of the territory of Switzerland. All domestic and international airports were closed down, grounding all planes, while all airline flights over Switzerland were diverted.

Simultaneously, the thermometer on the ground indicated a sharp and continuing drop in temperature. By 1.00 a.m. Friday, May 25th, it stood at 35 degrees Fahrenheit and was still falling steadily. At 2.17 a.m., with the thermometers now indicating just below freezing, temperatures varied only insignificantly throughout the land and snow began falling.

Nor is "falling" the proper word for what was happening. The snowflakes were tiny and came down so close one to the other and so fast that it was painful to the skin. Even in the thickest outdoor clothes the impact could be felt, quite apart from the impossible cold. Later it was estimated that between 2.17 a.m. that Friday and a sunrise that brought no light, some sixteen feet of snow fell. Switzerland began the day in darkness and ended in that way, as this same kind of painful ice-snow kept coming down. Throughout the land, temperatures plunged rapidly to arctic levels of 50 below zero and even lower. In some places up to ninety-eight feet of snow had fallen and there was no break in the weather - if that is what the phenomenon could be called.

Through the morning hours of Friday a fierce struggle of those on the ground against this elemental assault had been waged unsuccessfully. Short stretches of roads had been kept open for varying periods of time. By mid-morning, when it became apparent that the entire nation was engaged in a life-or-death struggle, a few thousand people from the western part of the country were evacuated by land into France. Some escaped in daring low air flights from runways that disappeared under snow in a matter of minutes. Here and there, at military installations already deeply buried, attempts were made to blast out, and muffled explosions could be heard. Many courageous Swiss had decided to leave the traps of their houses and tried to keep on top of the quickly rising snow level by using skis and snowshoes. This turned out to be the only practical method of survival. Still, only one in a hundred lived through the ordeal .... they were pounded senseless by the weight and density of the snow .... they froze to death. A single slip was enough to end a life, for once a man fell he could not get up quickly enough and was buried alive.

The snow cover thickened and a terrible silence settled over the land. The valleys filled and the mountains grew top-heavy with snow. Avalanches thundered into the valleys that rose to meet them. The deadly deluge continued through Saturday, May 26th, into Sunday. At 3.07 p.m. Sunday, May 27th, three days after the cloud had begun to change, the snow stopped. The cloud began to shrink as it had expanded, and the sun shone everywhere upon the land. But how the land had changed!

Germany, France, Austria, Italy, all of Europe - in fact, the whole world - held its breath as airborne observers cautiously ventured over Swiss territory and sent back their messages of a vast white cemetery in which the only crosses were the craggy mountaintops dominating shallow snow valleys. Here and there, at the highest altitudes, an occasional tree had struggled free from its load, a rare pinnacle of rock had pierced the suffocating burden. But no trace of man or beast. No trace .... no, wait, there, there! .... here and there in the exquisite Sunday wilderness - a spot, a dark smudge, moving, waving, beckoning, testifying to the indomitable human spirit! Indomitable? Some had survived, yes. But even for them surely this was the beginning of ....